Angelic Monks and Earthly Men

*Monasticism and its
Meaning to Medieval Society*

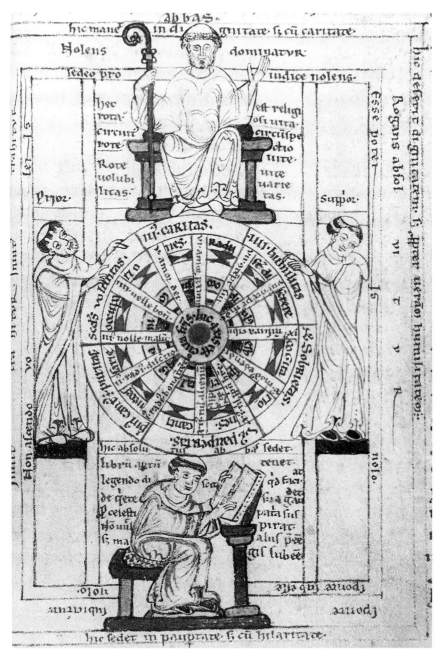

The wheel of true religion

(Thirteenth-century miniature from Hugh of Fouilloy's Liber de rota verae religionis.
Provenance: the Cistercian abbey of Aulne (Belgium, Hainault).
Brussels, Royal Libr., ms. II 1076)

Angelic Monks and Earthly Men

Monasticism and its
Meaning to Medieval Society

LUDO J. R. MILIS

THE BOYDELL PRESS

First published 1992 by The Boydell Press, Woodbridge
Reprinted in paperback 1999

The Boydell Press is an imprint of Boydell & Brewer Ltd
PO Box 9, Woodbridge, Suffolk IP12 3DF, UK
and of Boydell & Brewer Inc.
PO Box 41026, Rochester, NY 14604–4126, USA
website: http://www.boydell.co.uk

ISBN 0 85115 303 8 hardback
ISBN 0 85115 737 8 paperback

A catalogue record for this title is available
from the British Library

Library of Congress Catalog Card Number: 91–45505

This publication is printed on acid-free paper

Printed in Great Britain by
St Edmundsbury Press Ltd, Bury St Edmunds, Suffolk

Contents

Introduction

This introduction, like every other introduction, was written last of all. It was the culmination of several very fruitful months at the Institute for Advanced Study in Princeton, New Jersey, and the result of a mental preparation over ten, perhaps fifteen years. It was a long gestation. The introduction reflects the remarks and the objections of many persons with whom I have discussed my concepts, my goals, my definitions and my expectations. I will here try to outline the scope of my enquiry, as clearly as possible, in order to avoid misunderstandings. Indeed some people seemed offended at the very idea of the overall importance of medieval monasticism towards society being open to scientific re-assessment. Some had the impression that medieval monks led sixfold lives: that they prayed all day long, that they were (presumably at the same time) active in the fields, schools, hospitals, in the cure of souls and at princely courts. They do not sufficiently take into account the extent to which the overwhelmingly monastic origin of primary sources can lead us to overemphasize the impact of monasticism, or the degree to which such a view tends to be further enhanced by the Benedictine historiographical tradition which has been so dominant since the seventeenth century. School textbooks have been and still are largely responsible for spreading this image.[1]

It is always essential for an author to determine his readership. I expect it to be the interested, but not (or not yet) historically trained reader, in other words the layman in historical science. The book is especially written for students, as an intellectual attempt to evaluate critically the impact of an important religious phenomenon on society. The comparison of this approach to the classic histories of monasticism will prove, I hope, challenging and intellectually fruitful for them. I also have in mind the tourist, who visits Europe and who so often comes into contact with the splendid artistic achievements of medieval monks, as well as the faithful museum visitor, or even the reader of detective novels set in medieval abbeys.

---

[1] 'Ce qu'on apprend sur ce[t aspect] religieux des temps [médiévaux] quasi mythiques est d'ordre fort peu transcendental. On nous montre surtout une espèce d'épiphénomène dans ses concrétisations officielles . . . et dans ses effets non spécifiques (politiques, économiques, socio-culturels)' (*La religion dans les manuels scolaires d' histoire en Europe. Actes.* . . . Strasbourg, 1974, p. 111).

This book is not a history of the monastic orders. Many books have dealt with that theme, and some of them with notable success, thanks to the knowledge, the skill and the intelligence of their authors. I am, for example, a great admirer of D. Knowles' *The Monastic Order in England*,[2] and I genuinely enjoy C. N. L. Brooke's *The Monastic World*.[3] J. van Engen's article on the 'Crisis of Cenobitism' is rich and challenging[4] and I appreciate C. H. Lawrence's *Medieval Monasticism* as well as G. Zarnecki's *The Monastic Achievement*.[5] I do not intend to rewrite what they, and others, have so brilliantly treated. My purpose is to provide an *assessment* of what monasticism meant to medieval society, and not a history in the classical sense. Therefore I have taken a comprehensive view over a long, uninterrupted period. The attempt fits into the *longue durée*-approach of French historiography, necessarily so in my opinion, because mental influences and changes in society are too slow to be noticed over short periods. Therefore I leave the chronological divisions out of account insofar as this is intellectually possible. A chronological procedure is replaced by a thematic approach, for the notion and the aim of monasticism itself (the pursuit of spiritual self-fulfilment in a social context characterized by life in common) has remained unaltered from late Antiquity, all through the Middle Ages, until the present, even though the ways in which monasticism has been interpreted and realized have certainly changed.[6]

Generally speaking authors seldom try to define the notions they use, and that undoubtedly constitutes one of the scientific weaknesses of the humanities. Books on monasticism are no exception. This leads in my view to the use, in too broad and too vague a sense, of the word monasticism to include concomitant, though fundamentally alien, phenomena. To redress this lack of clarity I refer to the *New Catholic Encyclopedia*, where the following definition of monasticism is given: 'An institution of ancient and medieval origins, establishing and regulating the ascetical and social conditions of the manner of religious life lived in common or in contemplative solitude'.[7] We could try to define it ourselves as *a*

---

2 Cambridge, 1940 (second edition: 1963).
3 London (1974). The second edition (New York, 1982) was published under the title *Monasteries of the World*.
4 'The "Crisis of Cenobitism" reconsidered: Benedictine Monasticism in the Years 1050 – 1150', in: *Speculum*, 61, 1986, pp. 269–304.
5 London, New York, 1972.
6 For present-day monks, just as for their medieval predecessors, the basic characteristics of their life-style are praise of God, prayer and work, the latter being subordinate to the monastic vocation (G. A. Hillery Jr, 'Monastic Occupations: A Study of Values', in: *Research in the Sociology of Work*, 2, 1983, pp. 191–210).
7 New York, 1967, ix, p. 1032.

specific spiritual ideal and aim of perfection implemented as a life-style. This at least is what I propose to use as the standard measure, gauged according to the prescriptions of the monastic rules, and especially of the Rule of St Benedict, by far the most important and authoritative rule. I will further delimit the notion later on in this introduction.

My aim was to produce a concise book treating the entire medieval period, an objective which met with a certain degree of scepticism on the part of a number of my colleagues. This comprehensiveness certainly has disadvantages, as subtleties are lost (as I am well aware) and some statements may sound too un-nuanced. But are these not at the same time advantages? For, even if they are occasionally superficial, generalizations illustrate best how ideas, interests and groups interacted. The restricted length also implies an extremely reduced apparatus. This sacrifice is the price any author of a general survey must be prepared to pay. The evidence I use is, generally speaking, the same as that of other specialists although any author will be more familiar with some areas or periods than with others. We all share the feeling that when we start to quote primary sources systematically, we need to quote them *all*, in order to avoid some counter examples, *apparently* as solid, though in reality exceptional and thus non-representative examples. The author of a survey claims no indulgence from the reader, but offers him or her the guarantee of a scientific conviction, honestly acquired. My own is based on thirty years of investigating and analyzing primary sources. The opinions, matured during innumerable classes and lectures, *emphasize common rather than particular characteristics, similarities rather than differences*.

Furthermore, I wish to stress that I do not attach much importance (as is so often done in histories of the monastic orders) to the alternation of vitality and decay. They are not adequate categories in a comprehensive study of the impact of monasticism as a religious ideal, because vitality is mostly interpreted as the gathering of material wealth and secular power, whereas, religiously speaking, true vitality all but inevitably leads to precisely the opposite, namely to more seclusion, and thus to retreat from worldly matters. This apparent failure of categorisation seems to be the result of too vague a definition of monasticism. As we defined it earlier, monasticism itself is an objectified concept, and as such we consider it unaffected by the ups and downs of everyday life. When the meaning of monasticism is tied to such external and alien phenomena as for instance feudalism, then labels more properly applicable to these phenomena like 'flourish' and 'decay' are erroneously and unjustifiably transferred to monasticism itself. Phenomena such as land-ownership or political influence, are too often considered to be proofs of monastic social relevance. This, according to my definition, is mistaken. To use a metaphor, these phenomena are like ticks. Even if they live in symbiosis with their host, yet they remain separate and distinguishable entities. Nobody questions that monasteries were very great land-owners indeed, but this has, according to our definition, hardly anything to do with monasticism. We are looking for the *specific* impact of what we have called the *specific spiritual ideal and aim of perfection implemented as a life-style*, whereas the way in which estates were run was apparently the same as for other lords, both lay and ecclesiastical. Therefore, land-ownership by abbeys should be seen more as pertaining to feudalism or to the seignorial system, than to monasticism.[8]

I also need to stress what monasticism *certainly is not*. In discussions anecdotal events or circumstances have often been advanced to refute my theses. History is a very indulgent science, as all things have happened at least once. For my part, I try to see trends, and by definition a trend leaves exceptions out of account. In my opinion, monasticism is thus *not* considered to be the *enumeration of all the deeds of monks*, neither as individuals, nor even as communities. The deeds should be *general* enough to enter into the overall picture and moreover they should be a *specific* result of the monastic ideal. If we cannot blame or praise professorship for all the things professors do as spouses, parents or friends, why should we attribute to monasticism all the acts monks perform (for instance) as land-owners and lords?

Since I cover a period of a thousand years and, moreover, try to identify mechanisms, the great names of the history of monasticism are in a manner of speaking absent from this assessment.[9] Their individual achievements, however important they may have been (and unquestionably were), seldom enter in our scope. A bird's-eye view shows an active swarm, but barely identifies individuals. Unfortunately trends have a structural weakness when described in words instead of in graphs. The

---

[8] Georges Duby for instance used the monastic demesnes to describe how lay property functioned. The overwhelming analogy indicates that there is, generally speaking, no specifically 'monastic' system of exploitation. Hence this aspect cannot contribute to answering the question of what monasticism meant to medieval society (*Guerriers et paysans*. Paris, 1973, pp. 240–48). See also J. McDonald and G. D. Snooks, *Domesday Economy. A New Approach to Anglo-Norman History*. Oxford, 1986, esp. pp. 90–92, who were able to confirm statistically the analogy between monastic and lay agricultural management.

[9] Our scope is different thus from for instance J. Décarreaux, *Les moines et la civilisation en Occident. Des invasions à Charlemagne*. Paris, 1962 (Signes des temps, xiii): (p. 7) 'On a voulu surtout mettre en relief des personnalités. Pris comme tel, le monde monastique, spécialiste de l'humilité, compose une foule anonyme, un peu grise et rude dans ses premiers éléments. Son œuvre formerait dans l'histoire une trame cachée et, en ce qu'elle laisse apparaître, monotone, si, à point nommé, de grands conducteurs n'y marquaient leur empreinte'.

expressions 'general', 'ordinary' and others of their ilk infiltrate the discourse far too frequently (if inevitably). As a matter of fact historical language is poised here between two irreconcilable extremes, scientific exactness and an agreeable, readable style.

I have said already that I would further delimit my notion of monasticism. I gladly follow the authoritative opinion of D. Knowles, the *New Catholic Encyclopedia*, and W. O. Chadwick,[10] in that *only monks* are to be taken into consideration. It means that several religious expressions with a life-style apparently close to that of the monks are not included in this study. 'This opinion is too monolithic' remarked one historian after a paper. In the interest of exact concepts, I disagree. Canons and Mendicant Friars are not monks, and thus do not enter into our horizon except insofar as they help to delimit concisely the functions and appearances of monks properly speaking. Many of these other movements were the result of reformers' dissatisfaction with the social or religious meaning of monks, or towards what was considered to be their functional inadequacy. The canons were to a certain extent active in the cure of souls, because monks were not (or at least not on a sufficient scale for them), and because the training of the lower secular clergy was notoriously inadequate. Their choice of the Rule of St Augustine over that of St Benedict was a manifestation of a conception of religious life more open to the world. Their 'Augustinian tradition' broke the monopoly which Benedictine monasticism had represented for several centuries. The Mendicants, in turn, developed forms of socio-religious commitment, once again because monks were not sufficiently involved. The Dominicans followed the Augustinian model, whereas St Francis of Assisi suggested a Rule of his own for his friars. In both cases and in precisely the same way for other types of Mendicants, the rejection of the Benedictine ideal was a conscious decision, even though sometimes its influence is still perceptible. This new choice was not meant, however, as a censure of the *Benedictine life-style for Benedictines*. It meant that the interaction of their religious ideal with society was *per se* hardly possible. So the inclusion of all these opposite movements in one single word, monasticism, would do injustice to the specificity of their origin and goals, even when they shared similarities of observance and spirituality. I do not include hermits either, although I sometimes mention them.[11] Their appearance

---

10 *International Encyclopedia of the Social Sciences.* S. l., 1968, 10, pp. 415–19.

11 Hermits and the characteristics of eremitism have been studied in recent years on various occasions. In English see for instance H. Leyser, *Hermits and the New Monasticism. A Study of Religious Communities in Western Europe, 1000–1150.* London, 1984 (New Studies in Medieval History); W. J. Sheils (ed.), *Monks, Hermits and the Ascetic Tradition.* Oxford, 1985 (Studies in

was too fragmentary and transient (many were or became monks) to have a significant impact.

Thus two religious types enter into our monastic 'landscape'. First of all there are the early medieval monks, whether Celtic or Mediterranean, often with a very loose organization and a great diversity of views. Some of them regarded mobility (*instabilitas*) as a must and stressed the ideal of continuous exile. Missionaries of the early medieval period most often belonged to this group.[12] The second type are the Benedictine monks, who evolved from one of the Mediterranean solutions to monastic life. They, however, stressed *stabilitas*, the confinement to one's own abbey. In the Carolingian epoch, the ninth century, they overwhelmed the other movements and were to be religiously dominant for many centuries to come.

I hardly discuss nuns, and this requires some explanation, especially now that the study of female religiosity is such a fashionable theme. Nuns undeniably represented a substantial part of the monastic dwellers, but in tracing the impact of monasticism on society, the two major impediments which prevented monks from playing a larger role were present to a yet greater degree in the life-style of nuns. The first of these was their seclusion from the world, leading to an isolation far more pronounced in the case of nuns. Secondly the female monasteries served, even more than did the male monasteries, as repositories of a surplus of socially high-ranking children. When women began, in the later middle ages, to play a more conspicuous and distinctive role in religious life in general, Benedictinism had already been largely eclipsed as the leading solution of a religious life-style by the Mendicants and other (sometimes institutionally ambiguous) movements such as the Beguines.[13]

Finally I need a second definition: what is the meaning of *medieval society* in my subtitle? My focus is centered particularly on 'ordinary people', even though scientifically speaking, this is not really a viable expression either. It does, however, help us, to come closer to what I really mean. I am not interested in the upper class of society as such: in the nobility, in the clergy or, later on, in the wealthy and mighty merchants of the towns. I am looking for the ninety to ninety-five percent of the total population who lived a marginal life in every possible sense of

Church History 22), and G. Constable, *Monks, Hermits and Crusaders in Medieval Europe*. London, 1988 (a reprint of articles).

[12] P. O Dwyer, *Céli Dé. Spiritual Reform in Ireland. 750–900*. Dublin, 1981, pp. 111–13.

[13] There is an extensive literature on the Beguine Movement. The best and most recent, if succinct, evaluation is: W. Simons, 'The Beguine Movement in the Southern Low Countries: A Reassessment', in: *Bulletin de l' Institut historique belge de Rome – Bulletin van het Belgisch Historisch Instituut te Rome*, lix, 1989, pp. 63–105.

the word: social, juridical, material. The definition which the sociologist Arnold M. Rose gave of minorities is, without adaptation, practicable for the demographical majority with which I am dealing. It is 'a group of people who both think of themselves as a differentiated group and are thought of by the others as a differentiated group with negative connotations. Further, they are relatively lacking in power and hence are subjected to certain exclusions, discriminations, and other differential treatment.'[14] He continues: 'A minority's position involves exclusion or assignment to a lower status in one or more of four areas of life: the economic, the political, the legal, and the social-associational.' He recognizes moreover 'three types of attitudes of hostility or prejudice': first 'an attitude in which power is the main element'; a second 'attitude is ideological', and 'the third one is racist'. All three are applicable within the social pattern that characterized medieval Europe, if racist means, as the author suggests, the belief in a biological superiority of the (empowered) majority group.

The social minority group constituted, as I have suggested, at least ninety per cent of the population. As time progressed, its number certainly decreased, but only slightly. However limited this shift may have been, it was the result of those new economic possibilities that changed the social, legal and religious conditions in the second half of the middle ages. New groups could eventually compete in wealth with the traditional aristocracy. They could challenge its power and infiltrate its structure and life-style. These new groups then became, in their turn and together with the older ones, a social majority of the same type.

The demographical majority poses one structural problem for historians: lack of evidence. It would be easier to reconstruct how a peasant lived on the demesne of an abbey if he had left memoirs, and to evaluate the similarity or difference with life on lay estates if his neighbour had kept a diary. The silent masses never leave evidence of their own. In every society they must be studied through the bias of a dominant class.

The aim of this book is, as already said, to evaluate *the specific impact of the monastic ideal in the monks' behaviour towards ordinary people*. Our scepticism as to this impact will appear as a striking (and to the casual reader unacceptable) overthrow of firmly entrenched ideas. The reader must bear in mind, however, that I use the word monasticism in a more restricted sense than usual, even though in a more precise sense. I believe that our assessment enhances and purifies the worth of monasticism as a spiritual ideal, rather than denies it. It was no more, and certainly no less, than the best balanced path which Christendom had worked out towards a life dedicated to God. It is remarkable to see how monasticism could survive as a 'specific implementation of a spiritual

---

[14] *International Encyclopedia of the Social Sciences*, x, pp. 365–71.

ideal' notwithstanding all the 'ticks' which distracted its attention from its original and basic goal.

This book might never have been written without my term at the Institute for Advanced Study in Princeton, New Jersey, in early 1989. The working environment was exceptionally stimulating. The many contacts with colleagues from different countries and different scientific traditions were most enriching. The organizational and material provisions were perfect. I would especially like to thank my friend Professor Giles Constable for the intellectual support he gave to all of us in his group of medievalists. His reputation as an outstanding specialist in monastic history was already a challenge in itself. Among my colleagues at Princeton I would particularly like to mention Robert Lerner (Northwestern University, Illinois), William Courtenay (University of Madison, Wisconsin), Jean Dunbabin (University of Oxford), John Fleming (Princeton University) and Christine Smith (University of Georgetown, Fiesole, Italy) with whom I had stimulating conversations. I am very grateful to Julianne Kmiec who often helped me as a 'potential reader' of the book. I also wish to thank other friends, Professor Joanna E. Ziegler and Professor Virginia Raguin (both of Holy Cross College, Worcester, Mass.). They evaluated my ideas, especially the ones I defended in the chapter on art, with generosity and frankness. I am further grateful to Professor James McIlwain (Brown University, Providence, RI) and to Professor Martha Howell (then Rutgers State University of New Jersey) for the papers I was invited to give, and for the fruitful discussions with distinguished colleagues and a highly interested public afterwards.

On the other side of the Atlantic, more precisely in my home base, the University of Ghent, my graduate students will easily recognize the main features of the book. Many of them are the result of the open discussions held in several classes, spread over many years. I am especially grateful for what Dr Walter Simons, Luc Jocqué, Geert Berings, Peter Ruyffelaere and many others have contributed in this way. I owe special thanks to J. Lizabeth Fackelman and Peter Arnade for their editorial help. Thanks also to Professor Paul Tombeur and to Christian Ruell of *Cetedoc* (University of Louvain at Louvain-la-Neuve) for sending me computerized information on charters. Special gratitude goes to Professor Christopher Brooke, Professor Jill Mann (Cambridge University) and Dr C. L. Kruithof (University of Ghent) for their numerous pertinent remarks.

Quite naturally I reserve a special place in these acknowledgements for my caring wife Greta. She read the manuscript critically and she helped me (as she always does) to avoid major traps.

I will not forget the bright light of the New Jersey sky.

1

Our Written Information: from Recording the Exceptional to Recording the Usual

IS OUR KNOWLEDGE OF
THE MIDDLE AGES REPRESENTATIVE?

The long epoch from about 500 to 1500 which we call the middle ages can be roughly divided into two strikingly different phases. The first period covers the first six centuries; the last, three more centuries, considering one century, the twelfth, as a time of transition. The typology of the written historical documents by means of which we know the medieval period testifies to that evolution. Among the factors which help us to explain this phenomenon, changes in mentality may be considered the most important. A steadily developing, and hence a more socially organized, world needed an increasingly reliable means of communication. This meant that a more adequate system of record-keeping had to be available. It implied a shift from mostly oral to largely written transmission of data. The procedure of recording information allows one to overcome the limitations of physical memory and at the same time guarantees the quality of the transmission, that is its conformity with the original message. Things which are to be written down, however, need to meet one basic condition: they must be considered worthy of being recorded. For the producer of the document, as well as for the user, the message has to be important. Yet 'importance' is relative. As more and more was written down in the course of the middle ages, the notion of 'importance' underwent a change. Other subjects than those hitherto usual and traditional began to be considered worth committing to parchment or paper. More and more of what was previously 'less important' now came to be written down, even if the basic condition (sufficient importance) remained valid. As time progressed, a steadily increasing number of documents were produced. For the early medieval period all that was related to God and linked to Eternity was important, and only that. In the later period further points of interest came to be added, as the appearance of, for instance, business records attests.

It is obvious that the evolution of the use of writing is not merely an intellectual or mental phenomenon. It is also the result of an evolution in materials and skill. What was necessary for writing? We will not take papyrus into account here. It had nearly disappeared from the western European scene in the early middle ages. And wax? This was undoubtedly used most of all, especially for drafts, but as it is a perishable material, it was not in any way adapted for long-term preservation. A medieval wax-tablet is now an extremely rare and unexpected item, existing in only a handful of museums. Parchment was the material *par excellence* for adequate recording, thanks in large part to its durability. The ink also had to be of good quality so as not to vanish after a relatively short while. As a matter of fact, it was parchment, and not ink, which caused the major problem by its limited availability. As far as I know, no studies have yet been undertaken (if indeed they are possible at all) to calculate the precise proportions of the animal skins at hand used for the manufacture of, respectively, parchment, garments, equipment and the like.

As long as parchment was the only material used for durable writing (since wax need not be taken into account) there was a correlation between the available surface and the lay-out: the dimensions of the letters used, the frequency of abbreviations and of decorative or validating elements. When mental shifts imposed a greater use of writing, the existing correlation changed in consequence. On the other hand, there can be no doubt that a change in the correlation could equally well produce a shift in mentality.

Let us take the 'average' early medieval charter as an example: a large piece of parchment, with plenty of space left and many decorative and validating elements. A thirteenth-century charter is, generally speaking, much smaller, written in much smaller letters, with more abbreviations and less decoration. It becomes less solemn, less formal and more popular. The text itself, however, may be much more circumstantial. In other words, charters evolved toward more 'message' on less 'space'.

Once again, however, no calculations have been made in order to ascertain to what extent skin production was used for parchment, and what impact the raising of sheep had made (even if indirectly) on the development of writing. One could suggest that this link was very real, especially when we take into account the possibility that the proportion of the skins used for the manufacture of clothing may have dropped as the use of woven textiles increased. The early example of the English kings who used writing extensively for ephemeral administrative purposes from the twelfth century onwards, may be a convincing argument in favour of this point of view.[1]

[1] Cf. M. T. Clanchy, *From Memory to Written Record. England 1066–1307.* London, 1979.

It was the introduction of paper, however, which brought the great leap forward. In the early fourteenth century its introduction was mentioned in western Europe, and it spread quite rapidly all over that continent. Its cheaper, faster and easier production, as well as the printing techniques of the mid-fifteenth century, made paper an adequate means for the intellectual formation of what was to develop into 'modern society'.[2] A scholar who studies the typology of historical records can immediately point to the major difference existing between the types of documents current in the early and in the late middle ages, whereas a fundamental difference between the late medieval and the early modern periods could hardly be said to exist.

The availability of documents quite naturally depends upon their fabrication, but also upon their chances of survival. Here the material of the document itself is a factor, though a subsidiary one. Paper obviously has less chance of surviving than does parchment, in the same way that the thick, strong parchment of the earlier period has more easily defied the dangers of time than the more refined type used in later centuries.

Nevertheless, as a rule, entirely external factors determine survival or destruction. The depredations of fire and water, caused by nature or by man, can destroy any type of material, however sturdy. The manuscripts collected by Sir Robert Cotton, now in the British Library in London, for instance, are an astonishing example of the resistance of parchment to flames, having survived a disastrous fire in 1731, though the many archives and libraries devastated throughout the ages demonstrate their vulnerability, irrespective of the materials used.

Yet it is not war and the like which pose the greatest threat to documents. Other factors are much more dangerous. First of all there is loss of interest. As a rule, documents are kept as long as they are thought to be of any utility, present or future. Perhaps they are preserved beyond that moment, but then only insofar as storage space is readily available. When this is lacking, a selection will eliminate those documents which no longer serve a purpose or which are not expected to do so. To a certain extent, the second factor is linked to the first. What in fact do we mean by 'interest'? It depends on the potential continuity of the message and this in turn depends on the continuity of the person, group or institution involved. Obviously such institutions as monasteries occupy a favorable position in this respect. They are long-lasting, meant to be perennial, and so are their interests, for their members share the same goals and the same needs all through the ages. Finally topographical continuity is a major factor in the chances of preservation. Just as a lack

---

2   On the influence of writing on increasing rationality, see B. Stock, 'Schriftge-brauch und Rationalität im Mittelalter', in: W. Schluchter (ed.), *Max Webers Sicht des okzidentalen Christentums*. Frankfurt-am-Main, 1988, pp. 165–83.

of space can lead to selection and destruction, so can moving. Only those documents (and other objects) which are considered of actual or potential value will then be kept.

IS OUR KNOWLEDGE OF
MEDIEVAL MONASTICISM REPRESENTATIVE?

What is the place of monasticism and of monastic life with respect to the previous considerations? This has to be determined as clearly as possible, so as to be taken properly into account in making an evaluation of their social meaning. To what extent does a community of monks, that is people secluded from worldly affairs, need and use writing? As monks share a common life oriented towards the fulfilment of the religious ideal of perfection, a code is needed which expresses the content of the ideal itself and indicates the means of achieving this ideal. By 'code' we mean more than a mere rule. Supplementary comments, narrations or treatises, even when they are not written down but are transmitted only orally, are included when their aim is that of spiritual fulfilment.

Moreover, the monastic community is also a group with its own interests within society as a whole. This means that a clearly determined position within society has to be established in order to strengthen, to guarantee, to defend or to justify its position. These conditions can be secured by normative documents; they can also be secured by an adequate organization of the social setting. I have in mind the cultivation of lands, the management of possessions, in a word, administration. And the more administration there is, the more writing there is.

Such groups have rights and duties explicitly or implicitly formulated both *vis-à-vis* society as a whole, and with respect to other groups or individuals. Social history, however, tends to show that people are always as much concerned about their rights as they are heedless of their obligations. In other words, everybody has to know his or her *own* rights so that one can compel others to comply with the duties they have towards oneself. The protection of more rights requires an increased use of writing. Nevertheless, this general consideration as to how groups or individuals act should be mitigated. Opinions on morality or on social relations, or even perhaps individual characters, can induce people to exhibit a greater consideration for the rights of others, and thus contribute in one way or another to a certain kind of self-negation. The protection of one's own interests leads towards writing, self-negation does not. This is undoubtedly an aspect of the 'civilizing process' requiring close attention.

The last factor to be dealt with here is the 'importance' which the group attaches to itself. Here 'importance' has a very broad meaning. It can be related to the number of participants, to the attention the institution traditionally pays to the maintenance of its rights, or to the sum of rights which are expected to be guaranteed. Yet these points are liable to a subjective evaluation. As the religious ideal generally stresses abnegation, it might tend to reduce the importance which should be attached to the material environment and to social conditions. Under ideal circumstances 'importance' is for them the notion attributed to what transcends human and earthly life. This implies that their ties to external society were to be eliminated completely, or (to be more realistic) as much as possible. In this respect eremitical life is the most extreme. It implies the negation of all society as it rejects, at least in principle, contacts with neighbours. It refuses 'the World' and therefore excludes mutual contacts with this world.

Based on these considerations we can, theoretically, evaluate the importance of writing within monastic life and monastic communities. We must nevertheless keep in mind that the conditions discussed at the beginning of the chapter are of a more general nature, and hence pre-eminent. They are the first series of filters.

One principal idea dominates the social organization constituted by the monastery: the defence of its interests. This is quite generally shared by all other types of social organizations. Whereas most of them, however, limit themselves to material and social interests as a means of natural and cultural survival, the monastery primarily defends the existence of a transcendental meaning. The framework of its action is in fact both spiritual and material. Here we have deliberately used the term 'monastery' and not 'monasticism'. This differentiation is very easy to explain: abstract notions like the latter expression do not create written documents; only individuals within living institutions do.

What more can be deduced from what has already been stated? All the written documents, and thus all those preserved, are most likely to reflect the basic idea of self-interest. Take charters for instance: they nearly always served to confirm the rights of the institution they were meant for. Their side-effects, if not the essence of their existence, are therefore most likely to be system-confirming. The historian should be aware of this when he uses this documentation for the reconstruction of the past. It must be stressed that the less variation there is in the typology, and thus in the origin and the function of the documents, the more one-sided the information will be and the more misleading the reconstruction of the past.

5

CAN PROPORTIONS BE MEASURED?

In order to illustrate what we have just said, we can try to 'measure proportions'. We could try for instance to see, for a given area and for a given time, what proportion of all documents available are of monastic origin, and in particular how many of them were written or used by monks.

Such a calculation might prove a difficult undertaking. Moreover, the result might possibly prove misleading because of the degree to which monasteries were a significant presence in the selected area. Yet we can make a serious effort in this direction, at least for the medieval territories included in present-day Belgium, using for that purpose the data base built up by Cetedoc at the Catholic University of Louvain (in Louvain-la-Neuve). It now comprises all the charters written in, or dealing with, that area before 1200.

The results show that in the first period for which charters survive, that is 634–700, 47 out of a total of 48 (98%) have their origin or setting in a religious community. Throughout the following centuries the percentage remains significant, albeit decreasing. In the eleventh century it drops to 65%, rising again in the next to 74%.[3] It would be difficult to calculate how the proportion evolved afterwards, even for a smaller area. The number of sources (produced and still available) grew so much, that it becomes nearly incalculable.[4] There is no doubt at all, however, that the percentage of documents written in or for monasteries had diminished strikingly by that time. The use of writing had not only spread over larger groups within the Church, but had also steadily invaded new circles of secular administration. The general impression that such a shift had occurred could be confirmed by using the files of narrative texts, for the same period and for the same area, available at Cetedoc.[5]

All these statements point in fact in the direction indicated by M. T.

---

[3] The calculation by Cetedoc is based upon the *Nouveau Wauters*. Brussels, 1989, vol. i (microfiches). The renewed increase in the twelfth century is explained by the rise of new religious movements (for instance canons) and by a more rapid evolution within the Church in the direction of more writing.

[4] For example 31 charters for the last quarter of the seventh century, and respectively 74, 93, 169, 441 and 2767 for the corresponding periods of the following centuries (data calculated by Cetedoc).

[5] They are listed in L. Genicot & P. Tombeur (dir.), *Index Scriptorum Latino-Belgicorum Medii Aevi*. Brussels, 1973–1979, 4 vol.; cf. also P. Tombeur (dir.), *Thesaurus Linguae Scriptorum Operumque Latino-Belgicorum Medii Aevi. Première partie. Le vocabulaire des origines à l'an mil.* Brussels, 1986, 5 vol.

Clanchy when calculating an increase in the use of sealing wax by the English Royal Chancery.[6] What has been reported allows us to reach some important conclusions. We are now able to answer the question as to the extent to which we can reconstruct medieval history, and as to the extent to which we can become aware of the specific contribution of monks and assess the impact of their ideal. The overwhelming preponderance of documents with a religious origin inevitably signifies that it is difficult, at least for the early medieval period, to obtain a representative overall view of society.

The monks, who constituted something like *0.5% of the population*, were responsible for *from 65% to 98% of the written information*. When we add to this fact the consideration that documents are, and are intended to be, interest-supporting and system-confirming, it should be obvious that there exists a general danger that the importance of monastic influence will come to be over-emphasized. As a medievalist this is like wearing badly focused glasses . . . and it would be very unkind to remark that some of us hardly notice that we wear glasses at all. Let us be aware of the limitations and distortions which these artificial proportions can give in reconstructing the past.

For historians it is an advantage that in later centuries the proportion decreases. We are then able to reconstruct a more representative image of society. However, the risk of a distorting lens remains apparent. A diminishing percentage of monastic documents does not necessarily mean a corresponding change in the social impact of the monastic ideal or life-style. It only indicates a shift in the character (identity) of those who have mastered the skill of writing.

---

[6] *Op. cit.*, p. 43: from 3.63 lb. in the period 1226–1230 to 31.90 lb. in the period 1265–1271.

2

The Global Vision of the Created World

THE FULFILMENT OF GOD'S WILL

The most striking, if predictable characteristic of medieval society is the coherent place it gives itself within the global vision of Creation. The biblical words of Genesis and the Gospel of St John provided the framework of an unseparated, and unseparable, co-existence between God and man, between the spiritual and the material world, between life and death.

Life, and all things which existed, were considered as making sense. There *had* to be sense, as medieval society saw everything fitting into the broader panorama of what Almighty God intended by Creation and continued to intend into Eternity. Creation was, in essence, the expression of His own free will.

The fundamental principle of this way of thinking was quite simple: the God in whom the medieval Church officially believed was a unique God ('I am that I am'). This meant that He gathered within Himself all the characteristics thought of as positive qualities, and this He did in a perfect and complete way. God was perfectly good, perfectly just, and perfect in all other ways. The reflection and realization of His will could not be different from what He Himself was. According to Genesis, God looked on seven occasions at what He had created and He 'saw that it was good' (Gen. 1:4, 10, 12, 18, 21, 25, 31).

To this way of thinking the earthly world and earthly life could not be essentially different from life in Heaven as they were all the expression of God's will. They could differ only as a result of a discrepancy between Spirit and Matter. In fact, Christianity believed that the qualitative discrepancy between Spirit and Matter was only the result of Original Sin, committed by Adam and Eve. Man's free will, exercised in eating of the Tree of Knowledge of Good and Evil (Gen. 2:17), had destroyed the paradisal life God had created for them. Evil existed henceforth among Mankind. Before that, vanity (*superbia*), had already led to the fall of the Angels. The devils had therefore become the incarnation of Evil, the counterpart of the Good God. In sinning, they had also shown that they could make decisions contrary to the perfect goodness of God and His purpose, when He made Creation good. From the third chapter of

Genesis onwards, the gap is revealed between Heaven, described as especially delightful (in the Book of Revelation it became the Celestial Jerusalem) (c. 21), and the World on Earth. Childbirth would be painful, and labour necessary to provide food (Gen. 3:16, 17, 19). Man had disobeyed; God was angered and punished him.

I do not intend to pursue farther the theological details of Creation and Sin, but I must nonetheless stress some of the major characteristics, especially the religious opinion of Life. The medieval world view moulded by Christian doctrine had a negative attitude towards matter and was to a large extent pessimistic.[1] People thought that the ideal of Creation had vanished. Evil had struck, even though that man had been created good. Evil was not just a notion; it was a reality for which the Bible provided the *imaginaire*: Hell with its devils and fire, the deceptions and ambushes of the 'Great Enemy', and the perpetuity of pain for those who follow his misleading and devastating counsel.

The World, once good, had become bad. The description given by some early medieval writers, especially their predictions of the consequences of the Fall and the rise of Evil, testifies to the fundamental pessimism about the World of early Christianity. As suspicious as this religion was towards matter, it was positive towards the certainty of the final victory of Good, and thus towards the final reward. Generally, Evil was not regarded as sufficiently powerful to overcome God at the very end. Certainly, some movements can be distinguished within Christianity, for whom the fatal risk that Evil might win could not be denied.[2] Such movements never succeeded, however, in imposing their opinion on more than a limited constituency. Yet a movement of this type, known as Manicheism, had a remarkably long life, even witnessing a resurgence from the eleventh century onwards. Contrary to their ancient counterparts, these Neo-Manichees considered themselves mostly as Christian, although their opinion on Evil was not.

St Augustine of Hippo, the greatest among all patristic writers, played a major role, through his interpretation of the Bible, in moulding Christian theology. In his *Confessions* (x, 16) he tells how sinful his youth had been, and how he had come under the spell of Manicheism. He modelled Christian doctrine with a vigour comparable only to St Paul's, a model mainly concerned with free will and therefore with the relationship between God and Man. In his most outstanding book, *The City of*

---

[1] Cf. R. Lerner, 'Refreshment of the Saints: the Time after Antichrist as a Station for earthly Progress in Medieval Thought', in: *Traditio*, 32, 1976, pp. 97–144.

[2] Cf. E. Pagels, *Adam, Eve, and the Serpent*. New York, 1988, and P. Brown, *The Body and Society*. New York, 1988.

God (*De civitate Dei*), St Augustine constructed a theological view which has survived well into our own time. This view holds that the world of God is ideal, and the world of Men should imitate and reflect it. There *must* be a link between the two. The latter cannot be severed from the former. Therefore, the responsibility of rulers on earth is a responsibility towards God. They govern in God's name and by God's grace (*gratia Dei*, as it is called in rulers' titles), and at the end of their life they will be called to present their final reckoning. God will appraise what they did, as if He were the landowner in St Matthew's Gospel (20:1).

This view of an overall synthesis between the order in Heaven and the (dis)order on Earth took a long time to be known, disseminated, and accepted; and even longer to be put into practice. In fact only the Carolingian Emperors, Charlemagne and Louis the Pious in the late eighth and early ninth centuries, at least as far as western Europe is concerned, put St Augustine's view into practice or, to be more precise, aimed to do so. Their legislation which followed a period characterized by a predominantly customary legal tradition, breathed a sense of responsibility towards God. The same interpretation of government during the reign of the Ottonian Emperors by the end of the tenth century can be recognized with certainty. Both dynasties believed strongly that the Christian Roman Empire of Constantine the Great had to be renewed, and had to survive. The 'Renovation of the Empire' (*Renovatio Imperii*) was their task *and* their ideal. In fact it was ideologically necessary. In the traditional, teleological, vision of history (especially that based upon St Jerome) the Roman Empire was considered to be the last stage in the history of mankind. Were the Roman Empire to die, the consequence would be the end of Time.[3]

THE INELUCTABLE DECAY OF CREATION

The coming of the Messiah was, according to the Old Testament, the solution God presented for the salvation of mankind. In the New Testament the coming of Christ, the Son of the Living God, as a man on earth fulfilled that prophecy. 'He was in the world, and the world was made through him, yet the world knew him not. He came to his own home, and his own people received him not' (John 1:10–11). Hence, a final step was foreseen by God. His wrath would destroy all of Creation during Armageddon or the Last Judgment. A fundamental pessimism, however, looms over the hope for salvation. The God of anger can be seen on

---

[3] K. H. Krüger, *Die Universalchroniken*. Turnhout, 1976, pp. 23–30 (Typologie des sources du moyen âge occidental, 16).

the tympana of Romanesque churches. There He is the Supreme Judge, who separates the good from the evil on the Day of Doom. Thus, the whole history of mankind and Creation itself is one of gradual decay.

This ideology as such is not unique to Christianity. The Old Testament, and hence the Jewish tradition, knew 'Four reigns' parallelling the metals and their malleability. The prophecies of Daniel (Dan. 2:31–35), for example, present an image having a head of fine gold, chest and arms of silver, belly and thights of bronze, legs of iron and feet partly of iron and partly of clay. A stone rolled down, which smote the image and 'became a great mountain and filled the whole earth'.[4] Even Christ's coming and His salvation could not in fact change people's conviction in the inevitability of the process.

There had once been the ideal Garden of Eden, a society freed from the sorrows of life and at the same time imagined as the land of Cockaigne. Mankind had sinned and was banished from the Garden. The forces of Evil increasingly overran it and would only be overcome on the Last Day.

In terms of cultural history, then the process of time was considered to be one of a linear decline. Such an interpretation was, and in fact would remain, long lasting. All through the ages, up to the eighteenth-century period of Enlightenment, this interpretation of time was current, if not dominant. Only the rational thinking of the *philosophes* and the concomitant advance of the theoretical and applied sciences, would invert, albeit not completely, the linear direction of the supposed evolution toward decay. As a matter of fact, the Old Testament prophet's vision disappeared in that same century to become merely an element of the *imaginaire historique*. A line going obliquely down from the top to the bottom: this is how the medieval and early modern interpretation of the historical process can be visualized. Every step forward was felt to be necessarily a step downwards, and toward greater decay. The notion of 'progress', in its etymological sense of moving ahead, could in this view only be interpreted negatively. One step after the other was in fact thought to lead to a lower level. Hence 'progress' and 'decay' – which we generally use as antonyms – were synonyms to most of the pre-Enlightenment opinions. In such a context just two things could be hoped for: stability and restoration.

The first is stability. It means that no move be made at all. Staying on the spot is the guarantee of not falling. Evidently, the meaning was topographical; stability is a topographical ideal. It was imposed upon

---

[4]   E. Marsch, *Biblische Prophetie und chronographische Dichtung. Stoff- und Wirkungsgeschichte der Vision des Propheten Daniels nach Dan. VII.* Berlin, 1972; K.H. Krüger, *op. cit.*, p. 24–28.

the serfs, for example, who were not allowed to leave the manorial estates on which they worked. Escaped serfs, who found a base in the newly developing towns and boroughs, were pursued by their masters and easily recognized by their dialect. Hence stability also meant control. He who exerted power organized institutions in order to enhance this control. He himself, however, was not compelled to the limits of this control, as he belonged in turn to a higher system of imposed stability. The matrimonial policy is a striking example of how the ranking of intended stability functioned. Where we have evidence, serfs do not seem to be allowed to marry outside the group of their lord's serfs; or else they needed his consent to do so. But the lord was entitled to find a bride outside his region, and if he belonged to one of the great families, he certainly married a girl from far abroad.

Stability, furthermore, meant the preservation of a common memory. In a time when written documents were rare, the experience of social groups was guaranteed by what was transmitted orally. Movement of people interrupted the cycle of the transfer of knowledge and thus it was prohibited, or at least to be avoided. In moments of uncertainty the 'elders' of the community were consulted about the past, about the duties and rights of the lord and his serfs, or the precise boundaries of the lands. Elders could relay the ways in which major problems had once been settled: plagues, famines, and the like. They could perhaps remind people about rational solutions such as building dikes to prevent floods, or more likely they would remind people of inherited ritual: those processions or offerings that had proved succesful in reaching God or the saints, or the lingering survival of pagan divinities.

Stability, moreover, implied obedience. The moral value of obedience was socially explained by need, as actually experienced. For all that occurred in the past there had been a solution, and that solution was recorded in the memory of the elders. 'Trial and error' had perhaps been successful in the past, but it was to be avoided in the present. Never try new solutions! Common opinion, as shaped by the steady progress toward decay, held that new inventions were worse than the traditional systems to which one had become accustomed. Innovations would not be of any *utility* at all. *Inutilis* in both classical and medieval Latin, not only meant 'useless', it especially meant 'harmful'. Even St Bernard had to defend himself against foreseeable criticism: 'anything I say will be decried as an innovation'.[5]

Obedience, in this context, is *a* major – if not *the* major – clue to understanding how primitive, slowly changing societies functioned and

---

[5] Bernard of Clairvaux, *Five Books on Consideration. Advice to a Pope*. Kalamazoo, MI, 1976, p. 112 (Cistercian Father Series).

thus to understanding the society of the middle ages. The importance given to obedience is directly the inverse of the importance given to innovation. Traditional experience, the mortar of stability, would be hindered by an infringement of obedience; the results of new experimentation would not. Within a 'slow-motion world' such as the middle ages the entire educational system, by which I mean the means of adapting the individual to society and social behaviour, stresses obedience, and even submission.[6]

Whenever normative evidence exists concerning this phenomenon, it deals with the importance of the 'elders', the *seniores* as they are called. *Senior* (the elder) and *sanior* (the more sane) bear the same sense, even though they mean different things. We will have the opportunity to recall this problem later on. He who is 'older' is 'wiser' because of his age. He who is 'wise' is considered wise, even in his youth, when he displays the life-style proper to elderly people, a metaphor already used to describe the young St Benedict.[7]

Within monastic life both stability and obedience played an outstanding role. In the Benedictine tradition, and in some other monastic movements, stability constituted one of the vows. Vows are solemn promises that were, and still are, the pillars of the monks' religious life: vows of chastity, poverty, obedience (!) to the abbot, and stability. The first three are always and at all times present, despite different formulae or interpretations of religious life.

Monasteries had functioned therefore as small groups ('social categories') within the larger social framework. Although all such groups did not necessarily share similar goals (lay people, for example, aiming perhaps at individual wealth or power), the basic *ideals* were identical. In fact, if there was one thing that Christianity managed to impose on the middle ages, it was precisely the *theoretical* acknow-

---

6 Cf. L. Milis, 'Dispute and Settlement in Medieval Cenobitical Rules', in: *Bulletin de l' Institut historique belge de Rome – Bulletin van het Belgisch Historisch Instituut te Rome*, lx, 1990, pp. 43–63.

7 Gregory the Great, *Dialogi* (Grégoire le Grand, *Dialogues*, ed. A. de Vogüé. Paris, 1979, ii, prol., p. 126 (Sources chrétiennes, 260)): 'from the time of his childhood he had an old heart'. Cf. Bernard of Clairvaux, *Five Books on Consideration. Advice to a Pope*, p. 121: 'It is your duty . . . to summon from everywhere, and to associate with yourself, not youths, but elders, men who are old not so much in age but in virtue . . .'. This explains why sometimes younger monks or canons were elected as abbots. They had demonstrated an 'elderly wisdom' (cf. abbot Walter of Arrouaise, elected at age 25, who says about himself 'such a boy on the seat of the Holy Fathers', *Fundatio monasterii Arroasiensis*, ed. O. Holder-Egger, Monumenta Germaniae Historica, Scriptores, xv, 2, p. 1123).

ledgment of a shared value system. The Virtues, the expression of this system, could only be approached by way of control, and control made things as static as possible. It could not have been otherwise than that human wickedness, the result of the Fall, would be restrained in this way. The importance of obedience and stability inevitably enhanced the role played by the 'senior' monks. The abbot is, as the word etymologically means, the father, to whom all obey. St Benedict says in the Prologue of his Rule 'Listen, my son, to your master's precepts, and incline the ear of your heart. Receive willingly and carry out effectively your loving father's advice, that by the labour of obedience you may return to Him from whom you had departed by the sloth of disobedience' (Prol. 1–2).[8] The younger members of the community also have to consider what the older monks have to say. Even the abbot had to consult his *seniores* on special occasions (Ch. iii). The incomplete parallel between 'wise' and physically 'old', as we already stressed, is also found in St Benedict's marvellous Rule (Ch. iii, 3). Even if it breathes a paternalistic and conservative ideology, the text proposed – perhaps precisely as a result of this – a way of life characterized by remarkable equilibrium.

Second to stability was restoration. Preventing decay meant that the fatal line downwards had to be avoided, that a step backwards on the ladder had to be taken. Backwards meant at the same time higher and better. As a result of this mental attitude, which lasted until the eighteenth century, any change to be mentally acceptable, especially for the Church, had to be presented as a return to something past; certainly not the past as it historically had been, but as interpreted and imagined to have been.[9] Hence past meant a past idealized by men, coloured with imagination and seen through the filter of the unknown and the selection of reality. 'In our time things were better; now everything is going wrong.' We frequently read this kind of lament in medieval documents, and let us admit that it remains alive in everyday speech.

As a matter of fact, this ideological step back is reflected in the vocabulary used. All change had to be presented as the *re*storation of an old situation, as a *re*formation or a *re*naissance. Change needed to look back ideologically, even if in actuality it did not.

---

8 This and other quotations from the Rule are taken from the translation of L. J. Doyle, *St. Benedict's Rule for Monasteries*, Collegeville, MN, 1948.
9 B. Smalley, 'Ecclesiastical Attitudes to Novelty *c*.1100–*c*.1250', in: *Church Society and Politics*, ed. D. Baker. Oxford, 1975, pp. 113–31 (Studies in Church History, 12).

FUNDAMENTAL PESSIMISM
AND PRESUMED MONASTIC CREATIVITY

As the World was inevitably marching towards decay, just as inevitably the Day of Doom was approaching. A negative concept of matter, then, was a striking feature of the mental attitude of medieval religious people towards their own religious and cosmic setting.[10] Optimism *could* only be attained once the final stage, life in Heaven after the Judgement, was certain of being reached. But any certainty was obstructed by the fear that it would never be attained. Let us remind ourselves of that magnificent thirteenth-century sequence which was to remain the most touching part of the Latin funeral liturgy: the *Dies irae*. It expresses the feeling we discuss here in a frightened and frightening line: 'Cum vix iustus sit securus' . . . 'when even the just can hardly be secure'.

One may wonder whether the foregoing discussion has overstressed the importance of the underlying value system on actual behaviour. Perhaps life was more joyful than pictured in these pages; there were many feasts, tournaments for the nobility, intemperate meals for the urban guild-brothers, and fairs for the country folk in honour of their patron saint. This is all true, yet let us not forget that the pressure of Christian ideology was always present, reminding revellers that sin was embedded in every feeling of happiness, unless it was spiritual in character and directed towards God. Feeling comfortable in the earthly environment and taking satisfaction from it for its own sake was accepted as an escape but only on limited occasions, pre-established by tradition, the 'world upside down', as such occasions were to be known. Carnivals were meant to be moments of travesty, rooted in pagan times: people disguised as animals, or as members of the opposite sex. Christianity poured disapproval on these moments. Yet even so it could not eradicate them completely. The tradition behind them was too strong, and moreover these events functioned socially as release valves. Even now, when genuine carnivals survive but rarely, they tend to include, apart from the customary mask or disguise – albeit temporarily tolerated for the occasion – the uttering of 'reproach' to dominant bosses, spouses or parents, a venting of all the frustration accumulated throughout the year. The necessity of a once-yearly escape created a once-yearly

---

[10] As far as lay people are concerned, the validity of such an overall pessimistic view might be questioned (Cf. R. and C. Brooke, *Popular Religion in the Middle Ages, Western Europe, 1000–1300*. London, 1984, p. 155, and C. Brooke, *The Medieval Idea of Marriage*. Oxford, 1989, pp. 186–202). It depends in fact on the degree of penetration of the Christian doctrine.

tolerance. The continuity of social order, the (only partly adequate) expression of the dominating mental pattern, was guaranteed by regulated infringement; rule had to be preserved by regulated violation.

The *contemptus mundi*, the contempt of the world, is the dominant ideology of Christianity. It is the paradigmatic medieval religious ideal, even though it is stressed more explicitly in some periods (as for instance in the late eleventh and early twelfth centuries) than in others. When authors such as St Anselm of Canterbury or Conrad of Hirsau, published at that time treatises on the theme, this was only because to them, life had become too devoted to secular pursuits. In their eyes a fundamental change was an urgent necessity. Hence these writings expressed the conviction of decay. The mental system, already strictly formulated, had to be increasingly re-formulated as time went on.

Pessimism and rejection of the world are the key operative concepts in medieval religious thought. What do they imply for those who study the social dimension of religion, and more specifically that of monasticism? What was the contribution of angel-like monks to a society of earth-bound men? How could pessimism and the rejection of the world possibly have led to 'progress', as 'progress' was expected to end in decay? Was conservatism – preventing things from becoming worse – not the aim of the monks' life on earth? Was escaping the world – all year round, all throughout life – not the only 'sense' that monks could have operated render if they were to attain eternal life? If monks did play a social role (meaning oriented towards the World), was it not, then, the result of the impossibility of fulfilling the spiritual ideal (of being oriented towards Heaven)? Does it mean, finally, that perhaps it was only their weaknesses that kept monks among men and socially useful to them? These are the questions answered in the book.

3

The Sources of Material Wealth

THE RURAL SETTING

The Vow of Poverty

'This vice especially is to be cut out of the monastery by the roots. Let no one presume to give or receive anything without the Abbot's command,[1] or to have anything as his own – anything whatever, whether book or tablets or pen or whatever it may be – since they are not permitted to have even their bodies or wills at their disposal; but for all their necessities let them look to the Father of the monastery. And let it be unlawful to have anything which the Abbot has not given or allowed. Let all things be common to all, as it is written, and let no one say or assume that anything is his own' (Ch. xxxiii). These words of St Benedict very clearly stress the economic as well as the spiritual position of the monks. They are not allowed to have any private property, all possessions are shared and the abbot is responsible for the support of the monks and for the management of their collective property. In another chapter of his Rule the 'Holy Legislator' described what was to be done with the possessions of a new monk entering into religious life: 'If he has any property, let him either give it beforehand to the poor or by solemn donation bestow it on the monastery' (Ch. lviii). When young children are offered by their parents (we will deal with this practice later on) the latter have to take an oath that they will never give them anything to own for themselves. They can, however, make a donation which will become part of the common property. If the parents own nothing, they do not have to give anything, which means that according to the Rule a 'dowry' (as it is called later on) is not a condition for entering monastic life. These prescriptions are the result of what 'we have learned by experience'. What St Benedict had already noticed in his time would obviously remain the current and ever-recurring difficulty of monastic life: the struggle between the ideal of shared property and the reality of personal or family selfishness.

---

[1] I have changed *leave* to *command* in Doyle's translation, the Latin word being *iussio*.

The excerpts are very clear: the denial of private property does not imply in any way a materially poor life-style. In the middle ages the word *poor* did not primarily refer to the person without goods but to one who lacks power.[2] As the monk no longer has 'power even over his own body' (Ch. lviii) he is necessarily poor. Refinement in garments or even in food was not felt to be opposed to the letter of the Rule. Nevertheless such practices were to be considered dangerous to the authentic interpretation of St Benedict's words.

Great Land-Ownership

The Rule implicitly permits the constitution of a demesne, as it takes into account gifts made to the abbey. Though St Benedict first says that the possessions of the novice may be distributed to the poor, he takes it for granted in other chapters of the Rule that they were in fact to be given to the abbey. From early on the dowry seems to have become a general practice and even a condition of entry, unless the historical evidence can be shown to be misleading.[3] It could have happened, at least theoretically, that some people entered without any gift, and that this has left no trace in documents since these mainly record transactions of rights and goods. In the reality of religious common life, however, free entries are very unlikely and could only be occasional, as a lifelong subsistence without any payment to act as counterpart would have been seen as a burden for the community as a whole. That this was so can be proved indirectly. As the history of the monastic movement often shows, periods of intensified and deeper spirituality returned to the literal interpretation of the Rule. When this happened for instance very clearly in the late eleventh and early twelfth century, people without means seem indeed to have gained free entry into the monasteries. Within a short time, however (a few years, not more) a very strict system of segregation was introduced, mainly among the Cistercians, whereby the illiterate and 'common' members of the community were separated from the literate members, presumably of wealthier origin. The latter were the monks, called 'fathers'; the former were the *conversi* or lay brethren. They were

---

2   K. Bosl, *Armut Christi, Ideal der Mönche und Ketzer, Ideologie der aufsteigenden Gesellschaftsschichten vom 11. bis zum 13. Jahrhundert*. Munich, 1981, p. 6 (Bayerische Akademie der Wissenschaften. Philosophisch-Historische Klasse. Sitzungsberichte 1981, 1).

3   J. H. Lynch, *Simoniacal Entry into Religious Life from 1000 to 1260. A Social, Economic and Legal Study*. Columbus, 1976, describes how dowries in the sense of forced gifts were condemned by the twelfth- and thirteenth-century canonists, as the buying of a holy thing.

not allowed to become monks, an indication of a rigid and static discrimination pattern, offending perhaps our opinion on equal rights.[4]

Were the material wealth and the formation of vast demesnes only the result of dowries? The answer is no. When the first monasteries were founded in early medieval Gaul, before ever the Benedictine Rule had any real success outside its home base of central Italy, they adhered to the Christian conversion programme. Their foundation and endowment was usually through royalty, as the kings held themselves responsible for the transition of their people from paganism to Christianity. Very important endowments were procured. One of the most striking examples is the abbey of St-Germain-des-Prés outside the gates of Paris. Its ninth-century inventory of landed property described twenty-two domains, totalling some 32,700 hectares (80,600 acres), and this was only a part of their land holdings.[5] Much of it had already been donated in the Merovingian period as the abbey was founded c. 543. The Merovingian kings had inherited, in fact, the large Roman public (or 'fiscal') demesnes when they came to power in the fifth century. We cannot enter here into the discussion of how and to what extent forms of Roman administration and organization survived through the first centuries of the middle ages, but more and more historians agree that it was fairly general for lands formerly belonging to ancient large landowners to continue to be cultivated, even if the buildings of the manor (*villa*) were destroyed or abandoned as a result of Germanic incursions. The vast property of the royal dynasty, and undoubtedly of the higher nobility in general, both that of Germanic and that of Roman origin, seemed nearly inexhaustible. In the beginning at least. Otherwise, the large donations to several dozen quite rich and powerful abbeys scattered throughout Europe would not have been possible, much less the elaboration of the feudal system, which was supposed to recompense services and loyalty with land. In the end the landed property turned out not to be inexhaustible at all.

It is striking that abbeys or monastic movements in general benefited from the generosity of wealthy donors over long periods, mostly until the time when stricter observances arose. More gifts suggest greater riches and an increased number of monks, but this was not necessarily

---

[4] They commonly wore beards as a mark of class distinction; Cf. G. Constable's Introduction, pp. 128–30 to the *Apologia de barbis*, ed. R. B. C. Huygens, *Apologiae duae*. Turnhout, 1985 (Corpus Christianorum. Continuatio mediaeualis, lxii) and C. N. L. Brooke, 'Priest, deacon and layman, from St Peter Damian to St Francis', in: *The Ministry: Clerical and Lay*, edd. W. J. Sheils and D. Wood. Oxford, 1989, pp. 65–97 (esp. pp. 77–80) (Studies in Church History, 26).

[5] F. L. Ganshof – A. E. Verhulst, 'Medieval Agrarian Society in its Prime', in: *The Cambridge Economic History of Europe*, i, 1966², p. 303.

so, a statement which implies losses or bad management. Often monastic economic decline has been explained, by the contemporary monk as
well as by Church historians, as being the result of moral decadence and
not often enough of managerial incompetence due to the positive monastic ideal of 'spiritual absentmindedness'. Too often business ability on
the part of the monks has been taken for granted[6] and it has been
opposed to presumed short-sighted managerial stupidity on the part of
the nobles. The 'absentmindedness' testified to monastic fervor, but
jeopardized the material wealth with which nobles bestowed the abbeys
in order to gain Heaven. This means that many of the interventions of
lay people in monastic affairs, as lay abbots or advocates, were not
necessarily attempts at usurpation (as the documents, written by monks
and for monks, constantly wish us to believe).[7] These interventions may
just as easily be interpreted as the concern of lay people that their *financial* investment in the *religious* function of the abbey (helping them to
win Heaven) should not end up a bad investment.

In order to avoid this lay intervention, perceived as a hindrance, and
to guarantee spiritual, institutional and economic freedom, immunity
was often granted by the rulers. Abbeys and their possessions were
removed from the normal secular administrative and juridical framework in order to procure a large degree of autonomy for them. Monastic
(and more generally ecclesiastical) immunity became a recurrent, albeit
not a general, feature of the late Merovingian and of the Carolingian
period.

As the foundation of abbeys was a result of what we shall later on in
this book refer to as 'functional reciprocity', a rich aristocracy automatically meant richly endowed abbeys. All kinds of reasons, however,
were responsible for this concentration of power and wealth slipping
through the fingers of the very few hands which held it: feudalism, the
inheritance system, invasions, and inadequate communication. The result of feudalism was that landed property was transferred from a few
persons of higher social levels to a larger number of lower-ranking
persons (the king to his counts, the counts to their knights).[8] Inheritances

---

6 Cf. G. D. Gyon, 'L'état et l'exploitation du temporel de l'abbaye bénédictine
   Sainte-Croix de Bordeaux (XIe–XIVe siècles)', in: *Revue Mabillon*, n.s. 1, 1990,
   pp. 241–83: 'La mentalité économique des religieux a été souvent décrite,
   mais, telle qu'on la représente [. . .] elle paraît bien idéalisée' (p. 242).
7 F. J. Felten, *Äbte und Laienäbte im Frankenreich. Studie zum Verhältnis von Staat
   und Kirche im früheren Mittelalter*. Stuttgart, 1980, especially pp. 47–58 and
   305–07. In the eleventh and twelfth centuries 'converted' noblemen continued to manage the endowment they had given when entering monastic
   life (J. Wollasch, 'Parenté noble et monachisme réformateur', in: *Revue historique*, 104, 1980, pp. 3–24).
8 In England this centrifugal effect of feudalism was virtually nonexistent. The

were traditionally equally divided among the sons, which meant that even a very wealthy family might see its fortune break up in a few generations, in spite of the extreme importance of clan-solidarity. The invasions of the Vikings, the Muslims and the Magyars from the eighth to the eleventh century caused in large, if quite separate, parts of Europe devastation and loss of property through plundering or ransoms, even if these were perhaps less critical than is generally thought. The extent of the Carolingian Empire was too great in relation to its ineffective communication system. It stretched from just south of the Pyrenees to the borders of Denmark. This huge territory did not admit of any serious and efficient control, especially in times of insecurity. All these factors accelerated the decomposition of concentrated power and of concentrated land-ownership, two notions which are virtually synonymous at this period.

For monastic life this meant that, socially speaking, the average rank of founders or benefactors steadily decreased. From the post-Carolingian period onwards, let us say from the tenth century on, the extent of the endowments could no longer compete with what had been given to older houses. The wealth which the extremely rich abbey of Cluny (founded in 909) was able to gather might be cited as an objection. However, the original endowment of the founder William of Aquitaine was not actually much more important than what other, comparably wealthy, nobles donated to their abbeys. The many subsequent donations, stimulated by the fact that Cluny changed the system of autonomy, traditional among Benedictine abbeys into a centralized order, explains the enormous influx of riches, realised visually in its successive building activities. Generally speaking, newly founded abbeys were smaller than the older ones, in terms of land as well as of the number of their monks or of the importance of their buildings and precious manuscripts. As a result, Benedictine abbeys of the eleventh or twelfth century were seldom able to boast a demesne of more than a few thousand hectares. Moreover, this was also the result of the competition with the very determined Cistercian movement in which they were involved. This general discrepancy between the older foundations and the more recent ones was still apparent at the Dissolution of the houses in sixteenth- century Britain and eighteenth- or nineteenth-century continental Europe.

We have only spoken so far of landed property in general. In reality a whole range of different forms must be distinguished, for the most part chronologically determined. Often the older endowments were com-

system itself was worked out after the Norman Conquest of 1066, much later than on the Continent, and with a knowledge of what the disintegrating effects had been there.

posed of large agricultural units, Roman *fiscs* for instance, which normally stretched over several villages. The gifts could be smaller, but until the eleventh century they generally covered at least an entire manor, we would now say a village. This suggests at the same time that not only the land itself was given, but also the moveable property belonging to it: serfs and animals and equipment. The drain of possessions, the fragmentation of the estates (as a result of inheritance) and a greater competition among an increased number of religious houses made gifts from the eleventh century onwards smaller and much less prestigious. It was now only a parcel of farm land, or a family of serfs, or a waste-land which was to be handed over. In the thirteenth century and later the importance of gifts still continued to decrease. Then the rents of houses, for instance, were commonly given. The great number of lawsuits in the later middle ages and in the early modern period not only bears testimony to a more juridically minded society, or to an increased use of writing, but also to a basic need for abbeys to be more cautious about their possessions.

Monastic demesnes were normally composed of other types of income as well, such as tithes, parochial churches and seignorial rights. Tithes constituted, according to the Bible and to the legislation passed by the Frankish king Pippin *c.* 765, the tenth part of the crops, and were intended to be used for the subsistence of the clergy and of the poor.[9] In the post-Carolingian turmoil, however, they were most often usurped by local lords. Only the reforms under Pope Gregory VII stimulated, in the second half of the eleventh century, a restitution movement. In general the tithes did not then come into the hands of the parochial clergy, where they belonged, but they were most frequently given to monasteries. For several reasons the lords found this more favourable. The restitution was a new means of gaining Heaven, a much surer one when paid to virtuous monks than to ordinary clerics. At the same time their own reputation for generosity remained untouched, even if they only gave away illicitly gained goods. Third, the tithes were most often given to their 'own' abbey, the one their kin had founded, and in which children, or at least members of the family, were dwelling as monks or nuns.

The same feeling of unlawfulness burdened lay people owning churches. The ideas Pope Gregory VII had spread were intended to cope with the involvement of lay persons in ecclesiastical matters. According to him, the Church should be dominated by the clergy, and the Church itself should dominate Christian society as a whole. As neither popes nor bishops were materially speaking powerful enough to realize their

---

[9] G. Constable, *Monastic Tithes from their Origins to the Twelfth Century.* Cambridge, 1964, pp.9–31.

ideas, only spiritual coercion remained as a weapon in their struggle. In the same way that tithes were given mostly to monastic houses, so were churches. They very often did not pass into the hands of the bishops, according to canon law and ecclesiastical tradition those responsible for the cure of the souls. The abbeys normally considered the churches only as sources of supplementary income. They gathered the alms and the revenues stemming from liturgical activities and given or paid by the parishioners. When these churches were centres of a devotional cult, the monks derived income from the pilgrims. The abbey (and the abbot personally) normally held the title of rector (*persona*) of these churches. Priests, generally belonging to the secular clergy, were in fact in charge of the parishes as *vicars*. The system of rector and vicar still exists in the Church of England.

Moreover, part of the monastic demesne might well be composed of public or feudal rights. By this we mean such possessions as tolls on bridges and ferries, or mills, grinding being a seignorial privilege. We have now given a (certainly very superficial) idea of what the elements of monastic property were. It helps, however, to imagine how geographically scattered such possessions could be and actually were, how diverse in type and in period of acquisition. A concrete idea can be given for the abbeys of the Rheims area, whose demesnes have been studied in detail. St Rémy had possessions and rights in 189 different places, St Nicaise in 129, Notre-Dame de Mouzon in 115, and St Thierry in 91.[10]

Methods of Cultivation and Management

The figures given allow at least one conclusion to be made: each abbey normally had a demesne, which was at the same time typologically and geographically diversified. This was a way of approaching economic self-sufficiency. Was this only an ideal and an element of the spiritual seclusion, or was it also a reality? The more that economic activity in the middle ages was dominated by agriculture (and so it was, at least until the twelfth century), the more great landowners, ecclesiastical and lay, could rely only on their own production. Even if early medieval trade did not collapse to the extent historians traditionally assumed, it is obvious that it was mainly long-distance trade which was economically fruitful. The precarious transport of precious goods was counterbalanced by a sure gain. Agricultural products, on the other hand, could only be fruitfully shipped from the second half of the middle ages onwards as a result of better transport facilities. All this signifies that

[10] F. Poirier – Coutansais, *Les abbayes bénédictines du diocèse de Reims*. Paris, 1974 (Gallia Monastica, i).

when a landowner needed food, he had to create his own supply system. When he needed luxury articles, he could buy them.

Among the managerial systems in agriculture the so-called *manorial organization* seems to have been the most developed, even if it was mainly a characteristic of the region between the Rhine and the Loire rivers. Historians have long debated whether this *villa*-system, as it is also called, was of Merovingian or of Carolingian origin, and even to what extent late-Roman manors, the *latifundia*, may have served as model or antecedent.[11] Whatever the final answer may be, the system is best known in its 'classic' form, that is to say in the second quarter of the ninth century when it seems fully organized. It is difficult, however, to form any conclusions as to just how general the system really was, since the historical evidence is principally of monastic origin and deals mostly with monastic possessions. Scarcely any information on large lay landownership is available. Nevertheless legislative texts issued by Charlemagne describe how the royal manors were to be administered, and this in roughly the same way as the monastic *villae* were organized. Hence, it is very likely that there were no major differences with lay management, not so much because we believe in the strength of the Carolingian legislation, but because the system had a self-evident simplicity given the period and the social stratification.[12]

Polyptychs, a specific type of document, provide us with information on the juridical, social and agricultural organization of the system. The most famous is the one which abbot Irmino of St-Germain-des-Prés composed in the early ninth century. We are taught that the *villae*, demesnes, constitute the managerial unit. These are to be considered as the precursors of many (and in some regions of western Europe most) of present rural and, to a certain extent, urban communities. The philosophy behind this agricultural activity was to produce as much as possible for home consumption. A variety of lands, cultivated land as well as meadows (for cattle or sheep) and woods (for pigs and timber), was therefore necessary. Part of the agricultural unit was 'in direct exploitation'. Often a 'mayor' represented the owner locally. This happened when the latter was the proprietor of more than one *villa*, or when it belonged to a religious institution. The work on the fields was done partly by tied personnel living on the manor. The rest of the work was

---

[11] See Y. Morimoto, 'État et perspectives des recherches sur les polyptyques carolingiens', in: *Annales de l'Est*, 40, 1988, pp. 99–149.
[12] Yet L. Kuchenbuch, 'Die Klostergrundherrschaft im Frühmittelalter. Eine Zwischenbalanz', in: *Herrschaft und Kirche*, ed. F. Prinz. Stuttgart, 1988, pp. 297–343 (Monographien zur Geschichte des Mittelalters, 33) stresses some, all in all small, differences.

provided by free or servile tenants who lived on a number of small farms belonging to the manor. They had to pay for their holdings with their labour, which was normally required two or three days a week. Furthermore they had to pay rents or transport goods if they had horses or carts. When an abbey was the owner, the tenants were, for instance, required to supply wine which was necessary if only for the celebration of the mass. They therefore had to travel to other manors, sometimes hundreds of miles away. The rest of the week the tenants and the members of their family worked on their holding (*mansus*). The lands at their disposal were meant to keep them as self-sufficient as was the manor as a whole.

In the period between the ninth and the twelfth century some technological as well as managerial changes were introduced. The former improved production; the latter brought about the disintegration of the *villa*-system, to the benefit of the tenants. Four changes had an impact on the size of the harvest. A new type of plough was the first. A triennial instead of a biennial rotation of crops was the second (a changing field rotation of winter grain, summer grain and fallow). It allowed more land to be cultivated with a larger variety of cereals and vegetables and thus with less risk of a failed harvest. The third was, at least in northern Europe, the use of horses (instead of the slower oxen), and later on of the horseshoe. The last was the increased use of power, for example, that supplied by water-mills.[13]

These organizational changes led, as we have stated, to an improved position of the tenants, at least from the second half of the eleventh century onwards, as the traditional *villa*-system broke up. Direct exploitation was steadily abandoned; the duties of the farmers decreased, or were commuted into fixed payments (and as such susceptible to inflation). The mediocre productivity which was an inevitable result of the traditional system of imposed labour was certainly one of the major considerations in the change, even if no statistical calculation is possible. As far as can be conjectured from an examination of the sources, there were no, or only slight, differences in the organizational structure be-

13 Lynn White, *Medieval Technology and Social Change*. Oxford, 1962, (New York, 1966[2]), pp. 39–103; G. Duby, *Guerriers et paysans*. Paris, 1973, pp. 211–25. In a challenging article A. Verhulst, 'Agrarische revolutie: mythe of werkelijkheid', in: *Mededelingen Faculteit Landbouwwetenschappen Rijksuniversiteit Gent*, 53, 1, 1988, supports the opinion that the 'innovations' followed, rather than preceded, the population growth of the eleventh to thirteenth centuries. G. Ovitt Jr, 'The Cultural Context of Western Technology: Early Christian Attitudes toward Manual Labor', in: *Technology and Culture*, 27, 1986, pp. 477–500 is right to stress that monks (and Christianity in general) reacted to, rather than created the conditions for, medieval technological innovations.

tween ecclesiastical and lay estates. In fact, when charters inform us of lay manors being given to monasteries, no adaptations are recorded as being held necessary.

In the ninth century a normal tenant's holding covered an area of approximately 15 hectares (37 acres), on ecclesiastical as well as on lay (at least royal) estates. This is probably indicative of a similar standard of living, in both cases very marginal indeed. Some questions, however, can be raised as to whether a more adequate productivity on monastic land was to be expected or not. First of all: what was the impact of the manual labour which the Rule imposed upon the monks? Second: did greater riches lead to more agricultural investment, especially given the fact that mills were costly installations?

The monks' manual labour cannot have had any major effect on the total result of the harvest. This implies our scepticism towards the thesis expressed in Lynn White's book concerning the positive mentality towards labour, said to have characterized monasticism and to have improved 'labour ethics' in general. In fact the meaning of what St Benedict (and also the so-called Master) prescribed in a chapter 'On the Daily Manual Labour' (Ch. xlviii) did not at all point to production as a goal in itself. For both spiritual legislators the specific purpose was to fight idleness, because that was 'the enemy of the soul'. Manual labour was also an exercise in humility. Nearly all civilizations have considered work in the fields as inferior, and reserved for slaves or other underdogs. The red neck was a mark of disgrace to be avoided at all cost. One of the most important things the wealthy, and predominantly noble, monks had to learn was not to feel too proud to do manual, and hence servile work. It testified to their painfully gained humility, but nowhere did the Rule say that they had to work hard or that they were required to be productive. Moreover, in stressing humility as a virtue, the servile character of manual labour persisted. The meaning of the manual labour was thus primarily spiritual and not material. Could it have been material at all? Let us imagine an average abbey of thirteen monks with a landed estate of approximately 2,000 hectares or 5,000 acres, the equivalent of about five villages inhabited by a few hundred persons, a thousand at most,[14] three quarters whom would have been economically active. The thirteen monks had to live partly off the direct agricultural surplus produced by these people: yet only partly, because other sources of income, indirect ones this time, such as alms, provided them with more goods. Their own hours of working (six or seven in summer, less

[14] G. M. Schwarz, 'Village Populations according to the polyptyque of the Abbey of St. Bertin', in: *Journal of Medieval History*, 11, 1985, pp. 31–41. The average population density he gives is lower than that generally accepted.

in winter)[15] could represent hardly anything in the totality of all the labour done. The more so, when we remind ourselves that their work was interrupted by the Divine Office, and was necessarily performed in the immediate neighbourhood of the abbey, that their nutritional pattern was not adapted for heavy work on the land, that not every member of the community was physically able to work, that they underwent blood-letting several times a year, and that other activities (writing, household tasks, or maintenance works) were considered to be manual labour as well. Moreover, it is far from certain that St Benedict's Rule was always assiduously observed on this point. The influential Cluniac movement enhanced the importance of the liturgy in everyday life precisely to the detriment of manual labour.

Within Catholicism it became generally accepted that hard servile work helped to gain Heaven.[16] A link between 'servile work ethics' and monasticism, however, is not apparent. The biblical background for the former can be found in Gen. 3:19, in the need for mankind to earn the necessities for living 'in the sweat of one's brow' and was entirely dis-similar to the victory over idleness which was the target of the Rule. The first was in fact the sublimation of the bare need for marginal survival, the latter a moral weapon for the rich who could, in an economic sense, afford laziness.

The question remains whether monks made more investments for the infrastructure of agriculture, such as, for example, costly mills. The answer is very difficult to give as hardly any documents have survived concerning lay landowners.[17] Yet, we know that the seignorial right of

---

[15] A. de Vogüé, *La Règle de saint Benoît*. Paris, 1971, v, p. 600 (Sources chrétien-nes, 185).

[16] This way of thinking differs, however, from the labour ethics recognized by Max Weber among the early modern Protestant mercantile class (*Protestant Asceticism and the Spirit of Capitalism*, in Max Weber, *Selections in translation*. Ed. W. G. Runciman, transl. E. Matthews. Cambridge, 1978, pp. 138–73 (Translation of *Die Protestantische Ethik und der 'Geist' des Kapitalismus*. 1905). Weber's theory has been applied (in my opinion erroneously) by A. Kieser, 'From Asceticism to Administration of Wealth. Medieval Monasteries and the Pitfalls of Rationalization', in: *Organization Studies*, 8, 1987, pp. 103–23, speaking of a Puritan work ethic created by the monks.

[17] D. Lohrmann, 'Le moulin à eau dans le cadre de l' économie rurale de la Neustrie (VIIe–IXe siècles)', in: *La Neustrie. Les pays au nord de la Loire de 650 à 850*, ed. H. Atsma. Sigmaringen, 1989, pp. 367–404 (especially p. 396) (Bei-hefte der Francia 16/1) stresses the early appearance of water-mills. He very explicitly indicates that numerous mills existed long before the demesnes passed into monastic property. 'Domesday Book' (1086), the most complete survey in the middle ages of the resources of men and wealth suggests that, in England, mills occur on monastic and lay lands alike. It was normal for a

grinding implied that landowners in general were aware of the long-term economic and financial benefit they could derive from mills. Both monks and other possessors made sure that the compulsory use of mills was imposed on the inhabitants of their seigniory,[18] but there is no evidence that any spiritual consideration influenced the policy of the monks, and that is precisely the kind of question we are interested in.

Land Reclamation Activities

The aspects of the subject treated so far apply mainly to the period preceding the twelfth century. Religious involvement was therefore limited to the traditional Benedictine monks, the so-called black Benedictines, a name derived from their black habit. We must also consider the later period which is typified by a vast land reclamation movement. Church historians generally link this activity to the new orders, and mainly to the Benedictine order of Cîteaux. Is this connection really supported by the historical evidence, especially when one considers that many economic historians do not attribute to them the same significance? My purpose is to consider the data by means of a detour, this detour being the 'twelfth-century renaissance'. The expression, first used by Charles Homer Haskins in the 1920s, primarily encompassed intellectual life. Later on its sense was broadened to include all possible aspects of the society of that time which showed such an astonishing impulse of creativity. Demography, economy, institutions, religion, everything seemed to be in ferment. Society changed fundamentally between c. 1050 and 1250.

The explanation of this apparently sudden development is most often sought in economy and demography, as these are considered to be the major vectors of historical evolution. Historians, even when using the same evidence, become involved in long discussions as to whether the preceding period was, or was not, as dark as contemporaneous sources tried to make themselves and us believe. It would be hard to deny, however, that in the ninth century, in other words in the Carolingian epoch, evidence is already available of some land reclamation activity, which might point to both an increasing population and to a possible exhaustion of the soil. Yet nothing suggests any large-scale action whatsoever before the eleventh century. Earlier, more frequently in some regions than in others, the land reclamation movement became a main

village to contain at least one mill when water-power was available (Cf. R. Lennard, *Rural England. 1086–1135. A Study of Social and Agrarian Conditions*. Oxford, 1959, pp. 278–87).

[18] Duby, *Guerriers et paysans*, pp. 212–13.

feature of the vigour of the period between 1050 and 1250. When opportunities at home were lacking (the woods or marches between villages having already been cleared), large estuaries, sea-shores or dense forests were converted into arable lands. At a later stage a migratory movement even led to the colonization of large parts of Slav territory in central and eastern Europe. Such actions, requiring important investments, can only be explained if a demographical pressure really did exist. This is supported by the historical evidence: charters permit us to calculate, at least to a certain extent, the increase in population.[19]

The 'twelfth-century renaissance' was also characterized by a religious revival, the Gregorian Reform. As the expression is understood, it had two major aspects, the first being institutional. From the second half of the eleventh century onwards successive popes tried to 'liberate' the Church from lay interference. The second aspect was much more important, at least where contemporary trends in agriculture are concerned. Some people, both among the clergy and among the laity, were caught by religious enthusiasm and were seduced by what was called the 'Poverty of Christ'.[20] They tried to imitate what the Gospels reported of the life-style of Christ, and what the Acts of the Apostles described as the behaviour of the first Christian community in Jerusalem. This withdrawal from worldly affairs and riches came to be formulated as the slogan 'to follow naked the naked Christ' (*nudus nudum Christum sequi*) which could frequently be heard into the mid-thirteenth century. In terms of religious organization (even if these people very often rejected such structures altogether), a whole range of solutions between eremitism and cenobitism were experimented with. Some survived, other failed. As a rule, the experiments set up by clerics stood more chance of succeeding than those set up by lay persons. Yet this may only imply that the primitive goal (the *propositum*, as it was called) was, or had to be, changed or even betrayed. This happened systematically in a number of hermitages which later became important abbeys. Only the Carthusians, founded in 1084 in the remote reaches of the Alps around Grenoble, successfully combined an eremitical ideal with a cenobitical life-style. In the hilly landscape of Tuscany and Umbria two analogous

---

[19] R. Fossier, *La terre et les hommes en Picardie jusqu' à la fin du XIIIe siècle*. Paris, Louvain, 1968, i, p. 284 thinks that the annual increase must have been something like 0.28% in the third quarter of the twelfth century and 0.72% in the next quarter. For the first two quarters of the thirteenth century the figures are respectively 0.12% and 0.64%.

[20] Works on religious history, following literally the exaggerated discourse of the primary sources, often speak in terms of 'lots of people' or other similar ideas. It would be extremely audacious to advance figures, but to suggest that more than 1% of the population was involved would be exceedingly difficult to believe.

movements had already developed into religious orders decades before: Vallombrosa and Camaldoli. The formation of religious orders normally occurred according to a covenant between participating abbeys, or as the result of a policy of abbey-founding, whereby the 'mother-house' retained a certain authority over its 'daughters'. Some houses, in common with some orders, abandoned the predominant Rule of St Benedict and chose as the basis of their observance one of the Rules attributed to St Augustine (c. 400). This famous theologian had imposed common life upon his cathedral clergy in Hippo, in modern Algeria. Afterwards, during the Carolingian epoch, the so-called canonical movement had experienced a new impulse, and now did so again, at the end of the eleventh and the beginning of the twelfth century. Other reformers preferred to fix their attention more upon a renewed reading of St Benedict's Rule which stressed its original meaning. Although Cîteaux, in Burgundy, was not the only one to return to the literal observance (there is for instance the Savigny movement as well), it was by far the most important. In 1098 a number of Benedictine monks left their abbey of Molesme in order to create for themselves the possibility of living 'authentically'. After a while, and especially following the arrival of an active young man who stimulated his contemporaries with his dynamism, the movement developed and within a short time it competed with Cluny, whose appeal for a while it greatly surpassed. The young man would become known as St Bernard of Clairvaux. From the beginning the attitude of the Cistercians towards labour differed fundamentally from that traditional among the black Benedictines. The former said it was illicit to live from the proceeds of other people's labour. This was in stark contrast to the black monks, whose economic system and bodily survival depended precisely on what was produced by their farmers. Rents and tithes, the two main sources of income for Benedictines, were rejected by Cîteaux. As one of the primitive legislative texts of this order put it: 'The monks of our order have to draw their food from the work of their hands, the work on the fields and the raising of cattle' and it forbade the possession of 'Churches, altars, (income from) burials, tithes from other people's work or raising, villages, serfs, census from lands, revenues from ovens or mills . . .'[21] Although Cistercians thus did not share the opinion of the Benedictines on how to earn their living, their attitude was alike in that they did not 'intend to encourage productivity or efficiency in . . . manual labour'.[22]

Traditional Benedictine abbeys could be involved in the land reclama-

---

[21] *Les plus anciens textes de Cîteaux*, edd. J. de la Croix Bouton & J. B. Van Damme. Achel, 1974, *Summa Cartae Caritatis et Capitula*, ch. xv & xxiii, pp. 123–24 (Cîteaux. Commentarii Cistercienses. Studia et Documenta, ii).

[22] L. M. Sullivan, 'Workers, Policy-makers and Labor Ideals in Cistercian Legis-

tion movement in the same way as any other wealthy land-owner. It was an investment which after some years of risk and loss yielded much more than ordinary land did, less fertile and more exhausted as it already was by a long period of cultivation and an inadequate system of fertilization. Benedictine abbeys participated as landowners indeed, but not as a result of any spiritual consideration. There is no doubt that we should forget the image of their monks working the lands by themselves.

And what about the Cistercians? Their refusal to benefit from other people's productivity implied a manual labour program. Nevertheless, it does not in itself explain their participation in the reclamation movement. Two other conditions had a much more important influence upon what happened: their search for topographical isolation and the bargaining minds of the benefactors. The white monks' ideal (Cistercians wore a white habit of natural wool as a sign of humility) was to settle 'in the Desert'. It was no longer the true *desertum* of the anchorites of late antiquity, but a remote site, cleared for example in a wood, far from other human settlements.[23] In a treatise called *The Book on the Different Orders and Callings of the Church* (*Liber de diversis Ordinibus et Professionibus qui sunt in Aecclesia*) the twelfth-century author distinguished precisely between 'Monks who live close to men, such as the Cluniacs and the like' and 'Monks who remove themselves far from men, such as Cistercians and the like'.[24] Even if the latter claim to seek out a 'place of horror and great solitude', evoked in the Bible, the historical evidence sometimes admits only with difficulty the idea that the *desert* to which they were going was in truth so abandoned. It could be, then, a saying based only on spiritual policy. According to Constance Berman, for instance, the southern French Cistercians did not go into 'uncultivated wilderness', but rather they excelled in organization of cultivated lands.[25] Against what their own written tradition says, however, some cases are documented of Cistercian abbeys which were erected on the site of an earlier village, from which the inhabitants had been previously expelled.[26] The *Summa Cartae Caritatis*, one of the basic texts of the order,

lation', in: *Cîteaux. Commentarii Cistercienses*, 40, 1989, pp. 175–99 (especially p. 188).

[23] B. Ward, 'The Desert Myth. Reflections on the Desert Ideal in early Cistercian Monasticism', in: M. B. Pennington (ed.), *One yet Two. Monastic Tradition East and West*. Kalamazoo, MI, 1976, pp. 183–99 (Cistercian Studies Series 29).

[24] Ed. G. Constable & B. Smith. Oxford, 1972, ch. ii–iii, pp. 18–54 (Oxford Medieval Texts).

[25] C. H. Berman, *Medieval Agriculture, the Southern French Countryside, and the early Cistercians. A Study of Forty-three Monasteries*. Philadelphia, 1986 (Transactions of the American Philosophical Society, 76, 5).

[26] Cf. examples in R. A. Donkin, 'Settlement and Depopulation on Cistercian

stated: 'We are allowed to have for our own use waters, woods, vineyards, meadows, lands away from where secular people live'.[27] Most of the sites of the abbeys genuinely testified to their spiritual origin, as so many English ruins, such as Furness or Rievaulx, still show.[28]

This search for remoteness met happily with the wishes of benevolent donors. With the passage of time, less wealthy lords had increasingly been involved in the endowment of abbeys. Founding was a status symbol. It was moreover a spiritual necessity for the clan or the family, and obviously a costly operation. The founding of Cistercian houses was easier and less of a financial drain than that of traditional Benedictine ones. Cistercians often sought waste lands which at the time of the donation were of no value at all, even if they were reclaimed and yielded well afterwards. The benefactor did not instantly impoverish himself by such a bequest and the monks were made happy. Moreover, the spiritual gain the benefactor could hope for seemed better guaranteed. Cistercians were living a more severe life, an *arctior vita* as the texts said, than traditional Benedictines, and as a result they were considered to be more pleasing to God. They had taken a step backwards on the ladder of 'ineluctable decay' in reading the Rule literally. So, a donation to white monks (and to newly founded orders in general) was considered to be an excellent spiritual investment, and this was, together with sheltering their own, superfluous, clan members, the very reason for all that generosity. A double advantage, spiritual and material, for both of the partners, explains the countless number of gifts to a steadily growing number of houses towards the middle of the twelfth century.

The spiritual targets of monasticism meet here the great social and economic development of the 'twelfth-century renaissance'. The land reclamation movement had started at the latest in the eleventh century, but the share of the Cistercians, perceptibly spreading a web of houses from the second quarter of the twelfth century onwards, could not go further back than that time. The white monks took part in the land

Estates during the twelfth and the thirteenth Centuries', in: *Bulletin of the Institute of Historical Research*, xxxiii, 1960, pp. 141–64, and H. Thoen & L. Milis, 'Het site Ten Duinen te Koksijde: archeologisch, geologisch, historisch', in: *Handelingen van de Maatschappij voor geschiedenis en oudheidkunde te Gent*, 28, 1974, pp. 1–35, even if the later excavations at Ten Duinen itself do no longer permit us to consider it to be such a case (contrary to what the authors then believed). Cf. also S. Bonde & C. Maines, 'The Archaeology of Monasticism: a Survey of recent Work in France, 1970–1987', in: *Speculum*, 63, 1988, 4, pp. 794–825 (especially p. 800).

[27] *Les plus anciens textes de Cîteaux*, ch. xv, p. 123.

[28] D. M. Knowles & J. K. S. St John, *Monastic Sites from the Air*. Cambridge, 1952, pp. 78–85.

reclamation movement as a result of the monastic ideal they fostered but only as one among many participants. Incidentally, how many religious were actually involved? Statistically calculable records of Ten Duinen Abbey, by far the most important in Flanders, and well documented, enumerate some 430 names of monks and lay brethren for the period 1203–1259.[29] Five other, less populous, male Cistercian houses existed in the same county at that time. Numerically the movement did not involve more than a fraction of one per cent of the total Flemish population.[30] Similar results were obtained by Dom D. Knowles. For England he estimated about 15,000 religious persons (monks, lay brethren and canons) for a total population of 3,000,000. This represents for each of the three categories, the black Benedictines, the Cistercians and the canons, about 0.17% of the male population of the realm![31] So can their impact have been of such overall importance as has often been suggested, considering particularly that Cistercians longed for spiritual retirement and topographical seclusion?

The lay brethren who actually did the work on the fields, as the translation of the ideal of manual labour into reality, were a double substitute: on the one hand for the monks to whom (and to whom only) the Rule of St Benedict applied, and whose fast did not physically allow more than a ritualized participation in agricultural work, on the other hand as a substitute for the labour done by the tenants, free or servile, in the traditional manorial setting. The activity and the status of the lay brethren were spiritualized in the sense that working-people came to constitute a religious proletariat, illiterate and unversed, yet cloistered to remain so. The difference in origin and social condition between the *conversi* and the unfree servants living on the older manors presumably was not very great, although the living conditions of the former were better. Comfortable housing contrasted with poor shelters. In the concept of the Cistercian movement *conversi* constituted a step towards a society on earth which reflected society in heaven. According to the ideal of spiritual perfection those who were humble by force of circumstance (the brethren) were ruled by those who were humble voluntarily (the monks). In everyday life the pseudo-religious status of the *conversi* did not in any event turn out to be a sufficient and satisfying framework for acquiescing in their subservient position *vis-à-vis* the monks. The historical evidence of the period 1168–1200 records the existence of some

---

[29] *Cronica et cartularium monasterii de Dunis*. Bruges, 1864, pp. 37–51.

[30] Cf. the estimate in Chapter 5. The number of female Cistercians (both nuns and lay sisters) may have been higher at the end of the twelfth century, since the monks tried to limit what they considered to be a burden.

[31] D. Knowles, *The Monastic Order in England*. Cambridge, 1963, p. 679.

twenty revolts among the lay brethren, and thirty in the following century.[32]

The Cistercians, and especially St Bernard as their spiritual leader, preached the simplicity of St Benedict. They fulminated against the riches of the Cluniacs and their, for Cistercians intolerable, luxury, even if for the Cluniacs themselves this luxury represented a continuous appeal and praise addressed to God. The Cistercians, within decades, were trapped in the antagonism of their own spirituality. They lived in a (compared to other monks) modest way and continued to do so, even when after some time the worthless waste lands of the beginning were converted into high-yield farms. Moreover, the monks and lay brethren had only to feed themselves, without the everyday material burden of caring for a numerous family. The crops from the Cistercian lands had to be shared by fewer people. So, simplicity inevitably created wealth, and modesty led to surplus. For the Cistercians there was no other way left except commerce, charity or . . . the 'embarrassment of riches'.[33]

CRAFT AND COMMERCE:
THE ABBEY, THE MARKET AND THE TOWN

The tourist who travels in Britain and tries to avoid fast motorways in journeying from London to the north-west will certainly use sections of Watling Street. If he looks at an Ordnance Survey map he will immediately notice its long, rectilinear route and recognize it as an old Roman road. North of London it passes, on a hill, the pretty borough of St Albans. The place was, and still is, famous for the awesome beauty and the thrilling dimensions of its Benedictine abbey which was perhaps founded in the late eighth century by a king of Mercia. The complementary relationship between settlements and means of communication is apparent in this as well as in many other cases. Medieval, and especially early medieval, abbeys quite often searched for an accessible site along big (and hence old) roads meant to handle through traffic. This choice expressed certain basic needs, one of which was that for a feeling of security. Safety was in fact better guaranteed along major routes than when monasteries were built at more isolated sites, even though numerous narrative sources told stories of saintly monks murdered by brigands. Another reason for the choice was that some early abbeys needed easy contact as they played an active role in the conversion from pagan-

[32] J. Leclercq, 'Comment vivaient les frères convers?', in: *I laici nella 'societas christiana' dei secoli XI e XII*. Milano, 1968, pp. 152–76 (Pubblicazioni dell' Università cattolica del Sacro Cuore. Contributi. Serie terza. Varia. 5).

[33] Cf. L. K. Little, *Religious Poverty and the Profit Economy in Medieval Europe*. Ithaca, NY, 1978, p. 93.

ism. Their monks often left for other regions, far from their 'home base', tens, if not hundreds of miles away. One example is Corbie, in northern France, which founded a dependent house in Corvey, Saxony. The difficulty of contact, a major (if not the prevalent) problem of the time, was at least eased for monasteries when their site fitted into a broader, even if a relatively poor, communications system. In this system roads and stocks of goods were counterparts, in the sense that they both needed trading places, markets and eventually towns. As neither new roads nor bridges were constructed until the twelfth and thirteenth centuries (and even then much more as an exception than as a rule), roads normally never owed their existence to abbeys. They and their possessions could only provoke the extension of local, rural paths, as naturally formed as animal trails had been, and which were rarely the result of any systematic planning. As roads were scarce and badly maintained, central authority being usually absent, most transportation was by boat. Hence, donors or settling monks normally looked for a suitable place on or near the banks of a river. If possible they were also looking for an amenable site, which explains the choice of Roman spa resorts for monastic implantation. The names of Luxeuil-les-Bains, where St Columban founded his most important abbey, or St-Amand-les-Eaux, or Bath testify to the attraction of their water, considered beneficial to the soul as well as to the body.

Henri Pirenne in his remarkable studies on the evolution of medieval towns has already demonstrated that a diversity of optimal factors determined urban settlement. The most appropriate sites were those where two roads, or a road and a river, crossed, or where two rivers joined. Even if the fruits of recent historical scholarship allow us to refine his typology and his chronology, these general topographical conditions remain valid. The economic laws which govern easy communication and thus determine social interaction are alike in every period. Thus monasteries and towns, even if involuntarily, shared the same needs, and hence they looked for analogous topographical solutions. By chance they met. Many medieval villages and towns, large ones too, grew up around the impressive and secure buildings of monastic houses. Vézelay in Burgundy is a striking example of a small town which developed in the shadow of the abbey. In Tournus, on the river Saône, a hundred miles to the south, an impressive tenth-century wall enclosed both the abbey and its dependent town-like settlement. Even larger towns developed around a monastery, such as Arras around seventh-century St Vaast. It grew on the bank of a river, opposite the bishop's palace which prolonged the existence of a Roman city. Five centuries later Arras had become the most important and wealthiest town of the heavily urbanized county of Flanders. Yet one question remains unanswered: was monasticism itself, defined as a *specific*

spiritual ideal and aim of perfection, responsible for this urban development as such? Or were two phenomena (trade and town on the one
hand, religious life on the other hand) merely overlapping? The answer
is rather ambiguous. One can conjecture that many towns, whose origin
is currently linked to the presence of a monastery, would have come into
existence anyway, precisely because the site itself was so promising. An
example like Bury St Edmunds or St Riquier leads us to believe that this
was indeed the case,[34] and the flourishing of Arras is explained, not only
by its abbey, but also by the presence of a castle.[35] It is not the development itself that should be explained by the neighbourhood of a monastery, but rather the moment when the development started. It made no
difference whether it was a monastery or a nobleman's castle which
guaranteed security and consequently attracted commercial activity.
People who lived in the uncomfortable and unhealthy dwellings near a
monastic, ecclesiastical or secular stronghold only took into consideration what was to their advantage: that their activity in the workshop
was secured, and that they were given the occasion to survive, even if
conditions were marginal; that neither their own lord, nor another
would extort money from them. What they could hope for from the
monastic community, if this was their lord, was treatment where less
violence prevailed. Economically speaking, however, the difference between a secular and an ecclesiastical owner did not mean a great deal.

For subjects as well as for strangers, the concentration of people in the
abbey or in the castle represented a potential market for luxury products. Abbeys and castles constituted a concentration of non-productive
consumers, more or less significant according to their number. This factor largely explains, together with the feeling of safety, how market-
places developed in the neighbourhood of both and how some of both
became urban settlements in the same way. But our purpose is to consider the specific impact of monasticism as a spiritual ideal and so we
have to look for dissimilarities between monks and lords. When king
Ferdinand I of León, for instance, decided *c.* 1060 to donate annually a
thousand golden coins (*metcales*) to the abbey of Cluny (which amount
his son Alfonso was to double shortly afterwards), he apparently meant
to provide the monks with more, or more fashionable, garments than the
two tunics and cowls foreseen in the Rule (Ch. lv).[36] St Benedict had

---

[34] R. S. Gottfried, *Bury St. Edmunds and the Urban Crisis: 1290–1539*. Princeton,
1982, p. 82; R. McKitterick, 'Town and Monastery in the Carolingian Period',
in: D. Baker (ed.), *The Church in Town and Countryside*. Oxford, 1979, pp.
93–102 (Studies in Church History 16).

[35] G. Duby (dir.), *Histoire de la France urbaine*. Paris, 1980, ii, p. 70.

[36] L. K. Little, *Religious Poverty and the Profit Economy in Medieval Europe*, 1978,
pp. 64–65.

prescribed that 'the monks should not complain about the colour or the coarseness of any of these things, but be content with what can be found in the district where they live and can be purchased cheaply'. The refinement in such houses as Cluny explained the protest of the Cistercians some decades later when they stressed the literal observance of the Rule.[37] Other houses did not enjoy anything like comparable means. When the northern French abbey of Andres was burnt down, at some time in the twelfth century, it was the monks of Christ Church, Canterbury, who sent them old garments. The Cluny example proves that cloth was purchased, and not just turned over by the tenants of monastic lands as part of their payments. We can venture the explanation that the quality of the products woven by these people was too peasant-like and not at all in keeping with the living standards of the noble Cluny. For poorer houses there was no other possibility than that of using the wool of their own sheep (which Andres certainly raised on the shores of the North Sea) and to have it woven by household personnel. The real simplicity which was such a recurrent theme in St Benedict's Rule seems therefore more apparent in these smaller houses, although it was not the result of voluntary denial as such, but rather of a bare material necessity. Until the rise of the Cistercian movement, however, contemporaries considered the life-style of Cluny to be much more representative of 'genuine' monasticism, ritualized and only formally 'poor' as it was, than the real poverty with which small and powerless houses were faced. These were also more vulnerable to the claims local lords could easily lay upon them.

The gift of fortunes to Cluny, such as the one referred to earlier, implied trade and trade implied market-places where merchants and customers could meet. Precious goods were likely to be involved in the commercial circuit, for example those needed for the decoration of the church and the performance of the liturgy, such as incense and embroidered linen. Historians are better informed about long-distance trade in luxury articles than about local or inter-regional trade, even though written evidence rarely matches archaeological data. All excavations of abbeys (and of castles) show for instance quantities of potsherds of foreign and of local origin, but trade in terracotta is hardly mentioned in documents at all.

How urban *nuclei* developed from tiny gatherings of houses into larger towns depended on such elements as the site itself, the global communication system or the assurance of safety. The number of consumers within the walls was only one among these factors, and not even a very important one. Large abbeys did not necessarily attract large urban settlements. It is as consumers, rather than producers, that Benedictine

---

[37] B. K. Lackner, *The Eleventh-Century Background of Cîteaux*, p. 63.

monasteries seem to have made the greatest impact on economic activities. The payments of the tenants were, apart from (some) money and services, mainly in agricultural produce and less the result of any artisan activity such as weaving. Only the surplus could possibly come onto the market. Precise comparative figures can never be calculated (except perhaps once in a while for the later middle ages) but it is unlikely that trade of agricultural produce would have been important. The crop depended in general both upon the managerial system and upon the climatological conditions. For a systematic exportation of a surplus, or even for an occasional one, in the case of famine for instance, the transportation system was neither adequate nor sufficiently reliable, and as the management and the weather was locally the same, irrespective of the type of ownership, a surplus can have met with only a limited local demand. Thus, trade of agricultural produce was not very meaningful, either for local or for foreign consumption, even when monks needed money for buying cloth.[38]

What we have said so far in this paragraph only applies to the first half of the middle ages and thus only to the black Benedictines and their seignorial way of management and consumption. The new religious opinions of the 1100s dramatically shifted the economic orientation of monasteries. The Cistercians and some other reform movements rejected secular society and they withdrew into the remoteness they called 'desert'. To a great extent this change can be explained by a new-wave labour system, inspired by the literal reading of the Rule and exemplified in the use of lay brethren and in the creation of large farms called granges (*grangiae*).

The Cistercians involuntarily marked one of the great antagonisms between religious life and society in the 'twelfth-century renaissance'. Their withdrawal from secular life, in other words from towns and villages, fits into the ideal of agricultural activity which had already taken root some time before: that of leaving the long-cultivated lands, in order to extend the milestones of human presence. Even when their motives were different they shared a 'frontier mentality' with part of the rural population, looking for wider opportunities on fallow lands and in new territories.[39] But along with this rush into reclaimed areas, urban life

---

[38] D. Knowles, *The Religious Orders in England*, i. Cambridge, 1956, pp. 32–35. He stresses changes in the period after 1150 (pp. 36–40); G. Duby, 'Le monachisme et l'économie rurale', in: *Il monachesimo e la riforma ecclesiastica (1049–1122)*. Milano, 1971, pp. 336–49.

[39] A nice example of this 'frontier mentality' is given by the Cistercians of Poblet Abbey in Aragon, focusing their activity on land development in New Catalonia, the former Muslin territory occupied by the Christians in the middle of the twelfth century (L. J. McCrank, 'The Cistercians of Poblet as

was developing. The agricultural surplus, which became guaranteed thanks to the innovations already mentioned and in spite of the growth of the population, made markets and towns both necessary and possible. Urban crowds and their busy life were the very things from which the Cistercians were fleeing. Moreover, life in town and its concomitant activities, crafts and trade, were to evolve steadily into the most prominent feature of European society. The monks escaped from a phenomenon which sprang from the same vitality as their own. They withdrew from 'the World' and they did not wish to fit into the existing, if rapidly changing, organization of society. Their life-style was much more humble and simple than that of their black Benedictine colleagues. The agricultural yield from which they benefited was undoubtedly higher than that of the traditional exploitations once the waste and worthless lands they were given were brought into cultivation. The religiously inspired personal involvement of the working lay brethren certainly led them to perform better. The monks fasted more and had no family to feed. Religious ideals increased agricultural production and reduced consumption, invariably leading to a surplus. The market the monks tried to flee became the usual outlet for their products, functioning as an exponent of social interaction. They were eventually attracted by the market they had initially rejected. As the monks' vital needs were limited they inevitably enjoyed a favorable commercial balance. The costly, if not exorbitant, expenses of the black Benedictines, and more specifically of the Cluniacs, in building and decorating, had kept (and were still keeping) their money circulating. Georges Duby very forcefully demonstrated how a seignorial economy, documented in the context of religious orders, evolved from a domestic type to a so-called *money movement*.[40] Craftsmen had, in fact, to be hired to express and to realize the lavish and sumptuous dreams of these monks in the praise of their Lord. More spending, higher prices and less control over the agricultural revenues led to more money-renting since the alternatives, austerity and direct farming, were not envisaged. The Cistercians spent less and, whether willingly or not, they accumulated money, even if managerial imprudence could lead to cash problems. They are said to have played an important role in the wool trade between England and the Continent, although few comparative figures can be given as to what they and other ecclesiastical or lay producers exported.[41] Overstressing

---

Landlords: Protection, Litigation and Violence on the Medieval Catalan Frontier', in: *Cîteaux. Commentarii Cistercienses*, xxvi, 1975, pp. 255–83).

[40] *Guerriers et paysans*, pp. 240–48.

[41] J. E. Madden, 'Business Monks, Banker Monks, Bankrupt Monks: the English Cistercians in the Thirteenth Century', in: *The Catholic Historical Review*, 49, 1963, pp. 341–64; C. V. Graves, 'The Economic Activities of the Cistercians in

this activity from the point of view of 'ordinary society', however, would be wrong, perhaps not economically but certainly religiously speaking as 'this traffic . . . was in direct contradiction to the spirit of Cîteaux'.[42] Considering their numbers, how many of them could be seen on market-places, given the remoteness of their sites, the inadequacy of the roads and above all their heaven-oriented mentality, all this irrespective of the proportional importance of their production? Cistercian monks certainly had to deal with 'the embarrassment of riches' – and how limited were the solutions proposed to escape from this wealth, unwanted and unsearched for! No alternatives existed, other than practising works of charity towards those rejected by ordinary society or giving up the initial purity of their observance. By the end of the thirteenth century at least, the second alternative was real. By that time, however, the wealth in Cistercian houses had already noticeably decreased. The often marginal lands the white monks had been cultivating now yielded less than before as they were increasingly exhausted. The system of the lay brethren collapsed before the middle of the fourteenth century (in some areas even before that time) as the religious attraction of the order among middle- and lower-class people had ceased, and other spiritual solutions for them had been worked out, mostly within the framework of the mendicant movement. When the number of lay brethren shrank the cheap production-system vanished. Henceforward there was no longer any difference between the managerial approach of the Cistercians and that of the black monks. As the towns, the secular Church, and the central authority intensified their power, grafted on to the growing economic activities, the black and the white monks remained landowners, confined to the horizon of the countryside, in the same way as the nobility. And even when an abbey was the owner of most of the houses in town, or the most important rentier in the area, as was for instance the case for Bury St Edmunds, nothing was reflected in their ownership of what monasticism represented as a spirituality or as a code of behaviour. The monks acted as possessors, like every other owner, nobleman as well as burgher, not as knights of the Lord.

Medieval England (1128–1307)', in: *Analecta Sacri Ordinis Cisterciensis*, 13, 1957, pp. 3–60. According to the latter one sixth of the English wool production came from monastic demesnes, which neither means that it was completely monks' property nor indicates to what extent it was commercialized by them. D. Knowles, *The Religious Orders in England*, i, pp. 67–69 stressed the existence of the *collecta*, wool bought from small growers and gathered by abbeys. The clip of the Cistercians was marketed quite well in the late twelfth and thirteenth centuries, and sometimes already sold years in advance, provoking criticism from the General Chapter of Cîteaux (T. H. Lloyd, *The English Wool Trade in the Middle Ages*. Cambridge, 1977, pp. 288–317).

42 D. Knowles, *The Religious Orders in England*, i, p. 68.

4

The Monks' Attitude towards People

MONKS, NOBILITY AND COMMON PEOPLE

At a first stage the interest of monks in 'ordinary people' can be best evaluated through a close look at a particular type of historical source which they eagerly produced, annals. In some abbeys major events were written down, year after year and normally over a long span of time, sometimes covering centuries. The information obtained through their own experiences, from messengers, from passers-by, or through 'rumour' was finely sifted according to the criteria of their mental system, in order to select those things deemed important enough to be preserved for posterity. Annals thus allow us to reconstitute the mental as well as the social and geographical horizon of monks. That distinctions can be made between abbeys in the light of their geographical horizon seems obvious, as they were scattered all over western and central Europe. As far as the mental and social aspects are concerned, it is striking how remarkably stable they were through the centuries regardless of the orders or the countries to which the monasteries belonged. A concrete example, such as the *Annals of Vézelay* in Burgundy can clarify what the points of interests and the criteria for registration were.[1] The deaths and the successions of rulers of whatever kind, ecclesiastical and lay, represent the bulk of the information, more than three quarters of all the entries. Half of what remains deals with other ecclesiastical events, such as dedications of churches, or with military activities (such as those related to the Crusades), or with astronomical and meteorological phenomena (eclipses, floods, and the like). The reason that the latter events were noted could be one of human concern, in the light of their repercussions upon the harvest, and so upon the people's survival. Yet this feeling seems only rarely to have determined the noteworthiness of an event. In the *Annals of Vézelay* it did so only once,

---

[1] *Monumenta Vizeliacensia*, ed. R. B. C. Huygens. Turnhout, 1976, pp. 195–233 (Corpus Christianorum. Continuatio Mediaeualis, 42). There is no special reason (for instance the rivalry between the monks and the urban population) why we quote from these Annals, rather than from other ones. They mostly show a similar image.

Duke Arechis of Benevento supervising the construction of the Santa Sofia Church he favoured
(Twelfth-century miniature in the Santa Sofia chronicle. Vatican Library, ms. lat. 4939)

namely for the year 867, when fifty-six inhabitants of Sens are said to have starved on the same day. That entry, however, turns out to have been added much later, which means that the calamity only caught the monks' attention after some delay. When a bad harvest occurred and famine struck, and when the event was written down, no explicit concern or pity was expressed for those who suffered. Perhaps this lack does not prove that human concern was absent as such, but it certainly indicates that the death of individual rulers and dignitaries was felt to be much more important than the collective death of ordinary people. Another famine, also registered belatedly in the Vézelay Annals, that of 1042, lasted for seven years. It implicitly recalled the Bible, and that was the very reason why it was written down. Most of the time when celestial 'wonders' captured the monks' attention, they were interpreted as elements of God's transcendental planning and as indicators of His often wrathful and vengeful mood. The underlying idea of why these calamities happened, was always guilt and sin, and that warning alone guided the concerned hand of the writing monk.

Very little interest was accorded to ordinary people, and this statement is valid for all analogous texts. Thus the Vézelay monks thought it important to mention the birth of a boy whose pupils were marked with the words 'Man of God' and 'Good Man'. Yet, the question arises as to whether this event can be considered as dealing with 'ordinary people'. The only really 'common' example deals with the year 1156 in which the Vézelay burghers surrendered after an uprising against their lords (the abbot and the monks), a 'bad conspiracy', as the Annals called it.

One could argue, and correctly so, that we are looking for everyday people in a type of document which is, by its very nature, highly selective, and that it would be virtually a contradiction in terms to find them. In the first chapter I have already stressed that only exceptional matters were considered worthy of being committed to parchment. Although the possible objections are thus correct, they serve at the same time to confirm that ordinary people were not a prime preoccupation of the monks' minds.

How can this attitude be explained other than by considering the idealistic way in which monks looked at God? This consideration has to be taken into account in conjunction with their social and juridical status. The Rule of St Benedict did not discriminate at all between rich and poor among the monks. He took it for granted that both groups could (and in his lifetime actually did) join the community, and he forbade their monastic lifestyle to recall any previous social differences. According to the Rule (Ch. xxxiv) they all lived without private property, and they all depended on what the abbot bestowed upon them, which he did not do according to their descent, but rather according to their spiritual needs.

The humility which constitutes the foundation of monastic life was less ritualized by St Benedict than it was in explanatory commentaries, written in later centuries. The less ritualized the more authentic and demanding the feeling of humility undoubtedly was. Nevertheless, when dealing with the topic of hospitality the Rule already contrasted the rich and 'the very fear which they inspire' (Ch. liii) to the poor, although it was in the latter that Christ was to be recognized. The antagonism became enhanced when Christianity steadily established itself in realms built on the ruins of the Roman Empire and dominated by Germanic peoples, or in pagan areas, among Germanic, Celtic and (later on) Slav populations, as the religion took root at first only in the upper class. So, for a long time, it was always the nobility who cultivated the 'perfect way', even if they did not do so with exclusively spiritual purposes in mind. Founding and entering monasteries was, then, an expression of an upper class status and of the presupposed superior quality of this life-style. The notion 'rich', in its opposition to 'poor', gradually shifted to 'noble'. In the Carolingian period and in the centuries thereafter, *dives*, rich, was used as a synonym for *nobilis*, and had thus a broader meaning than that of material wealth. It implied certain moral and even physical qualities which were considered intertwined with power. Though this seems contradictory at first glance, being powerful was linked to being good, handsome and morally high-ranking, as the text of numerous saints' lives prove.[2] Moral standards were confined to the nobility and to its exercise of free choice. Being good was being condescending, a quality one could fulfil, activate or abandon at will. It made 'the others' more dependent, because any benefit they might derive from that goodness was arbitrarily offered.

In general, the nobility were responsible for the founding of monasteries and its members were their inhabitants. The general impression upon which this statement is based has been convincingly proved by C. Brittain Bouchard among others in a study on the intertwining of lay and ecclesiastical life in Burgundy.[3] Within the precincts of the abbey the poverty of the monks did not indicate at all the same thing as the poverty of the powerless masses outside. Monastic poverty meant spiritual simplicity and the absence of power and private property, and though it prevented the development of individual power, it was the result of a free option, and thus in itself an indication of strength.

We often forget, or do not sufficiently realize, that monasticism originated as a movement of lay people, somewhat suspicious of clerics. St

---

2 M. Heinzelmann, 'Sanctitas und "Tugendadel". Zu Konzeptionen von "Heiligkeit" im 5. und 10. Jahrhundert', in: *Francia*, 5, 1977, pp. 741–52.
3 *Sword, Miter, and Cloister. Nobility and the Church in Burgundy, 980–1198.* Ithaca, London, pp. 46–55 and 247–254.

Benedict explicitly warned against the 'self-exaltation or pride' of the (one or two) priests living within the community, and if they trespassed against the Rule, he wished them to be punished 'not as a priest but as a rebel' (Ch. lxii). Canon law did not impose restrictions on entering monastic life on unfree persons, as it did for the clerical order by prohibiting the ordination of serfs.[4] In reality the door of the abbeys remained closed. Later customaries explicitly prescribed that on the occasion of his entry, the novice be required to give assurance that he was and had remained unbound. Servitude, marriage or physical handicap barred one from acceptance.[5] Free, unmarried and healthy youngsters seem thus to have been, at least in writing, the appropriate candidates for religious life. The latter condition, however, was often infringed, as noble families used the abbeys to dispose of their surplus children.[6] The entrance of handicapped children is attested in several primary sources, as in Hirsau and Andres.[7] The Carolingian period, however, witnessed an increasing number of ordained monks, and consequently an enhanced feeling of superiority, the clerical order being esteemed higher than lay status. This evolution continued and at least by the thirteenth-century priesthood among monks had become general.[8]

RURAL PEOPLE

Charters and other documents, most often from abbeys, allow us a glimpse of ordinary medieval country folk. Basically they belong to two different categories, the free and the unfree. Social conditions, however, could and actually were mixed up with juridical status, implying that freedom did not necessarily mean a higher standard of living. The free ran the risk of losing their freedom to the noble class, especially when out of feudalism there developed the so-called seigniorial system which

---

4 *Dictionnaire de droit canonique*, v, cc. 453–54.
5 Cf. for instance *The Customary of the Benedictine Abbey of Eynsham in Oxford-shire*, ed. A. Gransden. Siegburg, 1963, 1, pp. 28 (Corpus Consuetudinum Monasticarum, ii). The most elaborate formula we know is the one in the *Caerimoniae Mellicenses*, iii, 1, in: *Breviarium Caeremoniarum monasterii Mellicensis*, ed. J. F. Angerer. Siegburg, 1987, pp. 145–46 (Corpus Consuetudinum Monasticarum, xi 2). The text as a whole is an enlarged version of the customary of Subiaco, applied in Melk Abbey, Austria, *c.* 1460.
6 J. Boswell, *The Kindness of Strangers*. New York, 1988, calls it a form of abandonment.
7 *Patrologia Latina*, 149, c. 635 (Quoted by Lackner, *op. cit.*, p. 66); *Monumenta Germaniae historica*, Scriptores, 24, p. 705 (Quoted by Boswell, *op. cit.*, p. 299).
8 C. N. L. Brooke, 'Priest, Deacon and Layman, from St Peter Damian to St Francis', pp. 69–70.

strengthened the legal and social control of the lords over the people living on their demesnes. Historians agree that, as a result of the collapse of central authority in the post-Carolingian period, this seigniorial system exerted heavy pressure on the free population. The rights of the landowners over their tenants were extended to the 'public' rights, including the administration of justice and the imposition of so-called *banalités* (such as enforcing the compulsory use of the seigniorial mill). The idealistic ethics of the Carolingian rulers who wished to create a just society and to prevent the 'poor' from being exploited, were, from approximately the late ninth century onwards gone forever (at least in France; in Germany this happened somewhat later). Owners had now become lords, and more than ever before labourers in their service became labourers in their power. The free population was steadily limited in their individual and social rights (for example, in the choice of a spouse) and they increasingly merged into the category of the unfree. Within the framework of the seigniorial system both free and unfree people were limited (perhaps more in practice than in theory) in their mobility, being bound to a manor-owned farm. They were also limited financially by annual payments and *corvées*, and by the claim of the lords upon a part or all of their inheritance. The unfree people, being indigenous and baptized, could not be sold individually as (heathen and imported) slaves still were in southern Europe or even in (early medieval) Britain. Nevertheless they were considered to be part of the rural equipment, and as if they were furniture were sold, bought or given away with the farms and the land which they worked. They constituted part of the land, and how could they be expected to have any quality, any superior human quality, since land was matter, and matter was in itself bad according to current theological concepts. However could unfree people have become monks since they did not possess the basic condition, freedom? Everything had to await the social improvements of the twelfth century when the economic revival generated more freedom.

St Benedict prescribed care and attention towards the poor – that is, the powerless – and towards pilgrims only 'because it is especially in them that Christ is received', and not for the persons themselves. There are no indications that in the following centuries when the notion 'nobility' implied goodness and 'unfreedom' ugliness, nobles could psychologically take a step towards sharing the life of the poor, even in the monastic system where voluntary poverty was essential. Neither nobles nor monks were interested in the freedom of the people. The feeling of the monks was based first on the opinions they shared with the social group they belonged to, the nobility, and secondly, on their spiritual conviction that the abandonment of individual freedom was essential to gain eternal life. Freedom could not be an issue in a society which was psychologically and sociologically strictly hierarchic, in which the transfer of obedience was expected to be counterbalanced only by the ideal of justice and the ideal of responsibility.[9] Could a monk who, on entering the monastery, chose to abandon his freedom and even his own personality, be expected to care about the social and juridical status of ordinary people? Moreover, the social order was what God had imposed, and when it worked badly, it was the result of human sinfulness and depravity. Disorder could only be overcome by self-denial and escape from the material world, and not by social action. Above all, monks regarded unfree people as possessions of the abbey, and thus of the legacy which they, as monks, had received from their predecessors and were expected to hand down, enriched and not impoverished, to future generations.

In the preceding chapter, one of the conclusions was that monastic estates were run in basically the same way as lay estates. This suggests that the tenants of both types of lords were treated in the same way,[10] and there is in fact no indication of general exodus of people towards monastic lands in hope of a better life. The payments and *corvées* were similar and as burdensome in either case. Obviously, the social and economic system as a whole would not work if there were any striking difference. Monks belonged to the class of landed proprietors, with analogous interests and analogous mental attitudes. The best dependent tenants could hope for was that their families and mainly their women should not be subjected by their lords to physical violence, and it is plausible that this occurred less frequently on abbey lands. Charters of monastic origin sometimes testify to lay lords behaving badly and arbitrarily towards their subjects, and to the fact that abbeys tried to bring these unfortunate people under their own jurisdiction. Were they really helping with the intention of making these people happier, and of guaranteeing them a safer life? That is not exactly what these charters reveal. Tied people were a source of conflict among landowners, lay and monastic, and when the latter try to gain control of the unfree, it seems it was in order to increase their own wealth, and not from concern for social conditions. Monks regarded life on earth as a passage-way to eternal life, and consequently the more unfortunate and difficult one's time in the world, the greater the chance of gaining Heaven. Thus, the monks' psychological attitude fitted in with the social stability which the dominant classes deemed necessary, and which they tried to enforce.

---

[9] L. Milis, 'Dispute and Settlement in Medieval Cenobitical Rules', in: *Bulletin de l'Institut historique belge de Rome – Bulletin van het Belgisch Historisch Instituut te Rome*, lx, 1990, pp. 43–63.

[10] S. Moorhouse, 'Monastic Estates: their Composition and Development', in: *The Archaeology of Rural Monasteries*, edd. R. Gilchrist & H. Mytum. Oxford, 1989, pp. 29–81 (esp. p. 58) (BAR British Series 203).

A Cistercian monk mowing
the grain

(Twelfth-century miniature
from Gregory the Great, *Moralia
in Job*. Manuscript from Cîteaux.
Dijon, Bibliothèque municipale,
ms. 170 f. 75)

Above. A farmer flailing sheaves of grain

(Thirteenth-century illustration from Matthew
Paris' Chronicle. Cambridge, Corpus Christi
College, ms. 16, f. 79r. Courtesy of the Master
and Fellows of Corpus Christi College,
Cambridge)

Right. A monk and a lay worker cutting
a tree

(Twelfth-century miniature from a Cîteaux
manuscript. Dijon, Bibliothèque municipale,
ms. 173, f. 41)

It appears obvious in such a system that not only lay lords, but also abbeys, attempted to exercise control over the marriage pattern of their tenants. Weddings outside one's own seigniory were restricted. Nevertheless unfree male farmers could choose a spouse of free status inside the seigniory with the intention of improving the legal position of their progeny, traditionally inherited 'through the uterus'.[11]

The so-called *'sainteurs'* or *'tributaires d'Église'* are a specific type of unfree people bound to a monastery.[12] Charters often phrase gifts to abbeys as personally and literally made to their patron saint. When human beings were offered, it produced the juridical fiction that the saint himself was their lord, rather than the abbot or the convent. He represented lordship, with the monastic community merely acting as his executive staff. Moreover, he represented continuity, whereas the monks themselves were viewed as transitory. Hence this sort of 'gift' was actually more of an offering. It gained a higher degree of security, both for the giver (such a gift represented a better spiritual investment), and for the receiver (there was more fear of a spiritual sanction, and thus less risk of usurpation).

Offering *sainteurs* to such a patron saint was a way of freeing people, but it did not imply complete liberty. Their tied status was changed into a 'less tied' one, under a new, a holy lord. One could not gain complete liberty, for this was at once a quality with which one was born, and a life-style. The charters mostly present these donations of *sainteurs* as alms. Occasionally, however, they can be seen in a more amiable light. The tied person bought his freedom from his (former) lord, but as liberty was inaccessible as such, he passed under the control of a saintly lord. Other *sainteurs* were of free origin, and dedicated themselves. They abandoned a risky and precarious liberty for a more sheltered existence, in exchange for a certain control. And often the question remains open as to whether this dedication was really the people's own choice or came about through some form of (economic) pressure from the monks' side. At any rate, *sainteurs* thus constituted a category of 'less tied' persons, illustrative of that continuous movement in history (even at a time of idealized stability) of some people climbing, and others descending the social ladder. The *sainteur* phenomenon seems to be linked to the increased mobility which became noticeable from the 1050s onwards. Hence, it can be considered, at least in some cases, as a means of

---

[11] E. Coleman explained how this ploy worked on the ninth-century estates of St-Germain-des-Prés ('Medieval Marriage Characteristics: A Neglected Factor in the History of Medieval Serfdom', in: *The Journal of Interdisciplinary History*, ii, 1971–1972, pp. 205–19).

[12] P. C. Boeren, *Étude sur les tributaires d'Église dans le comté de Flandre du IXe au XIVe siècle*. Amsterdam, 1936.

regularizing the legal position of fugitive serfs. If necessary, their new lord could cope with the claims of the former lord, on whose lands they were born. At the same time enough freedom of action was guaranteed within the new framework of developing commerce, crafts and towns. From the point of view of the *sainteurs* themselves, this offered an opportunity to progress socially, and for at least some of them juridically as well. For monasticism stability and the veneration of the saint were matters of concern.

URBAN PEOPLE

The town can be considered as the antonym of monasticism, even if the *Book on the Different Orders and Callings in the Church* distinguished a separate category of monks living in close proximity to lay people. Burghers, especially in those towns which developed as a result of the twelfth-century renaissance, identified Benedictine monasteries with land ownership and consequently with the static feudal organization of the preceding centuries. Ordinary people did not themselves leave many documents. The reconstruction of their mental world thus remains relatively hazardous, and susceptible to generalizations. Yet it is very unlikely that mutual sympathy characterized the relationship between towns and abbeys, as the above-mentioned uprising of the Vézelay burghers witnesses. The best one could suppose is a love-hate relationship, on the side of the urban people proved by both generosity and irritation. To the newly developing society, monks were representatives of 'the old order'. They enjoyed privileges which in any case were often inimical to urban interests. Monks, or their personnel, were accustomed to make use of roads and rivers without paying toll, a token of royal or seigniorial generosity. For both lords and monks the service of God implied material benevolence. In this way, however, monks distorted, at least to a certain extent, a fair economic system; moreover they took this for granted. That monks were to be esteemed higher than ordinary people was a truism so deeply ingrained as to be virtually innate. Their descent and their religious function made them highly respected and, until the advent of the Cistercians, no contradiction was felt between their religious function as servants of God, and the accumulation or display of riches and power.

Some of the towns of antiquity had survived the difficult dawn of the middle ages, most often as centres of ecclesiastical organization; some had developed out of early medieval 'wics', and some were newly founded in the central middle ages. Urban activity, however, as a vector of dynamic social life was certainly a new phenomenon, and new things, as we know, were considered to be bad, and viewed with distrust. The town stood for all that monasticism most resolutely rejected: promiscuity, profit, mobility and ambition. It infringed all of the vows: chastity as well as poverty, stability and obedience. A mental harmony could not be envisaged. There were tangible economic and social rivalries between the static interests of the landowning and seigniorial class on the one hand, and the striking dynamism of the growing urban population, in search of an expanding economic frontier, on the other.

One could not expect monks to sympathize with or even to appreciate the struggle going on for emancipation and for more freedom, which, moreover, challenged their very position. When abbeys found themselves embroiled in this struggle, and occupied a position of sufficient strength, they fiercely opposed urbanism in the same way other privileged institutions or persons evidently did. Vézelay is again a good but an extreme example, when in the 1150s the burghers revolted, entered the abbey and harassed the monks. The latter did not consider at all the villeins' claims for more freedom and more social modernization, the apparent issue of the uprising. They begged the king of France to intervene and to suppress the rebellion, which he promptly did. The Pope wrote that 'For new diseases, new antidotes should be prepared' (*Novis siquidem morbis nova convenit antidota preparari*). Moreover, some burghers had started to construct houses in stone. They had the 'arrogance' (*superbia*) to do so, vying thus with the Church and the nobility, whose power they challenged.[13] The privileged classes considered this to be an intolerable abrogation of a long-standing and consequently equitable social situation.

Does this imply that burghers saw monks only as their opponents? This would be difficult to believe. In fact it was only rarely that most people had any opportunity of meeting monks. The latter represented only a tiny portion of the total population, and were, moreover, expected not to leave their abbeys. Monasticism imposed seclusion. When a monk had been sent on a journey the Rule did not allow him 'to tell another whatever he may have seen or heard outside' (Ch. lxvii). Moreover, monks often lived in the countryside and, except for merchants, noblemen and important Church people, journeys were not a characteristic of medieval life. Only in the later twelfth and early thirteenth centuries did the population of some towns have any opportunity of seeing Cistercian lay brethren conducting transactions at the marketplace. Nevertheless, this contact, however limited it may have been, helped form the negative view of monks current at that time.[14] The

---

[13] *Monumenta Vizeliacensia*, pp. 386–91.
[14] A superb example of the negative image is the wolf in the twelfth-century Ysengrimus poem, where he represents the greed of monks (*Ysengrimus*, ed. J. Mann. Leiden, 1987, pp. 10–20 (Mittellateinische Studien und Texte XII)).

Merchants and their customers

(Twelfth-century miniature illustrating Hildegard of Bingen's description of her vision, *Scivias*. Wiesbaden, Hessische Landesbibliothek, ms. 1 (lost since 1945); manuscript facsimile 1927–1933 in St Hildegard's abbey, Eibingen. Photo courtesy of das Rheinische Bildarchiv)

Pilgrims visiting St Dunstan's tomb

(Late Medieval 'drollery'. London. British Library, Royal ms. 10 E IV. Copyright the British Library)

attitude and feeling of the townsfolk was even ambivalent towards the thirteenth-century mendicant friars with whom the urban population could identify itself so much more easily than it could with monks. The impression of monks outside their monastery, or friars too much outside their convent, formed an easy butt for the gossip and imagination of lay people.

THE WORKS OF MERCY

When the sociologist Léo Moulin dealt with the charitable activities of medieval monks in a book published some ten years ago, he did not hesitate to call them 'Social Security', asserting that at that time 'the totality of [social] services so familiar today were dispensed completely by religious people'.[15] The quotation gives the impression that *the* (or at least *a*) major purpose of monastic life was to provide adequate food, shelter and medical care for people in distress. Is this image of 'the works of mercy' correct and, if so, were they practised by monks as a goal in themselves, a result of human concern, or as a path towards self-sanctification?

Their origin is in the Gospel of Matthew (Mt 25:35–40), where the Apostle reports a conversation between Jesus and his disciples. Christ's saying that 'anything you did for my brothers here, however humble, you did for me', was to become the theoretical cornerstone of behaviour within Christian doctrine. In a later chapter we will show its influence upon the system of moral values. It is our purpose here to consider how monks viewed 'the works of mercy' in theory and in practice. For this we will turn first to St Benedict. In his Rule, our gauge, he distinguished four categories of persons of whom the greatest care should be taken: the sick, children, guests and the poor (Ch. xxxi). The cellarer (the monk responsible for the food supply) and the abbot (who is the person ultimately responsible) are warned that they will have to render an account to God for all these people on Judgement Day. According to Chapter xxxi human concern in itself is not an issue. In deploying social activities the monks think of themselves and of attaining eternal life in Heaven. This is the basic meaning of monasticism and should not shock the reader, who is perhaps not always aware of the subtle distinctions

See also G. G. Coulton, *Five Centuries of Religion*, i. New York, 1929 (1979), who speaks of 'unpopularity' (p. 396); H. Roussel & J. Trotin, 'Invective aux clercs et satire anti–cléricale dans la littérature du moyen âge', in: *Acta Universitatis Wratislaviensis*, 265, 1975, pp. 3–36 (esp. pp. 8 and 22–23).

[15] *La vie quotidienne des religieux au moyen âge. Xe–XVe siècle*. Paris, 1978, pp. 290–93.

between medieval Benedictinism and subsequent, more socially active religious movements. In another chapter (Ch. xxxvi) it is said: 'Before all things and above all things, care must be taken of the sick', but this exclusively concerns sick members of the own community. When in the next chapter care for old men and children is stressed, it is with monks and oblates in mind. As far as social care is concerned, only Chapter liii focuses on people from outside the community. All guests should 'be received like Christ', although a closer reading makes two things clear. First, that 'guests', also the 'domestics of the faith and [. . .] pilgrims', refers only to important people whose arrival 'is announced'. Secondly, that the way in which they were received was ritualized. The washing of hands and feet could hardly be said to have had cleansing or physical relief as its main purpose. It was meant to purify the person spiritually before he entered the immaculate space of the angelic monks. Out of the twenty-four verses of this chapter, only half of one deals with the poor (Ch. liii, 24). The tiny place these people occupied in this Rule, together with the ritualized form in which monastic ideals were traditionally cast, made 'works of mercy' in the sense of social commitment highly marginal.[16] The ritual itself kept actions from being socially effective. To what extent for instance was the recurrent risk of starvation attacked by the solemn supper which charitable institutions traditionally offered to twelve poor old men on Maundy Thursday, an oft-cited example of fundamental relief?[17] That their feet were washed and a meal served to

---

[16] It is difficult to follow W. Witters, 'Pauvres et pauvreté dans les coutumes monastiques du moyen-âge', in: M. Mollat (ed.), *Études sur l'histoire de la pauvreté (Moyen Age – XVIe siècle)*. Paris, 1974, i, pp. 177–215 (Publications de la Sorbonne. Série Études, 8), when he states that 'Cette œuvre [= St Bene-dict's Rule], basée sur le principe de la réception de tout hôte comme le Christ, refuse des distinctions sociologiques et combat la tendance naturelle à en créer' (translation: 'This book [St. Benedict's Rule] based upon the prin-ciple of receiving every guest as Christ, rejects sociological distinctions and fights the natural tendency to create them') (p. 213).

[17] Cf. M. Rubin, *Charity and Community in Medieval Cambridge*. Cambridge, 1987, pp. 246–47 (Cambridge Studies in Medieval Life and Thought. Fourth Series). Little, *op. cit.*, pp. 67–68 gives some examples of charity in Cluny, among which a 'king's meal' to be served daily to one pauper. E. Lesne's book on *Histoire de la propriété ecclésiastique en France*. Lille, 1943, iii, which is still a classic work, gives the example of St-Denis, the royal abbey *par excel-lence*, and thus one of the richest within the Kingdom of France (p. 180). Every day five paupers are received and fed. At Easter they get clothes, whereas on Maundy Thursday twelve men have their feet washed and a meal served. Very often, if not most of the time, the almoner's service ac-count from which these expenses are paid, is endowed by private persons with the special purpose of caring for the poor (Cf. B. Harvey, *Westminster*

them had no meaning save as a liturgical commemoration of Jesus' humility and his Last Supper.[18] Helping poor people out of their misery was not at issue for the monks, whose attention was focused on the after-life. An idealized reciprocity within the social system kept the discrepancy alive between 'those who possessed' and 'those who did not'. Structural relief, by which we mean relief coping with more than immediate needs, would have reduced poverty, and consequently undermined the ideal of charity itself. It would have jeopardized the continuity of the ideal and, therefore, it would have narrowed the path to Heaven, already so narrow. Ironically 'those who possessed' could only reach beatitude if misery continued to exist. These words are not an anachronistic assault of a twentieth-century historian on medieval monastic charity, but the paraphrase of the very words of one of the leading religious legislators of the early middle ages, Cesarius of Arles. In his Sermons, read in monasteries all through the medieval epoch, he put it this way: 'If nobody were poor, nobody could give alms and nobody could receive remission of his sins.'[19] The survival of poverty was then a necessary counterpart of condescending philanthropy, practised in the same way as it was in the nineteenth or twentieth century by wealthy business people.

The Rule of St Benedict does indeed show just how marginal the ideal of helping already was. Old habits put aside by the monks were 'to be put away in the wardrobe for the poor' (Ch. lv). What was the social meaning of such an act? Half a per cent of the population stored its old clothing (with the intention of giving it away someday), from a wardrobe already (as a result of the monastic ideal itself) scantily filled. Moreover later sources revealing how monastic life really worked prove (and we refer to an example already given) that voluntary poverty always had priority over economic poverty: in 1130 the monks of Christ Church, Canterbury, sent their old garments to the monks of Andres,

---

Abbey and its Estates in the Middle Ages. Oxford, 1977, p. 30 and *passim*). In those cases the monks should be considered much more the mediators between those who give and those who receive, than active participants in a social deal. P. D. Johnson, *Prayer, Patronage, and Power. The Abbey of la Trinité, Vendôme, 1032–1187*. New York, London, 1981, pp. 156–64 enthusiastically mentions (small) examples of charity not really any different from what happened in other abbeys.

[18] The liturgical meaning of the Works of Mercy is stressed by M. Mollat, 'Les moines et les pauvres', in: *Il monachesimo e la riforma ecclesiastica (1049–1122)*. Milano, 1971, pp. 193–215.

[19] *Sancti Caesarii Arelatensis Sermones*, ed. G. Morin, i. Turnhout, 1953, ep. 25, p. 112 (Corpus Christianorum. Series Latina, ciii).

when their abbey burnt down.[20] Voluntary poor were 'better poor' than the real ones. They were better deserving of help. Spirituality proclaimed its supremacy over economic realities.[21] This attitude explains the competition between these two groups of poor, which steadily increased in the thirteenth century when the mendicant orders made their appearance on the religious scene.

What was the importance of the help monks gave at the gate of their abbey? One reads in narrative or devotional literature of astonishing quantities of bread which were said to have been distributed. It is methodologically legitimate to express doubts about historical sources of this sort as the figures they give are largely coloured by imagination and exaggeration. These doubts do not imply that abbeys were not involved in charity (the Gospel of St Matthew was forceful), but that such an activity, when it went beyond the letter of the Rule, arose from an individual's effort towards spiritual fulfilment and human compassion. The Rule and later customaries are very clear. They did not envisage a system of relief which would have affected the financial and material means of the monastic community itself even though benefactors' donations were often especially intended for alms giving. Customaries prescribe that some, usually fixed, quantities of food or other items should be distributed to a fixed number of poor. In this respect the Statutes of Adalhard of Corbie (822) are useful evidence, as they are steeped in the ideal view of the Carolingian period of a religiously organized secular society. The number of monks in Corbie, one of the most important abbeys of the period, is estimated to have been between 150 and 200.[22] What was their regular social commitment? Among the poor who presented themselves at the gate of the abbey, fifty loaves of bread were distributed, made from less than four pounds of maslin, wheat or spelt. They were thus the same size as what we would now call a roll. The poor also received some beer, and (presumably on special occasions) some cheese and bacon. Those who could pass the night in the poorhouse were the luckiest of all. They got a roll and a half out of this basket of fifty. In order to cover these expenses, a fifth part of certain tithes and of the alms received (estimated at four pence, which represent 6.6 grams

---

[20] William of Andres, *Chronica Andrensis*, ed. I. Heller, in: Monumenta Germaniae Historica, Scriptores, xxiv, p. 698.

[21] In many historical studies the concept of simplicity is designated rather confusingly as 'poverty', apparently the result of Matt. 5:3, 'Blessed are the poor in spirit' (cf. R. Grégoire, 'La place de la pauvreté dans la conception et la pratique de la vie monastique médiévale latine', in: *Il monachesimo e la riforma ecclesiastica (1049–1122)*. Milano, 1971, pp. 172–92).

[22] W. Horn – E. Born, *The Plan of St. Gallen*, I, pp. 342–45.

of silver) was expected to be distributed at the gate.[23] Studies of the expense pattern of Benedictine houses (necessarily for the later middle ages as earlier evidence is lacking) confirm in figures what the Corbie text suggests: that the practice of charity was a marginal phenomenon.[24] The almoner of Christ Church, Canterbury for example, who as such was responsible for the care of the poor, spent only half of one per cent of his income on external poverty relief in the period 1284–1373.[25] Naturally, one should not reproach the medieval monks for this attitude,

[23] *Statuta seu Brevia Adalhardi abbatis Corbeiensis*, ed. J. Semmler. Siegburg, 1963, pp. 365–408 (esp. pp. 372–73) (Corpus Consuetudinum Monasticarum, i) (translated in Horn – Born, *op. cit.*, iii, pp. 103 ss.). Cf. A. Verhulst – J. Semmler, 'Les statuts d'Adalhard de Corbie de l'an 822', in: *Le Moyen Age*, 68, 1962, pp. 91–123, 233–69.

[24] The twelfth-century Customary of the regular canons of Saint-Victor mentions, as work of mercy only the distribution at the gate of the remainders of the refectory in as far as they had been touched. Untouched food returned to the cellarer (L. Jocqué – L. Milis, *Liber Ordinis Sancti Victoris Parisiensis*. Turnhout, 1984, Ch. 12, pp. 43–44).

[25] Rubin, *op. cit.*, p. 247. Other examples, based on modern calculations too, and much more reliable than the verbalism of narrative sources and the theory of normative texts, point in the same direction. Cf. *The Book of William Morton, almoner of Peterborough Monastery. 1448–67*, ed. W. T. Mellows, P. I. Kings and C. N. L. Brooke. Oxford, 1954, pp. xxvi–xxviii (Northamptonshire Record Society 16), pointing out how very little was spent on external alms. R. Snape, *English Monastic Finances in the Later Middle Ages*. Cambridge, 1926, pp. 110–18 stated that less than five per cent of the income of abbeys was spent on alms-giving. He stressed that this came mostly (as we have already stated) from special private endowments. R. A. L. Smith, *Canterbury Cathedral Priory. A Study in Monastic Administration*. Cambridge, 1969, p. 47 calculated that only 0.52% of the almoner's income went to the poor, apart from distributions of corn or occasionally cloth, in the period 1284–1373. The author also refers to other English examples. In the early fifteenth century St Peter's Abbey, Ghent, one of the oldest and richest in the Low Countries, distributed an annual amount which was the equivalent of only 220 to 452 times the daily wage of a bricklayer's mate, whereas other categories of distribution (food, cloth) tended to be symbolic. The sum represented 0.12% to 0.45% of the annual income of the abbey, astonishingly near to the 'social aid' of the Dukes of Burgundy (0.14% to 0.28%); public authority did not indeed enjoy a reputation for generosity (W. P. Blockmans & W. Prevenier, 'Poverty in Flanders and Brabant from the fourteenth to the mid-sixteenth century: sources and problems', in: *Acta historiae Neerlandicae*, x, 1978, pp. 19–57 (esp. 43) and W. Prevenier, 'En marge de l' assistance aux pauvres: l'aumônerie des comtes de Flandre et des ducs de Bourgogne (13e – début 16e siècle)', in: *Recht en instellingen in de Oude Nederlanden tijdens de middeleeuwen en de Nieuwe Tijd. Liber amicorum Jan Buntinx*. Leuven, 1981, pp. 97–120 (esp. 113) (Symbolae A 10).

because other, larger and more adequate concepts of 'social security' are standard nowadays. Nevertheless one needs to correct the exaggerated and often uncritical image so widely held of their charity, that of vast crowds of poor people swarming daily about the gate, while father porter generously distributes bread. What did the thirty-six pounds of bread distributed daily by the Cluniacs mean in terms of structural relief,[26] considering that, due to the benevolence of rich donors, these monks built three consecutive huge churches in a span of two centuries. The last church was the largest and the most sumptuous ever built in the middle ages, a proof of how the monks' gaze was directed towards Heaven. The fact that figures in narrative sources always have to be approached with caution (and not only the number of enemies reported killed in battles past and present) is one of the first things drilled into history students in their classes on historical methodology. It has only rarely been applied to the field of religious studies, not even to investigate whether or not the figures given are (materially or topographically) possible at all.[27] How, for instance, could a vast crowd be fed at the gate of a Cistercian abbey when it was (as usual) settled in 'the desert', far away from towns or villages?

It is necessary, however, to stress how specific religious concerns had an impact on the significance of alms giving. Therefore we turn to the monks of the Cluniac order known for the spiritual care they took of the dead. Their necrologies, registers containing the names of about 48,000 deceased monks and benefactors, clearly witness this activity.[28] According to the Cluniac customaries, one poor man had a meal served during the thirty days following the death of a monk, as well as on his 'anniversary'. In the middle of the twelfth century this tradition had become a considerable financial burden, when, according to the calculations of J. Wollasch, three to four hundred monks were expected to distribute annually eighteen thousand meals. Their abbot Peter the Venerable complained that 'there is always a crowd of guests and the number of poor people is innumerable', a statement sufficiently convincing to justify his decision to limit the aid to fifty daily meals. One should neither underes-

---

[26] The example is given by L. Moulin, *op. cit.*, p. 291. How far the evaluation of charity may be influenced by personal involvement is illustrated by the recent and undoubtedly wrong and unreliable statement of a Cistercian author that hungry people were dying at the gates of Benedictine houses, whereas his own predecessors generously helped them (J.-B. Auberger, 'Spiritualité de l'architecture cistercienne du XIIe siècle', in: *Visages cisterciens*. Paris, 1990, pp. 64–72 (Sources vives, 33)).

[27] Cf. for example L. Moulin, *op. cit.*, esp. pp. 290–95.

[28] J. Wollasch, 'Konventsstärke und Armensorge in mittelalterlichen Klöstern. Zeugnisse und Fragen', in: *Saeculum*, 39, 1988, pp. 184–99.

timate nor underscore its importance as we are dealing here with the richest abbey of the middle ages, spending more than any other on building.

Monks were involved in the care of the sick. This is too sweeping a generalization and needs more subtle distinction. As a rule, black and white Benedictines only organized a hospital for the members of their own community, where sick and elderly monks could benefit from a less rigid observance and a more appropriate diet. For their own convenience they were secluded from the community itself, if possible in a separate building or at least in a separate dwelling. But not only for that reason. Their looser life-style, which was characterized by the consumption of meat, bathing facilities, and the temporary suppression of the imposed rule of silence, was to be kept outside the conventual rhythm. The risk of spreading contagious diseases was another explanation for this seclusion. The astonishingly vast dimensions some of the infirmaries had (generally built east of the cloister) should not make us believe that they were meant for sick people from outside the community. Afterwards, however, in the fourteenth and fifteenth centuries, when the monastic population decreased, parts of the infirmaries happened to be let out, at least in England, as retirement flats for wealthy people, paying corrodies.[29]

When, in the ninth century, the Carolingian emperors planned social welfare with a lot of idealism but few effective means, they proposed the foundation of asylums for the elderly, for orphans and the like. Although we know how important abbeys were in the blueprint these rulers made of an ideal society on Earth, they did not seem to delegate tasks either of the management or of the sick people's care itself to Benedictines.[30] Examples undoubtedly can be found of hospitals run by monks.[31] When monasteries had anything to do with hospitals, it was mostly as owners, administering them from the distance. When it existed, such a hospital only seldom formed part of the monastic buildings. Generally it was situated in the neighbourhood or even far away in another town or another village. It was most often founded by secular or ecclesiastical benefactors and bestowed on the abbeys afterwards. The staff did not as a rule belong to the monastic community itself and when its members lived according to a religious observance, they mostly followed the Rule of St Augustine, even when the owners were Benedictines. St Augustine's Rule was in fact more appropriate than the one St

---

[29] On the Continent it presumably was a later phenomenon.

[30] *Capitula e lege romana excerpta* (A. Boretius (ed.), *Capitularia Regum Francorum*. Hannover, 1883, i, pp. 310–11 (probably the year 826)).

[31] D. Knowles – R. N. Hadcock, *Medieval Religious Houses. England and Wales*. London, 1971[2], pp. 310–40 (esp. p. 311).

Benedict wrote, as it was more open to secular affairs, and shorter too, leaving more room for interpretation. To be more precise, they lived according to one of the Rules attributed to St Augustine or, as D. Knowles stressed, they even followed a looser life-style based on such a rule. The personnel, composed of brethren and sisters, was directed by a master or a prior or a warden who were not monks (or nuns). It is rare to find Benedictines directly involved in curing the sick. In the late middle ages it happened once in a while that 'friars' or 'sisters' (with a life-style and status often not clearly identifiable) adopted the Cistercian observance, while continuing to exercise their former social function. The Bijloke-hospital in Ghent is a nice example of such a change from sisterhood to Cistercianism in the 1230s.[32] Although proofs of monastic management can be found quite regularly, the care of the sick itself was at the most a marginal activity and never served as a common way of implementing the biblical command to 'love thy neighbour'.[33] Medical care for outsiders was not a goal of the Benedictine movement and this explains why in the later middle ages networks of Augustinian friars or purely secular establishments (mainly in towns) provided a more adequate health service.

What about hospitality? We have already referred to what St Benedict said in his Rule. Rich and high-ranking people could make use of the guest facilities of the abbeys, and what it sometimes could mean, later on, can be gathered from the lavish (post-medieval) rooms of the Carthusian monastery outside Florence. Towards the poor and pilgrims, so we are told in the Rule, the greatest care was to be shown. This is shown to be, if only partly, a reality by the installation of a network of monastic houses along roads. We have particularly in mind those on the route to Santiago de Compostela in northern Spain, one of the most popular of all pilgrimage routes. Every night pilgrims could find solace in one of the monastic houses after another dangerous and painful day on their long journey to the shrine of St James. We should, however, have no illusions as to the extent of such hospitality. This hospitality only existed towards pilgrims, and even then there were real limitations![34] In other

---

[32] G. Van Acker, 'Abbaye de la Byloque à Gand', in: *Monasticon belge. Tome VII. Province de Flandre orientale*, 3. Liège, 1980, pp. 329–53.

[33] The twenty-six English, Welsh and Scottish hospitals and hospices enumerated by D. N. Bell, 'The English Cistercians and the Practice of Medicine', in: *Cîteaux. Commentarii Cistercienses*, 40, 1989, pp. 139–74 (all of them with a very different history, scope, organization and monastic status) do not convince us 'that the Cistercians were more deeply concerned about the local population than one might suspect'.

[34] The bizarre early fifteenth century visionary Margery Kempe slept in inns on her way to Jerusalem, Rome, Compostela and Wilsnak (Brandenburg,

words, the relief system only functioned for those who freely chose exile and hunger, with God and their salvation in mind. Once again voluntary self-denial was esteemed of a higher level than involuntary suffering. The merchants whose presence on the roads steadily increased from the eleventh century onwards were not the guests expected by the standard of the Rule. Their economic activity (involving as it did material gain, which was seen as both religiously and morally unacceptable) made them unwelcome, and so undoubtedly did their personal behaviour. They would have disturbed the monastery as a haven of peace and piety.

Nor were the hospitals or guest-houses intended as shelters for the homeless, at least not in the sense that they were a means of resolving that social problem. The aforementioned ninth-century Statutes of Corbie, one of the most important abbeys of the time, allowed twelve men to sleep in the poorhouse, and even when this was a sign of kindness, it was in no way an attempt to overcome the need. More effective, though still inadequate, measures for the succour of the homeless were only taken from the late twelfth and the thirteenth centuries onwards, and then usually in an urban environment.[35] Hospitals were founded and endowed by the urban magistrate or by wealthy people but only rarely by the nobility. They functioned usually with a nursing staff recruited from religious movements outside Benedictinism. The charity of the late middle ages remained, if to a lesser extent, ritualized. It undoubtedly reached more people, fortunately, I would say, at a time when more need was felt. First an increasing, and afterwards a decreasing standard of living implied a more intensely felt poverty. It seems as if urban indigent people could not be so easily cared for through the solidarity of kin or community as in the predominantly rural context of the previous centuries unless systems of charity were organized.[36]

Monks fasted a great deal. One might wonder what the (socially indirect) effect of this voluntary starvation could have been on the availability of food and thus on the survival chances of the poor. This can provide us with an easy and illustrative exercise. If monks (approximately one half of one per cent of the total population) ate half of what other non-indigent persons did, and the portion saved were to be distributed among 10%, 20% or even up to 66% of the total population

---

Germany). See L. Collins, *Memoirs of a Medieval Woman. The Life and Times of Margery Kempe*. New York, 1983[2].

[35] G. Maréchal, *De sociale en politieke gebondenheid van het Brugse hospitaalwezen in de middeleeuwen*. Kortrijk, 1978 (English summary on pp. 309–12) (Anciens Pays et Assemblées d'États – Standen en Landen, lxxiii).

[36] M. Rubin, *op. cit.*, pp. 49–53.

(depending on the period and on the area), then, obviously, the subsistence effect was virtually nil.[37]

Monasticism was an ideal for longing for heaven and as such it was largely absent from the systems of charity which were worked out to cope more effectively with real needs. The monastery was a dream of unreality in which the free choice to abandon self-will ideologically dominated its behavioural pattern. All denial was emphasized as a sign of poverty, which in turn was a sign of humility. This historical statement corresponds to the teachings of the Cluniac abbot Peter the Venerable who preached entrance into the way of poverty, particularly of that spiritual poverty which consists rather in the practice of humility than in the renunciation of earthly goods.[38] The monks' belief in the superiority of spirituality elevated this humility to social pride. Paternalism, even displayed with the best intention possible, as it is here, could not have functioned otherwise.

THE IMPACT ON THE DEMOGRAPHIC SITUATION

To question the demographic impact of monasticism may seem a fruitless exercise. Monks and nuns led a celibate life, and even if some transgressed their vow of chastity, this cannot have had the slightest influence on the birth rate. The question, however, can be put in a more pertinent way. Even when hard evidence is lacking, we may suppose that an important part of those entering monastic life were of noble blood, their number and proportion varying in time and space. A demographic effect, if an indirect one, should be apparent within the noble class, emphasizing the fact that 'God's calling' fitted in astonishingly well with the interest which the noble kinship groups had in not dividing their property between too many offspring. The influence of monasticism on the demographic situation of the nobility can be evaluated, even if roughly: something like 1% of the total population (monks and nuns) taken from a social class which can be estimated to have represented a maximum of 3% or 4%.[39] In other words, one quarter to one

---

[37] The figures are given in K. Bosl, *Armut Christi*, pp. 9–10 for fifteenth-century Augsburg.

[38] G. Constable, *The Letters of Peter the Venerable*. Cambridge, Mass., 1967, i, p. 16, Letter 9. – Cf. M. Peaudecerf, *La pauvreté à l'abbaye de Cluny d'après son cartulaire*, in: M. Mollat (ed.), *Éudes sur l'histoire de la pauvreté*, i, pp. 217–27 (spec. p. 227, but with incorrect reference).

[39] Ph. Contamine, 'The French Nobility and the War', in: *The Hundred Years War*, ed. K. Fowler. London, 1971, pp. 137–45. (reprinted in: *La France au [sic] XIVe et XVe siècles. Hommes, mentalités, guerre et paix*. London, 1981). He gives

third of the members of noble families were subject to monastic celibacy and spiritually imposed infertility. These figures, even if not in themselves entirely reliable, are nevertheless meaningful, as they are the result of an accumulation of other approximations. Since one portion of the nobility was absorbed by monastic life, and yet another part by a clerical career within the secular Church (as bishops, canons and the like), obviously a significant proportion of the noble youngsters of each succeeding generation were demographically neutralized. They were cast in the religious and ethical mould Christianity had worked out. Nobility found in the abandonment of the married status by part of its members an excellent means of restricting its numbers and its consequent risk of impoverishment. We may call it a deferred method of birth control. That handicapped children were placed in monasteries is further proof of this tenet, supported by archaeological evidence.[40] For the nobility, monasticism and its organizational structure were useful as a means of guaranteeing a dominant position in society. Thus monasticism functioned as part of the self-perpetuation of the ruling class, even though the goal of monasticism was of a completely different nature. The mutual link made monastic houses wealthy and powerful, although such an evolution obviously menaced the spiritual aim of St Benedict and of the other monastic legislators. However manifest and convincingly appropriate the link seemed (and emphatically so in the secondary literature), it constituted a structural impediment endangering the realization of genuine monasticism. How can St Benedict's original settlements of Subiaco or Monte Cassino be recognized later in such powerful abbeys as Monte Cassino itself, or Cluny? The many reforms of Vallombrosa, Camaldoli and Cîteaux, among others, looking back at the 'original purity' and aiming at its restoration, prove how difficult such an identification had indeed been.

From the material, and even from the spiritual, point of view we can quite easily understand that abbeys limited the free admission of candi-

figures ranging from 1.3% to 3.7% according to the (French) regions and for the Late Middle Ages.

[40] The malformations of the (recently excavated) skeleton of Abbot Lambert IV of the Flemish abbey of Ename (*c.* 1200), as well as the written records about his physical weakness and his psychological dependence on important people (*Annales abbatum monasterii Eenamensis*, ed. U. Berlière, in: Documents inédits pour servir à l'histoire ecclésiastique de la Belgique. Maredsous, 1894, i, p. 122), are a likely proof of such a case. In a revealing article Anthony Molho, 'Tamquam vera mortua. Le professioni religiose femminili nella Firenze del tardo medioevo', in: *Società e storia*, 43, 1989, pp. 1–44, considers physical or mental handicaps a major reason for young girls entering religious life in late medieval Florence.

dates, so that the number of monks was kept stable. For ordinary abbeys an abbot had authority over twelve monks. This referred to the number of the apostles and had a symbolic meaning, although larger abbeys greatly exceeded this number. Smaller houses, more specifically the dependent priories, often housed only three or four monks.[41] Even if every generation of monks brought in a new set of dowries, their theoretical maximum number currently remained unchanged for several reasons, most of all for the sake of preserving wealth, and thus ensuring a decent standard of living. Poverty in the monastic sense of absence of private property and absence of power was not allowed to lead to poverty in its literal sense. This was, at the same time, a means of keeping the monastery a haven for a select group, even if one where the members could have been rejected individually by their own social group. This suggests the inevitability of a re-styling of this type of abbey from the moment the social dynamism of the second half of the middle ages broke up the existing equilibrium. Otherwise it would have been outclassed by new and better adapted houses or orders. The fact that strictly and exclusively noble abbeys existed throughout the middle ages and the early modern period, especially in Germany, does not invalidate what we have said. On the contrary. They were and remained an expression of this class, of its expectations and of its needs, but as a rule their spiritual role (and do monasteries have any other role to play?) was very limited indeed, reflecting the impact of their class, which was in any case decreasing.

So 'modern times' asked for 're-stored' or 're-formed', adjusted, solutions. The 'twelfth-century renaissance' marks the break. Several major factors influenced the rise of new religious movements, new orders and new houses. The religious landscape of, let us say, 1150, was dramatically different from that of 1050, and it was to change even more in the century to come. First of all, a shift in the social status of the abbey founders is apparent, and this led naturally to demographic repercussions, since there was such an obvious link between founders and monks. All through the eleventh and following centuries lower-ranking noble people, and later even urban burghers, spent money settling monks or nuns. This phenomenon was part of a much larger movement which one can hardly call democratic, but which meant, at any rate, that financial means, power and a feeling of 'what should be done to be

---

[41] Horn – Born, *op. cit.*, i, pp. 342–45 often give, in our opinion, questionable figures for the great Carolingian abbeys. Reliable (and high) figures are enumerated by D. Knowles, *The Monastic Order in England*, pp. 713–14 for the big English Benedictine abbeys. The estimated average, however, is between 11.8 and 13.5 monks per house (D. Knowles – R. N. Hadcock, *Medieval religious Houses. England and Wales*, p. 489).

fashionable' became more widespread. And even when kings continued to found abbeys in the twelfth century, as so clearly happened in England and Scotland, the importance of the initial endowment was normally lower than in earlier centuries. Consequently Benedictine houses steadily lost their international character, and among the newly founded houses few could compete, either in wealth or in number of monks, with the venerable ones of times past. Nevertheless Benedictine abbeys remained select places, where entry was difficult for those who did not belong to the right social or kin-linked group. One of the possible responses to the population growth (and to a similar increase in the number of candidates) might have been for existing abbeys to accept more monks. It would have meant for them, however, a certain restriction in their life-style, as they increasingly had to share possible endowments with more fervent and thus more attractive movements. This would in any case have gone against the grain for a monastic life so firmly rooted in nobility, and consequently the fixed quotas normally were not raised.

New groups arose. As for the founders, they were generally less important, their means more limited, and consequently the endowments they could provide were correspondingly less generous. Very often it became more profitable, in the sense of the relationship between material investment and spiritual return, to go outside the Benedictine movement. At a time when the Gregorian Reform stressed the restitution of Church property (churches, tithes) 'illicitly' held by lay owners, it seemed for them at least as appropriate to found, for instance, secular chapters. As in monasteries, superfluous children of their own could function here as canons, but in contrast to what generally happened in the case of Benedictines, the former could ensure their own living with the income from the cure of souls in which they were involved. Erecting a chapter was thus less expensive and less of a drain on the founder's financial resources. At the same time it was in their eyes, religiously speaking, equally fruitful as the foundation was the tariff paid for moral guilt.

First, as I have said, there was a shift in the social status of the founders. A second phenomenon is the deeper religious feeling, coming down now from the elitist group of the first period of the middle ages to lower (but still 'upper middle class') categories. More places had to be made available for the fulfilment of an increased religious motivation. On the one hand, traditional Benedictinism was select and entry therein difficult. On the other hand, new experiments, outside the monasteries, were mostly transitory. The eremitical settlements, for instance, normally became, after a relatively short time, abbeys or priories, or simply disappeared. The Church, more and more cast in an institutional and juridical mould, was wary of experiments. New movements had thus to fit into a framework which the Church could both recognize and approve.

According to this logic, the Cistercian movement met all possible conditions, as did the regular canons of Prémontré, Arrouaise, St- Victor and certain other orders. These borrowed much of their organizational pattern from Cîteaux, and their spirituality was very similar. They all fulfilled the basic condition of the official Church that new forms of religious life must continue to work within the precincts of cloisters. Only when approved could their lifestyle hope to be successful. In an increasingly dynamic society the new movements had to be more open to people, and the major means of accomplishing this was through the emergence of 'lay brotherhood', even though its members, the *conversi*, were not monks. Moreover, as we know, the cost of foundation was less. Most often abbeys of Cistercians and of regular canons started with a very poor endowment which they had to extend themselves through 'fund raising' and efficient management. A religious life-style considered decent was no longer 'the rich poverty' it used to be among black monks. Estimates for England as well as for Flanders[42] show that even though the absolute number of religious people increased, their relative number remained about the same, as a result of population growth. The opening of religious life to a larger segment of the population (now including lower nobility, wealthy peasants, and perhaps some townsfolk) made it possible for these categories to achieve the same demographic effect that the higher nobility had earlier reached. The *oblatio*-system, leading youngsters to enter, continued to work, except in those very moments of religious revival. At the same time, however, the establishment of primogeniture prevented the division of inheritance. Certainly, this system, from the point of view of kindred, removed the risk of impoverishment, and this was very important, but it did not resolve the problem of what to do with those children not first-born. For them the same solution as in the previous period was apparently chosen: entering the monastery and thus removing the possibility of offspring. Nevertheless, since the proportion of religious people in relation to the total population does not seem to have increased before the thirteenth century, the demographic impact of the phenomenon described for the twelfth century varied only a little from that in the preceding period. A growing difference was that the possibilities of demographic restriction, and thus of protected patrimonies, steadily came within the reach of an enlarged elite. For the vast majority of the population nothing had changed. Their limited chances of entering their supernumerary children as *conversi* (supposing that these chances were

---

[42] See D. Knowles, *The Monastic Order in England*, p. 679, D. Knowles & R. N. Hadcock, *Medieval Religious Houses. England and Wales*, London, 1972[2], pp. 489–90, and my own figures in the next chapter.

real), did not have any tangible effect on the size of their social group. We are in fact speaking in terms of fractions of percents. Moreover, just as black Benedictine houses had come to limit the number of their monks, the new ones eventually did so also. By the late twelfth century, for instance, this fact provoked dissatisfaction with the limited possibilities of entering into religious life, especially in the case of women. I am not sure whether one should prefer to say that the discontentment arose 'among women' aspiring religious life, or 'on behalf of women', as it is not apparent who exactly made the choice of their life-style. Was it their own decision, or was it commonly made by their fathers and families? The personal involvement seems to prevail when the new movements bloom, but when the charismatic vitality fades, the second possibility is more likely; it was not at all against the canon law prescription of free choice, which was formally and solemnly respected when taking vows. The continuing evolution of the demographic situation, social relations (a reduced inequality) and a more interior faith made the changes towards new religious observances, now of the thirteenth century, easy to understand. The mendicant orders and such movements as the beguines corresponded better, not only socially and mentally but also demographically, to this changed society. From then on, at least in its most important and active areas, Europe had become (socially, not demographically) predominantly urban. The general trend for some centuries had been to create more vacancies to comply with the double phenomenon of population growth and a greater calling to religious life from 'middle class' levels. The result was that new monasteries were and remained less wealthy than the older ones had been and that they were less glamorous (taking for granted the riches of the Cistercians). Founding houses was less expensive, and the spiritual result, salvation, seemed even more assured. More people hoped to reach Heaven at a lower rate of investment.

5

Value Systems,
Christian and Monastic

CHRISTIAN VALUES AND ETHICS

In this chapter I will try to measure the impact of monasticism on medieval 'mentality'. I understand this to be the system which governs our feelings and our ideas, insofar as it is culturally determined, which means socially acquired. Hence it constitutes a part of the notion 'culture', in the broad sense of this word, as it was used by E. B. Tylor as early as 1871 and afterwards refined.[1] 'Culture' also includes modes of behaviour, and according to some, even the products which are its results.

Our concept of mentality thus consists of values organized into a system. The feelings and the ideas which it governs are 'expressions' of the mentality; they 'show' what the mentality looks like. Acts are themselves the results of feelings and ideas. They are 'expressions' too, undoubtedly as illustrative, but only at a secondary level. There is in fact an intermediary level of feelings and ideas themselves. The filter to be used must be of cultural origin, by definition, even if there exists a certain vagueness as to the delimitation of what is naturally determined and what is culturally acquired.

A Society Modelled after Monastic Ideals?

In order to know if monastic ideals did influence society we have to describe those ideals. We have to penetrate the value system which governed the monk's life of seclusion and denial. To begin this chapter, I would like to turn to St Benedict, by far the most important of all monastic legislators. His Rule, written in approximately the mid-sixth century, is very concise and in a very clear style which leaves virtually no opportunity for ambiguous understanding, even if different inter-

---

[1] According to Tylor 'Culture [. . .] is that complex whole which includes knowledge, belief, art, law, morals, custom, and any other capabilities and habits acquired by man as a member of society'.

St Benedict in his cell tempted by seven nude girls

(Fifteenth-century miniature in John of Stavelot, Vita beati Benedicti abbatis. Liège, 1432. Chantilly, Musée Condé, ms. 738/1041 f. 135. Photo courtesy of Giraudon)

pretations have been given all through the centuries. It prescribes a life in community, it stresses its spiritual aim (perfection), and it shows how the intrinsic tensions which would hinder the fulfilment of this goal should be avoided.

Other monastic counsellors were Cassian and the so-called Master. John Cassian came in the late fourth century from the Near East – the first roots of cenobitical and eremitical life were in fact located in Egypt and Syria – to Gaul. He wrote two books, namely the *Institutiones*, a Rule imposing prescriptions, and the *Collationes*, 'Talks' between old and venerable abbots and younger disciples. They are not a rule as such, but more like spiritual guidelines, serving as a model for a monastic lifestyle. The other legislator is the unidentified, so-called Master, model or follower of St Benedict.[2] In the Celtic World several other monastic movements and rules flourished and their followers were responsible for the conversion of large parts of England and continental Europe.[3]

If we want to know what the value system of medieval monasticism was, it seems most appropriate to use St Benedict's Rule as a point of departure, since this was the dominant one, and in exclusive use between roughly 800 and 1100. It is expressed most explicitly in four chapters out of a total of seventy-three. Chapter iv is called 'What are the Instruments of Good Works?', v 'On Obedience', vi 'On the Spirit of Silence' and vii 'On Humility'. Chapter iv is by far the longest. It is a list of seventy-four *instrumenta*, which means tools. They have a general purpose, and are usually based on the New Testament. There are, however, some which do not have biblical backing.

We do not have to go through all of these 'sentences', as one might call them after the formally (not intrinsically) analogous texts from antiquity, such as the *Distichs of Cato*, a text which was, as we will see, one of the most popular school-books of the middle ages.

The deeper meaning of St Benedict's sentences is love and trust towards God: this both starts and ends the enumeration. The other sentences pad out these basic certainties. They can be summarized as follows. We must love God. This implies love of one's neighbour, even if he does evil to us. We must escape and avoid all sins in act as well as in thought. We should have in mind the final confrontation with God, that is to say the moment of death, of the Last Judgment and of Hell. Prayers

2 The question of which text is the earlier remains a problem under discussion. M. Dunn, 'Mastering Benedict: Monastic Rules and their Authors in the Early Medieval West', in: *The English Historical Review*, cv, 1990, pp. 567–94, supports the priority of St Benedict.

3 M. Richter, 'England and Ireland in the Time of Willibrord', in: P. Bange and A. G. Weiler (ed.), *Willibrord, zijn wereld en zijn werk*. Nijmegen, 1990, pp. 35–50 (Middeleeuwse studies, vi).

are the path which leads towards salvation. Individual will and pride must be tamed. Hence obedience must be observed, as it holds us back from evil tendencies and acts. The list is not clearly structured, and sometimes the same idea is expressed in several sentences. It might suggest that the Master compiled his chapter from various models.[4]

Perusing the whole of the seventy-four sentences in chapter iv, we see that some are directed at Christian society in general. This is the more likely for the first nine, where the Decalogue is paraphrased. 'Do not commit adultery' is one of these. Even though it can be used metaphorically in a monastic context, it refers in fact to married people, and not to monks. Other sentences are addressed only to a religious community: the one which stresses the necessity for listening willingly to holy reading (55) for example, or the one which refers to the presence of an abbot (61). This serves to underline the ambiguity in the conception of this list. The Master, and Benedict, at times explicitly, at others implicitly, show the general Christian value system, with only a few specific references to its monastic implementation.

The other three chapters, on obedience, silence and humility, constitute an appendix to chapter iv.[5] Together they form a single unit in the sense that they serve to impose a transcendental as well as a social system based on authority. One must obey! This implies silence, and silence implies humility. These are undoubtedly general values within Christian ethics, but they are emphasized more when they are intended to function in the closed and hierarchical monastic community.

The question of where and how the Christian value system differed from the traditional late Roman system, and how it transformed accepted views on the ideal functioning of society, can be answered by comparing St Benedict's system with the *Brief Sentences* (*Breves Sententiae*) of the *Distichs of Cato* (probably written in the third century).[6] The most obvious parallel can be seen in the importance attached to God from the very beginning of both texts. In both this is followed by respect, if not love, for one's neighbour. This is a structural analogy. A resemblance can also be perceived in the content of the values: love your parents (2), do not lie (44), do not get angry (45), do not envy another's goods (54). Some of the points stressed in the Christian model are the inevitable result of its absolute and uncompromising character. The

---

4 *La Règle du Maître*, ed. A. de Vogüé. Paris, 1964, pp. 364–75 (Sources chrétiennes, 105–07).
5 Cf. the excellent pages of A. de Vogüé, *The Rule of St. Benedict. A Doctrinal and Spiritual Commentary.* Kalamazoo, MI, 1983, pp. 77–90 (Cistercian Studies Series 54).
6 *Disticha Catonis*, edd. M. Boas & H. J. Botschuyver. Amsterdam, 1952, pp. 11–30.

personal equilibrium hoped for in the *Sententiae* (feast seldom, 18; sleep enough, 19; keep away from prostitutes, 25), was reinforced in the monastic observance, and even to a large extent in the Christian life-style ideal for lay people. The prescriptions became: do not feast, do not sleep, live in chastity, for otherwise the Devil will defile you. The major difference between the Roman and the Christian concepts lies in the sense of social interaction. Christianity is not concerned with social structures or the smooth functioning of society as a goal in itself. If society is organized, this is only a transient situation of no substantial importance at all, soon to give way to God's eternal Order. Such points, for example, as obedience to the law court (5), to magistrates (11), or the military defence of the country (23), present in the *Distichs* find no counterpart in Christian ethics. Another difference appears in the respective attitudes towards learning. The individual, personal fulfilment, stressed by the *Sententiae*: read books (26), remind yourself of what you read (27) and instruct your children (28), is not, in general, emphasized in the Christian value system. Simplicity of the mind is the attitude it normally adopts: not learning acquired through books, but the acceptance in faith of God's message. This attitude, however, seems to have been the result of an evolution, for in monastic rules and in the *Vitae* of early medieval monastic saints the importance of study does not seem at all incompatible with an ideal religious life-style – on the contrary. We can understand this analogy by examining the early medieval belief that words are only worth writing down when they have an eternal value. Ordinary people only came into contact with books as part of the religious tactics of missionaries. And even then, it was not the content, but the magical function of the written word which explains their use. Nevertheless Christians saw nothing at all incompatible with their doctrine in the *Distichs*, precisely because of the large degree of agreement between the two. This explains why the *Distichs* were used as a school textbook for so long, being finally abandoned only in the nineteenth century.

The Content of the Value System

The Seven Sins for all

What most students of the Christian value system find noteworthy, is the importance attributed to sin, which is largely the responsibility of St Paul. The word sin occurs in fact as many times in his *Letters* alone as in the rest of the New Testament. The pessimism as to the final fate of all Creation is an explanation, albeit an inadequate one, since this belief is shared by other cultures or religions who do not know sin in the same sense. In this respect one must emphasize the difference between the violation of a taboo and a sin. Both are wrong and should be avoided, but the former is only an exterior act, involving no moral guilt. The evolution of the concept sin from mere act to thought and feeling is one of the most striking changes undergone by Christian ethics up to the twelfth century. We can see it happen through, for instance, the evolution of those taboos (concerning purity) enumerated in the Biblical Books Leviticus and Deuteronomy; they become sins in the so-called penitential books, early medieval manuals used by priests on the occasion of confession.

Christianity fundamentally believed that mankind was corrupt and inclined to evil since the Fall. That is why the monastic legislators thought a 'workshop' was necessary to elaborate a good 'art' or 'craft', in order to shape a good product, a man 'of steel', oriented towards God. Mankind descended from Adam and Eve, and was held responsible for their sin according to the solidarity principle of kinship-organized societies. This means that hereditary evil was present in every individual (naturally with the exception of Mary).

The Rule of the Master gives an enumeration of all the vices in chapter v. This list was completely dropped by St Benedict, presumably not because it was too exhaustive, but because he made his monks read Cassian who provided a more systematic list, with which we will deal later on. The Master distinguished thirty-three vices, grouped into nine categories, suggestive of symbolic combinations.

Nevertheless, the 'Seven Sins' became the standard notion, seven being a symbolic number as well. These seven, taken together, represent altogether the totality of evil. It implies that the enemy, the Devil, should be engaged by virtues, also numbering seven, in order to restrain the works of sin to the same, full extent.

The 'Capital Sins' were, both in the Western context and within a monastic setting, enumerated for the first time by Cassian.[7] His inspiration came from such older, Greek authors as Origen and Evagrius. Cassian is largely concerned with the description of these sins. His *Conlatio v* deals exclusively with the (eight) principal vices. Even greater is the importance he attributes to them in his *Cenobitical Institutions*.[8] This text is composed of twelve books or chapters, of which eight are dedicated to the description of the following vices and the remedies against them: gluttony, lust, avarice, anger, sadness, sloth, envy and

---

7   *Conférences* [= *Conlationes*], ed. E. Pichery. Paris, 1955, vol. I, pp. 197–99, (v, 10) (Sources chrétiennes, 42).

8   *Institutions cénobitiques*, ed. J.-C. Guy. Paris, 1965 (Sources chrétiennes, 109). An admirable selection has been translated by O. Chadwick, *Western Asceticism*. London, 1958, pp. 190–289 (Library of Christian Classics, 12). A fundamental study has been written by M. W. Bloomfield, *The Seven Deadly Sins: An Introduction to the History of a Religious Concept*. East Lansing, 1952.

finally pride (*gula, luxuria, avaritia, ira, tristitia, acedia (anxietas cordis), invidia,* and *superbia*). As we have said, most of the time one speaks of the 'Seven Sins', even though eight are enumerated. In which case *pride* or *vanity* was the eighth, not as the least important, but precisely because it was considered so fundamental that it was seen as the source of all the others. It was a sin, *the sin,* against the omnipotence of God himself.

Cassian's list was used by Pope Gregory the Great (*c.* 600) in his *Moralia in Iob.*[9] Both exercised an important influence on later religious ethics, although even independently of Gregory other (slightly later) authoritative authors also copied Cassian's list: Isidore of Seville, presumably Columban, and the Penitential of Cummean, authors from different horizons (Spanish and Irish) and writing different types of texts.

It is very significant to consider St Francis' thirteenth-century opinions on vice and virtue, and the dissimilar classification he made. Although he was a religious legislator, he was not a monastic one. The movement he created reacted against monasticism, traditional and reformed, in prescribing for his followers a charismatic life-style more embedded in society. His followers were to live in individual, absolute poverty, renouncing private property as monks did, but also rejecting material possessions as a community. The brethren had to beg for their daily survival, just as real, non-voluntary paupers had to do for theirs. In a hymn to the virtues, the *Admonitiones,* St Francis opposes virtues to vices.[10] Eleven vices were opposed to eleven virtues: fear, ignorance, anger, perturbation, cupidity, avarice, worry, instability, hostility, superfluity, and obduracy (*timor, ignorantia, ira, perturbatio, cupiditas, avaritia, sollicitudo, vagatio, inimicus, superfluitas, induratio*). It seems a rather haphazard list, probably as a result of St Francis' positive teaching aim.[11]

Sins for all . . . that was the subtitle we used. In fact, the whole concept of the Creation was negative as a result of the Fall. Mankind was bad, and only by living very severely and devoutly, was there any chance of being saved for eternity. Since the Fall, vice had gained priority. The vices were to be combated primarily by a virtuous life.

---

[9] *S. Gregorii Magni Moralia in Iob. Libri XXIII–XXXV,* ed. M. Adriaen. Turnhout, 1985, pp. 1610–12 (liber xxxi, c. clv) (Corpus Christianorum. Series Latina, 143B).

[10] *François d'Assise, Écrits,* edd. Th. Desbonnets *et al.* Paris, 1981, pp. 114–15 (Sources chrétiennes 285). Cf. also the *Salutatio virtutum* (ib. pp. 270–73).

[11] It is very striking that *lust* is not mentioned at all. This does not mean, however, that it did not have any importance within his value system. Chastity is already dealt with in the first chapter of Francis' First Rule, as one of the religious vows.

The Seven Virtues for some

The statement just made implies that the virtues, as weapons in the war against the vices, were very difficult to manage. Once again, we could go through the whole evolution of their content and their number, but the result would be very similar to what we have seen respecting the vices. The Rule of the Master gives in Chapter iv a list of twenty-eight virtues. At the head are the virtues of Faith, Hope and Love, the so-called theological virtues.

Throughout the Carolingian epoch, however, theologians, very often commentators in search of allegories, looked for the 'Seven Virtues'. In an effort to use Ancient philosophy the three aforesaid virtues were combined with the four known since Socrates: *prudentia, fortitudo, temperantia* and *iustitia* (prudence, fortitude, temperance, justice). The humanism of the Ancient philosophers, and of their ethical system as such, fitted in completely with what Christianity intended to teach. Yet, there was a major difference: the vices and also the three virtues addressed Mankind in its totality, whereas the four 'cardinal virtues' did not address the same audience. These were meant to support the actions and to strengthen the position of an élite. Not everybody, for instance, was expected to be strong. Obedience, yes obedience, was considered to be necessary in any social organization, whereas strength was a quality conferred only on the ruler. So was justice, and so were the other two. Many medieval writings, theoretical as well as practical, stress the link with rulership. It was still interpreted in that way in the late medieval wall-paintings by Ambrogio Lorenzetti in the *Palazzo pubblico* of Siena, where they are placed in the context of 'Good Government'. In fact, much more than the vices, the virtues came to be impoverished by reducing them to seven.

St Francis, however, and once again I refer to the verses in his *Admonitiones*, distinguished eleven virtues:[12] *Caritas, sapientia, patientia, humilitas, paupertas, laetitia, quies, meditatio, timor Domini, misericordia, discretio* (Charity, wisdom, patience, humility, poverty, joy, serenity, meditation, the fear of God, compassion, discretion). St Francis' combination points much more towards the practical religious life of his brethren, than the 'Seven Virtues' would have done. Its expression is very like a manifesto.

We are aware that this survey of medieval views on the virtues and the vices could be enlarged and completed, that the study of their

---

[12] Just as lust was not mentioned as a vice, neither was chastity mentioned as a virtue. One might be able to explain this, at first view obvious lack, by considering chastity not a goal in itself, but only as a means to the accomplishment of an unlimited love towards God.

St Benedict censuring a monk who had concealed presents received
from nuns

(Twelfth-century miniature from a Liège manuscript of Gregory the Great's *Dialogi*.
Brussels, Royal Libr., ms. 9916–9917)

The Vice of Luxury beaten by the Virtue of Sobriety

(Ninth-century miniature from Prudentius' *Psychomachia*. Provenance: Saint-Amand
Abbey, France, Nord. Brussels, Royal Libr., ms. 9987–9991)

76

evolution and sources could be improved.[13] The result, however, would be identical: that is to say that there was no list which clearly delimited, once and for all, either the vices, or the virtues. On both sides of the moral border, there was a handful of 'sentences' or labels, meant to regulate the position of men *versus* God, and of men *versus* men. Only occasionally was the monastery highlighted as the specific context within which these virtues were to be practised.

If sins were for all, virtues were only for some. Those 'some' are meant to be an élite, religious as well as social. This élite is first a religious one: those who had been called by the Lord to live in the monastery and who were praying to Him day and night. This is an idealistic view which does not correspond to reality, for a religious élite could hardly be distinguished from a social one, nobility, as long as the static *ordo*-theory prevailed according to which everybody should remain in his group of origin. This *ordo*-conviction governed the reflections on the stratification of men, and hence on their integral (social and juridical, as well as religious) positioning, throughout the greater part of the medieval period.

Virtues were considered the only way, though a difficult one, to reach God. Only some people would be able to succeed. The monastery showed which way should be followed, the only possible one according to the monastic legislators and reformers. Cassian, the Master, as well as St Benedict and many others, speak of a perpetual battle with the Devil, the personification of evil.

But, again, is the monastic value system specific or non-specific? If it is non-specific, it is general for the whole of the Christian society. As we saw already, the answer is obvious: the value system is non-specific. Since the path to God was so narrow, and monks were believed to be best able to approach Him; as life on earth and life in heaven were part of a coherent cosmo-religious system, and monks were trying to imitate the celestial atmosphere in the Divine Office, those values valid within the monastery were necessarily valid outside the monastery as well. These values outlined a clear programme for imitation: the more they were observed, the better they could lead towards the final reward. So the value system covering monastic life also functioned for the whole of the Christian society as a means of salvation. As shown, monasticism did not really have a specific, distinguishable value system, other than what any society in search of a good relationship with its Lord and its neighbour, could formulate, but it stressed certain of the ways to fulfil this relationship. The fact that these ways – geared as they were towards an unnatural, uni-sexual and permanent common life – were, ideally,

---

[13] For instance on the influence of Ambrosius Autpertus on the *Glossa ordinaria* (*De conflictu vitiorum et virtutum*), *Patrologia Latina*, 40, c. 1092.

also imposed on the lay society, and even expected to be followed, was much more striking than the identity of the values themselves. It was the evident result of a belief in the perfection to be achieved through monastic ideals. The world would only function righteously when it succeeded in living according to the value system it shared with monasticism, and moreover only if it did so in the same way. This explains why sexual denial among spouses, inherently a contradiction in terms, could be held up as an ideal.

Submission for the humble

Vices are for all; virtues are for an élite. What remains for the humble? The answer is short: the consolation of submission. This statement belongs much more to the theoretical framework of the values than to everyday practice, and I would not be surprised if social historians were to challenge the existence of such a resignation. Nevertheless, a society built upon an ideology of inequality can only maintain its equilibrium if greater force is used by the dominant group, or if the discrimination is mentally accepted by the dominated group. The humble will at least remain submissive as long as they (obviously also implicitly) agree to the existing situation, and will only take action against this when other circumstances disrupt the existing stability. By this I do not necessarily mean revolutionary action, but rather action leading to the possibility (for some) of moving into a situation where more opportunities are available, more wealth can be amassed, and more power can be attained. At that time the economically successful *humiles* would have been considered by the leading order as succumbing to the vice of pride or vanity, because in so doing they interfered with the immutability of a social order based on a divine plan.

So a mentality which considers resignation a positive trait is a necessary element in the continuation of this kind of society. This could give one the impression that humility was devised by the leading group as a means of maintaining the system. I imagine that examples of such an attitude can be found throughout the history of mankind and of Christianity. Humility, however, is already present in Christ's message itself, as one of the major values. He preached the acceptance by the poor of the established social order. The basic explanation for this ideology of humility is that little importance is attached to all that happens on earth. Only life in heaven has meaning; and it means everything, it *is* the absolute importance. There is no middle way. Thus, in this sense, being poor is a much easier way to live than being rich. Christ used the parable of the camel and the eye of the needle (Matt. 19:24, Mk 10:25, Lk. 18:25).

In Christianity humility thus became not only a means of accepting an unequally structured society, but a goal for part of the élite as well. When vanity was the great danger that menaced them, only the opposite humility could save them. The most striking example is the importance at various times in the course of Christian history of the phenomenon of the *paupertas Christi*. This is a poverty embraced voluntarily after the model of Christ's life-style, living the life of the poor, with all its frustration, humiliations, its sufferings of all kinds, freely, through choice rather than by necessity. The self-imposed practice of fasting is voluntary starvation; the refusal of a home and continuous pilgrimage is voluntary exile; the hermitage is a voluntary prison. In this manner poverty, not as a necessity but as a freely chosen option, realizes the ideal of humility and the way to heaven shown by Christ Himself.

All this implies that the humble person, down-trodden as he socially was, had one major advantage over the rich: that his way towards God was the easier one. It forced the rich man to look for an alternative, if he wished to have any hope at all for life in Heaven. That alternative was precisely religious life, not only as a means of individual salvation, however important this may have been, but also for the collective salvation of the abbey-founding clans. The abbeys played a major role within the kinship structure of the primitive society we are dealing with.

The Diffusion of the Value System

What role did monks play in the diffusion of their interpretation of the value system? Did monasticism have the means of accomplishing such a goal? The answer depends on another question: how often and in which circumstances did 'the medieval man' see monks? Estimates for Flanders (roughly and taking into account all the possible speculative weaknesses), for instance, show that only 0.42%[14] and later 0.28%[15] of the population were monks. These results give an indication of how seldom one could have had contact with monks, the more so since their basic

---

[14] The Benedictine population is estimated at 419 in the twelfth century: 5 great abbeys x 50 monks and 13 smaller ones x 13 monks. (Cf. with some reservation U. Berlière, 'Le nombre des moines dans les anciens monastères', in: *Revue bénédictine*, 41, 1929, pp. 231–61 et 42, 1930, pp. 19–42). After the rise of the Cistercians the total number of both black and white monks may have been as high as 800. The population of Flanders may have risen from a hundred thousand to two or two and a half hundred thousand inhabitants. In the case of (in reality impossible) extremes: 200 monks for a population of 350,000 and 800 monks for a population of 50,000 gives no significantly different percentages: 0.06% and 1.6%.

[15] The decrease in the percentage of monks does not mean a decrease in the number of persons living according to a religious rule in general. One should count the regular canons, who are technically speaking not monks, but whose observance has much in common with monasticism. This could point precisely in the direction of an overall status quo.

attitude towards the world was to escape from it! Were monks able to exercise any direct influence on the earth-bound population, in view of their life-style, which was oriented towards heaven? Did Christ's message of 'going and teaching all nations' (Matt. 28:19–20) apply to them?

Let us examine Gaul, where the first phase of conversion to Christianity had taken place in the late Roman period. In the transitional centuries from Antiquity to the middle ages the Church had collapsed there, or survived only with great difficulty. It is undoubtedly true that the first missionaries who came to re-convert Gaul were monks arriving from the British Isles, or from southern France. They were expected to support the efforts of the Merovingian kings to convert the populace, after Clovis himself had been baptized just at the end of the fifth century. These monks were not Benedictines, as this movement was then still confined to central Italy and just about to be introduced into England c. 600. This conversion was necessarily superficial: first of all because the Christian religion itself was still very external and formal, except in the minds of the great Fathers; secondly, because the missionaries could not accomplish anything more than gaining influence over external attitudes, rather than any inner conduct. Social life had to be christianized first, and therefore spectacular collective baptisms were organized after a very quick introduction to the doctrine. In fact, baptism and conversion were not the results of individual choice. Converted leaders imposed baptism upon the members of their group. Saints' lives call those kings *obdurati* who persisted in their pagan idolatry. Traces not only of pagan practices, but of practising (unconverted) pagans survived for some centuries, even up to the eighth century in areas which belonged to the older parts of the Frankish realm, and as such 'officially' converted to Christendom when Clovis was baptized. Each people went through the same sequence of conversion levels, although the moment and the relative chronology could be very different. It is obvious that such peoples as the Frisians and Saxons, or the Vikings and Slavs, came into contact with the Christian world later than the Goths or even the Franks had done, yet the steps in the conversion process were identical.[16] First of all the Church always imposed, hand in hand with rulership, a new external, collective behaviour. The strength and the truth of the new religion therefore had still to be proven, in order to convince the pagans. This was made possible by profaning or harrying their places of worship, and by thus discrediting the omnipotence of the (satanic) idols. For the pagans to be converted, and for the conversion to persist, the

---

[16] L. Milis, 'Monks, Mission, Culture and Society in Willibrord's time', in: P. Bange and A. G. Weiler (ed.), *Willibrord, zijn wereld en zijn werk*, pp. 82–92, and L. Milis, 'Pureté et sexualité', in: *Ville et campagnes au moyen âge. Mélanges Georges Despy*, ed. J.-M. Duvosquel – A. Dierkens. Liège, 1991, pp. 503–14.

missionaries needed signs, things to astonish the multitude, the literal meaning of the word miracle.

The second step in the conversion process was intended to adjust the individual, external attitude of men. The scholar who has a thorough knowledge of the hagiographical sources easily recognizes this new stage, and knows that it bears witness to a more advanced, that is sophisticated, religious behaviour. In this stage the role of the monks in the conversion process had already been played out, not by weakness as such but as a result of an evolution in the monastic concept. The triumph and monopoly of Benedictinism in the Carolingian epoch and the centuries to come stressed monastic stability and this was at odds with missionary activity.[17]

Only afterwards, that is some centuries later, did the third step in the Christianization process influence the *inner thoughts and feelings*. This stage was not so much a social phenomenon as a psychological one. The moulding into a Christian value system signified, and continues to signify a process which must be renewed in each generation, and indeed, for every individual, since ethics belong to the domain of culture and not to that of nature. Moral standards have to be culturally acquired, they are not naturally determined. This is, as we have elsewhere referred to it, a 'process without an end'.[18]

This change from a pagan society to a Christianized one needed systems of control to be fruitfully realized. The 'social control' over the external behaviour of the individual, as well as of the group, was the easiest to organize. People's attendance at mass can indeed be verified; yet what they are actually thinking about during mass is difficult to perceive. Hence, the more the conversion progressed, the more the need arose for an increasingly elaborate system of 'cure of souls', *cura animarum* as it is called. The Christian must be continuously monitored along his way to acquire and observe a Christian life-style.

By far the most effective control system elaborated by the Catholic

---

[17] Assessing the role of 'minsters' in the cure of souls in Anglo-Saxon England, S. Foot, 'Parochial Ministry in Early Anglo-Saxon England: The Role of Monastic Communities', in: W. J. Sheils and D. Wood, *The Ministry: Clerical and Lay*. Oxford, 1989, pp. 43–54 (Studies in Church History 26), states: 'There is . . . no reason to presume that any early minsters would have felt themselves bound by Benedict's insistence on *stabilitas*, and so prohibited from involvement in external ministry' (p. 48). The word minster 'encompassed all communal religious institutions from the wealthiest of the royal double houses to the meanest of priests' cells' (p. 45) and cannot be considered as a monastery with the connotations this word later had and still has today.

[18] L. Milis, 'La conversion en profondeur: un processus sans fin', in: *Revue du Nord*, 69, 1986, pp. 487–98.

Church was confession.[19] It is not the original late-Roman public confession, which only dealt with a general repentance. It is the individual confession, where the sins, the offences against doctrine and ethics, must be privately enumerated in front of a priest. This system undoubtedly developed in Celtic monastic penitential practices, where a monk or hermit confessed his sins to his 'soul-friend', as the texts call this moral guide. The same religious figure slipped into St Benedict' s Rule (iv, 50), apparently independently of the Celtic tradition, but presumably inspired by a similar practice within Orthodox monasticism. The bad thoughts, about which the Master spoke, had to be confessed to the spiritual elder. Slowly but steadily the system became general, to the point where the Lateran Council of 1215 decreed that everybody had to confess once a year to the parish priest. It was one of the most, if not *the* most, important step taken in order to enforce the Christianisation of hearts and minds. The Church imposed upon its members the free opening of their intimacy. For us, now, it means that this system, created to control monks, was generalized for all people. It implied at the same time that the mental control, first exercised over monks by other monks, came to be exercised over everybody by the secular clergy responsible for the spiritual care. Monasticism itself, which had elaborated this type of confession, was no longer involved as it began to be commonly applied. The authorship of the texts governing this practice, first penitential books, and afterwards confession manuals, shifted accordingly from monks and the like to clerics.[20]

Could there have been another way in which monks influenced the spread or the maintenance of faith? One thinks of the pilgrimages which were organized to visit monastic churches and which must have had an evangelizing effect. As a matter of fact, a good many pilgrimages were set up by monks for the veneration of the saintly relics they preserved and sometimes their churches were built according to the ceremonial practice of pilgrimages.[21] There was also a great deal of rivalry between

[19] On the link between confession and the spreading of new opinions, see for instance M. M. Sheehan, 'Choice of Marriage Partner in the Middle Ages: Development and Mode of Application of a Theory of Marriage', in: *Studies in Medieval and Renaissance History*, i, 1978, pp. 1–33. On confession, also in other civilizations, see A. Hahn, 'Sakramentelle Kontrolle', in: W. Schluchter (ed.), *Max Webers Sicht des okzidentalen Christentums*. Frankfurt-am-Main, 1988, pp. 229–53 (esp. pp. 244–53).

[20] Cf. J. Longère, 'La fonction pastorale de Saint-Victor à la fin du XIIe et au début du XIIIe siècle', in: *L'abbaye parisienne de Saint-Victor au moyen âge*. Paris, Turnhout, 1991, pp. 291–313 (Bibliotheca victorina, i).

[21] J. Hubert, 'La place faite aux laïcs dans les églises monastiques et dans les cathédrales aux XIe et XIIe siècles', in: *I laici nella 'societas christiana' dei secoli XI e XII*. Milano, 1968, pp. 470–87.

monasteries over the possession of relics, leading to more attendance and thus more money. On the other hand quite a number of pilgrimage centres only became abbeys as a result of the existing practice. There the aim could be double. First a spiritual one, to improve the solemnity of the perpetual and continuous Divine Office, and secondly a material one, to build up more wealth.

It is difficult to make any estimates, or even to get a general impression of the participation of 'ordinary people' in pilgrimages. The current impression of the pilgrimage to Compostela for instance, is that large crowds were on the roads, a kind of anticipation of modern tourism. And pilgrims certainly were numerous. There is historical evidence enough in the records of the major pilgrimage centres. But what did these numbers represent relative to the number of European towns and villages from which the pilgrims came? To give a concrete example: when in 1494 the burghers of Ghent who had made a pilgrimage to Compostela, gathered and founded a St James Confraternity, they were something like forty-seven.[22] At that moment the population of Ghent may be estimated to have been at least fifty thousand. Thus 0.1% had made the trip to Spain.[23] What the average man knew about those great pilgrimage centres, was thus determined by what these rare travellers had told him, directly or indirectly, with all the attendant exaggeration and anecdotage.

Yet I am convinced that the monastery-based pilgrimages really did exert an influence on medieval man. I have no doubt about that, but I think that it should be sought more in local centres. To continue with examples from Ghent, we could mention the annual procession from St Bavo's abbey to Sint-Lievens-Houtem, some hours' walking. This example of local success is supported by English and French pilgrimage centres, showing that half of the devotees returned home the same day they left, and that three quarters came from within a radius of 60 kilometres (or 37 miles).[24] How must this influence then be concep-

[22] P. Trio, *De Gentse Broederschappen (1182–1580)*. Gent, 1990, 152–55.

[23] Analogous figures, for instance for (French) pilgrims crossing the St Bernard to go to Rome for the first (and successful) Holy Year of 1300, have been calculated by G. Berings, 'Transport and Communication in the Middle Ages', in: *Kommunikation und Alltag in Spätmittelalter und Frühneuzeit*, ed. H. Kühnel, Krems, 1992 (in press). The same author quotes the figures of English Santiago pilgrims in the fifteenth century. In ordinary years 200 to 300 worshippers crossed the Channel, in holy years some 1275. The total population of England is estimated in 1485 at 2,250,000 inhabitants (C. Clark, *Population Growth and Land Use*. New York, 1977, pp. 82–83), implying a participation of less than 0.01% in ordinary years and slightly more than 0.05% in holy years.

[24] G. Berings, *op. cit.*

tualized? For example, one might imagine the general atmosphere, with songs, candlelight and incense. One might also think of spiritual exhortations, given to the faithful visitors. One would expect the text of these sermons to have been preserved. For the first half of the middle ages, however, up to about 1200, the number of surviving sermons written for ordinary lay people is scanty. For England before the Norman Conquest there are many, written in Anglo-Saxon, but within a Continental context almost all that survives are texts read before monks and sometimes before nuns. This lack has a double meaning. First, that the monks or clerics, the *literati* who mastered writing, did not judge these sermons important enough to copy. Second, that preaching was not an activity linked to monasticism. St Bernard stressed this point very vigorously when he fulminated in one of his letters against a monk who claimed liberty to preach and the duty to do so: 'He can and should know that the duty of a monk is not to preach but to mourn.'[25]

A more lasting influence of the pilgrimage would certainly have been exercised, I suppose, by the souvenir, as the material reminder of the religious experience. The medals or the shells, sewn on to hats or on to a garment come to mind; and later, the woodcuts, pinned up on the wall.[26]

In neither of these cases, however, was the role of the monasteries exclusive. They shared a practice (the pilgrimage) and its expressions with the other institutions which performed liturgies and stimulated devotion. Their primary goal, that of living devoutly and reclusively, made them both appropriate and worthy keepers of the shrines. But this activity opposed solitude to the crowd, and these were in fact antagonistic.

What about the indirect action of monks? Benedictine abbeys are known to have possessed many churches, mostly (and I have already stressed this) as a result of the Gregorian Reform movement.[27] Late medieval surveys, known as *pouillés*, give us the means of making a numerical evaluation, but they do not help to resolve the question of whether the monks really cared about the spiritual state of their parishioners. Abbeys considered the possession of parishes as one of their

---

[25] *The Letters of St. Bernard of Clairvaux*, transl. B. Scott James. London, 1953, Letter 393 (traditionally letter 365), p. 465. (I have changed the inaccurate translation 'to pray' into 'to mourn', the Latin words of the original text being 'plangentis officium').

[26] Cf. Petrus Christus' painting 'Panel with female donor', Washington, National Gallery, *c.* 1455.

[27] Cf. R. A. R. Hartridge, *A History of Vicarages in the Middle Ages*. New York, 1930 (1968), with special emphasis on Great Britain. The importance of the restitution movement has been illustrated by, for instance, M. Aubrun for medieval France (*La paroisse en France des origines au XVe siècle*. Paris, 1986, esp. pp. 81–85).

sources of income: part of tithes, of the alms and of the oblations.[28] They shifted the purpose of the biblical institution of the tithes to their own advantage. Tithes were intended to maintain the paupers, and monks were poor, yet voluntarily. Tithes were also intended to maintain the clergy responsible for the flock, which as a rule monks were not. The monastic community, or the abbot, appointed the parish clergy, but generally they do not seem to have occupied themselves with parochial tasks.[29] Even if there are many examples of pastoral care provided by monks, and even if a theologian like the Benedictine abbot Rupert of Deutz claimed the right to do so,[30] it was never a system, and the practice was contested as contrary to the meaning of monastic life.[31] Since the beginning of ascetic life, monks were considered to be 'dead to

[28] G. Constable, *Monastic Tithes from their Origins to the Twelfth Century*. Cambridge, 1964 (mainly pp. 99–135, 'Monastic possession of tithes in the twelfth century').

[29] J. Avril, 'Recherches sur la politique paroissiale des établissements monastiques et canoniaux (XIe – XIIIe s.)', in: *Revue Mabillon*, 59, 1980, pp. 453–517, esp. pp. 458 and 461: the Council of Clermont (1095) established the separation between the *spiritualia* (cure of souls) and the *temporalia* (material aspects and revenues). The spiritual control over the parishes was exercised by the archdeacons, not by the abbots, even if these parishes were abbey property. The same author expressed the same idea in: 'Moines, chanoines et encadrement religieux des campagnes de l'Ouest de la France (fin XIIe – début XIIIe siècle)', in: *Istituzioni monastiche e istituzioni canonicali in Occidente (1123–1215)*. Milan, 1980, pp. 660–78 (esp. pp. 672–73). As far as Cluniacs are concerned the conclusion has been drawn by G. Constable, 'Monasteries, Rural Churches and the Cura Animarum in the Early Middle Ages', in: *Cristianizzazione ecclesiastica delle campagne nell' alto medioevo: espansione e resistenze*. Spoleto, 1982, pp. 349–89, esp. p. 369, that 'As a rule, however, the pastoral work in Cluniac churches seems to have been performed by clerics appointed by the abbey for this purpose'. For the Cistercians we refer to C. H. Berman, 'Cistercian Development and the Order's Acquisition of Churches and Tithes in Southwestern France', in: *Revue bénédictine*, 91, 1981, pp. 193–203 (esp. p. 202).

[30] J. Van Engen, *Rupert von Deutz*. Berkeley, 1983, p. 326. P. Johanek, 'Klosterstudien im 12. Jahrhundert', in: J. Fried (ed.), *Schulen und Studium im sozialen Wandel des hohen und späten Mittelalters*. Sigmaringen, 1986, p. 57 (Vorträge und Forschungen, 30). The First Lateran Council (1123) reacted against attempts on the part of monks to acquire pastoral rights (*Conciliorum Oecumenicorum Decreta*. Bologna, 1973, c. 16, p. 193). Cf. C. E. Boyd, *Tithes and Parishes in Medieval Italy. The Historical Roots of a Modern Problem*. Ithaca, NY, 1952, p. 265.

[31] B. H. Lackner, *The Eleventh-Century Background of Cîteaux*, pp. 127–29. Gratianus describes the rights of the monks in a restrictive way (*Corpus Iuris Canonici. Decretum*, p. ii, c. xvi).

the world' indeed.[32] The vicar of a parochial church, even when an abbey was the owner, was normally recruited from the secular clergy, and what one could hope for, religiously speaking, was that the monks would be more inclined to choose the best prepared candidates than would lay patrons. There is, however, not enough supporting evidence that it actually happened. When on occasion a monk put in an appearance in the parish church, it was to inspect the state of the building and to collect the money (elements of the *temporalia*) and not to inquire as to the religious standards. The control of the *spiritualia* was indeed numbered among the prerogatives of the local bishops. A proof of what has just been said, can be found *a contrario*: it has never been established that in times of crisis a greater degree of orthodoxy or a more fervent religious feeling were to be found in those parishes owned by monks than in other parishes.

The abbot of Saint-Denis outside the gates of Paris, Suger,[33] ruling the kingdom of France in the absence of the crusading Louis VII, is often cited as an example of the social importance of monasticism. There is no doubt that other examples could be found of monks having had an influence on individual rulers and on rulership in general. Abbots often appear at the courts of the kings and princes, but not normally as permanent members. We do not intend to deny their impact but only to show that, if they did play a (mostly hidden) political role, such a contribution, once again, was non-specific.[34] Monasticism, in the precise sense I use it, might have influenced rulership insofar as it helped to spread the idea that the terrestrial 'City' should function according to the image of the celestial one, as St Augustine's doctrine of the Two Cities envisaged, and that monastic life represented the most heavenly way of life on earth, hence that most worth imitating. Nevertheless this kind of influence, even if it was real and easily documented (for instance in the Carolingian vision of the world), remains very indirect and is limited to political theory. In comparison with such an individualized means of interior modelling as confession, it represented very little for

---

[32] This concept exists already in the fourth-century *Apophtegmata Patrum* (*Patrologia Graeca*, 65, col. 71–440, for instance col. 317).

[33] See on Suger's role as an abbot, G. Constable, 'Suger's Monastic Administration', in: *Abbot Suger and Saint-Denis. A Symposium*, ed. P. L. Gerson. New York, 1986, pp. 18–32 (reprinted in G. Constable, *Monks, Hermits and Crusaders in Medieval Europe*. Oxford, 1988).

[34] See for instance J.-F. Lemarignier, 'Structures monastiques et structures politiques dans la France de la fin du Xe et des débuts du XIe siècle', in: *Il monachesimo nell' alto medioevo e la formazione della civiltà occidentale*. Spoleto, 1957, pp. 357–400 (esp. p. 367). In the French royal charters of the period 996–1031 there are only 3 abbots among the 177 witnesses (which means 1.7%).

ordinary people. This stresses again the elitist and escapist viewpoint of monasticism. The attitude of the mendicant friars was different. They were to use confession systematically as a means of infiltrating the mind and the heart. From the first decades of their existence they were already chosen by the rulers as personal confessors, and they imposed themselves as confessors on ordinary people. The grip they had upon mentality and behaviour was the opposite of the Benedictine ideal.

Similar qualifications can be made about the monastic influence exercised through writing. By far the majority of early medieval texts are of Benedictine origin. The greater part of the authors followed the Rule, and the greater part of the copies were made for their abbeys. But then again the central question arises. What was the influence of these texts on 'ordinary people'? The catalogues of numerous medieval libraries have been preserved, thousands of manuscripts are still extant, but very few can really have had any practical meaning for that part of the population we are interested in. Only when these works referred to the value system and only if monks actually had the means of popularizing them, might they have had any effect. The 'living example' is analogous. The saintly life of the monks, even their religious heroism (that is to say their extreme forms of asceticism) could only be known if the door of the monastery stood open.

So, when we have surveyed all the possible means of mental influence open to monasticism, the result appears to be quite poor. The late medieval success of the mendicant orders can be attributed precisely to the fact that *they* were interested in people. The well-entrenched urban class, more and more important, could identify much more easily with these brethren, even if conflicts and reciprocal misunderstandings were real. They went out on the street instead of staying in their 'shrine'. When society became more mobile as a result of increased urban and commercial life, monasticism continued to aim for seclusion, faithful to its spirituality. Socially speaking, it had always been élitist and therefore marginal. Now it faded religiously speaking, insofar as social changes were stimulating a different religious sensibility. Monasticism had been created to demonstrate the fundamental insignificance of the evil world. Its purpose had been to institutionalize indifference towards the earth and the rejection of sinful matter. From now on other solutions were worked out, outside traditional monasticism.

RECIPROCITY, A SOCIAL FUNCTION

'Baldwin, earl of Devon [sends his] greetings to Hildearius, abbot of Lyre and to the whole community of that same church. That you should know that I gave, for the love of God, for the redemption of my sins and for the remedy of my soul, to the abbey of St Mary of Lyre and your church and you, who serve God and St Mary there, all the churches, your tithes, lands, people, possessions, income and profits on the Isle of Wight.'[35] This text is an excerpt taken from the foundation charter of the Benedictine priory of Carisbrooke. It gives a spiritual explanation for the juridical act with which charters generally deal. Such documents are usually written to confirm gifts, and they notify that land *x* or revenue *y* have been given for what is usually called *the benefit of my soul and that of my ancestors*. Little attention, however, is paid to this and similar formulae. They are often overlooked as 'useless clichés', as if clichés were without meaning. Why should they exist otherwise? It is precisely to these expressions, superfluous to positivistic historians, that we should turn to find the major social reason for the existence of medieval monasteries.

Some primary information is useful in order to understand how medieval society was ideally perceived. It was Adalberon of Laon who formulated in the second half of the tenth century the theory of the three *ordines* within society. This tripartition, however, was a much older, yet subjacently existing system. According to Georges Dumézil it went back as far as prehistoric Indo-European society.[36] Three categories of people are to be discerned: those who work on the land to produce food, those who fight to give security, and those who pray to guarantee eternal life, or as it is said in Latin, in reverse order: there are *oratores*, *bellatores*, and *laboratores*. On the Continent of Europe this image of society was only overturned with the French Revolution of 1789, whereas in Britain there are remnants still alive of two privileged 'Estates', the clergy and the nobility, gathered in the House of Lords. The third one (we could call them 'the others') are represented in the 'House of Commons'. This word originally meant 'groups of ordinary people', say the remaining 95% of the population which did not belong to the privileged élite.

We should, however, bear in mind that, if society as a whole was expected to function according to this tripartition, the élite had to guarantee the functionalism of its own superiority. This implies bipartition, a mutual relationship, linking the two parts of the privileged body. For them to remain an élite, both parts had to interact, to support reciprocally their survival on earth as well as in heaven. This system was completely related to the concept of kin organization.

As to the importance of this social form in the middle ages, there can hardly be any doubt. When one considers the toponymy of innumerable

---

35 *The Cartulary of Carisbrooke Priory*, ed. S. F. Hockey. S.l., 1981, p. 9 (between the years 1142–1147).
36 Cf. G. Duby, *The Three Orders, Feudal Society imagined*. Chicago, London, 1980 (*Les trois ordres ou l'imaginaire du féodalisme*. Paris, 1978).

early medieval settlements, whatever the cultural, linguistic or ethnic background may be, their 'large family' origin is apparent. Even strolling through Rome, for instance, one is struck by the cul-de-sacs named after the 'extended families' which once lived there. The role of the *vendetta* or feud as a social phenomenon can only be explained in this light. When the nuclear family developed so far as to become the 'normal' one, we are already speaking of the twelfth or even of the thirteenth century. Socially speaking this development was the result of increasing personal mobility, which was in its turn the result of an enhanced economic dynamism. In the long run the dislocation of the clan was inevitable, but the process was a very slow one indeed which has not yet entirely died out (cf. royalty, business families, mafia). The Church, with its changing vision of marriage as a sacrament, and with its more severe restrictions on incest,[37] both followed and stimulated this evolution.

In a clan system one major objective governs the attitude of the members: the collective, not the personal interest. This idea can help us to evaluate the relevance of monasticism to clans. The clan is out to achieve its collective profit. In the system of solidarity which operates as a result the clan's lay members guarantee its survival on earth, whereas its religious members guarantee its survival in heaven. The monastery is one of its functional keys. It is hardly an overstatement to call many monasteries kin property. The terminology devised by German historians for this type of monastery, and which has been adopted by others without translation, is enlightening in this respect: they all speak of *Eigenklöster*.[38]

Other, more specific, goals are mostly advanced to explain the generosity of the noble founders of these houses: piety, for instance (yet without really giving anything away, for they usually kept some control or other over the finances), or the 'waste-basket function', to deposit superfluous children there. All these aspects fit into the functional reciprocity model of the kinship society.

One might object that not all abbeys were founded by wealthy patrons, and that I leave no place here for 'vocation' or genuine religious feeling. I do not deny the existence of houses which were founded solely under the influence of religious sentiment, but these most often remained without an endowment of any importance. Abbeys with mighty and wealthy founders fitted into a powerful kin system and were sure to be rich. To take just one example: in the early seventh century, when the Merovingian king Dagobert founded the abbey of Elnone, later called St

---

[37] In the middle ages incest was a much larger notion than nowadays. It did not therefore have the same connotation of perversion.

[38] See for instance E. Searle, *Lordship and Community. Battle Abbey and its Banlieu. 1066–1538*. Toronto, 1974. The first chapter is entitled 'The Conqueror's Eigenkloster: Exemption and Dependence' (pp. 21–35).

Amand, in northern Gaul, he provided it with an old Roman fisc, over 9,000 hectares (over 22,000 acres) of land, just for starters.

Another objection is that all this is not limited to monks alone. In fact, many ecclesiastical institutions (abbeys of regular canons, or chapters of secular canons) were established with the same idea in mind and for the same purpose. This might be true, but none of them were as wealthy as the traditional black Benedictine abbeys which were founded in this way. That later houses were less richly endowed confirms, rather than disproves, what we have found: kindreds which were financially speaking less important later followed the example set by mightier ones in earlier times. Yet there was another factor. Some religious movements did indeed consciously react against the material riches of the abbeys, for instance the eleventh-century *paupertas Christi* movement, out of which the Cistercians arose. Certainly, their link with nobility and kindred was less pronounced, as they had been driven by the ideal of the freedom of the Church, the *libertas Ecclesiae*, which was so much in vogue at that time. This did not mean, however, that wealthy benefactors stopped founding or supporting new houses. On the contrary. 'Functional reciprocity' implied that the solution considered as the most efficient should be chosen, and religiously speaking this solution was at that time considered to be the more fervent and thus more God-pleasing 'reform' movements. So there is an apparent antagonism. While the reformers rejected the earthly roots of the wealthy monastery, rich and less rich people solicited them to accept such gifts. In reality only a few settlements persevered in their voluntary poverty. The wave-like presence of eremitism, coming and going, is illustrative of the permanent longing for the poverty of Christ, so vivid among religiously motivated people.

Let us return to functional reciprocity. The way it works is quite simple: 'We look after you on earth, you look after us in heaven.' Protection and security in the world is the barter paid for salvation of the soul.[39] So paradise or damnation after the Last Judgement is neither

---

[39] B. H. Rosenwein & L. K. Little, "Social Meaning in the Monastic and Mendicant Spiritualities', in: *Past and Present*, 63, 1974, pp. 4–32 and B. H. Rosenwein, 'Reformmönchtum und der Aufstieg Clunys', in: W. Schluchter (ed.), *Max Webers Sicht des okzidentalen Christentums*, pp. 276–311 insist upon the role Cluny played in the pacification of medieval society. A. Becker, *Papst Urban II. (1088–1099). Teil 2. Der Papst, die griechische Christenheit und der Kreuzzug*, Stuttgart, 1988, p. 276 stresses that this role should not be exaggerated. A nice example of how monks indirectly influenced peace, is given in the *Historia miraculorum in circumlatione per Flandriam* (Complete text edited in *Acta Sanctorum Belgii*. Tongerlo, 1794, vi, pp. 295–309). When the eleventh-century monks of Lobbes in Hainault made a tour through Flanders with the

determined by predestination nor the result of a highly moral life-style on the part of the individual. Heaven is for sale. Heaven is bought. And anyone who does not have money, should be consoled with the idea that he is the poor man in the parable of the camel and the needle. But for the wealthy, how difficult is the way to escape damnation! In a society where exteriority is the ruling force, winning heaven might also be only the result of an exterior act. One tries to figure out the price, and one pays. It is the insurance contract which makes life more comfortable, and gives security for life hereafter. No personal interior commitment is involved. The whole system fits into the early medieval legal tariff system where lives, injuries and the like are indemnified by paying. So were sins, enumerated as they were in the long lists of the penitential books, with their unrealistic tariff of redeeming practices of abstinence, and with more realistic commutation lists, converting abstinence into payable good works or devotional acts. The late medieval practice of selling indulgences is reminiscent of that attitude, rather than a new phenomenon, as one often thinks.

The development of the idea of 'perception of the interior' constituted the major change. This is linked to the increasing importance of the individual, of individual responsibility, conscience, the transition from taboo to sin, the belief in sins-before-the-act – in short, it is linked to everything that stresses individuality rather than sociability. A clear chronological, geographical or social division cannot be indicated. It is the result of a long evolution, and the new system only became apparent in the second half of the middle ages. The role of the Church is obvious in this respect. The generalized practice of confession, that most personal and confidential moment in the year of a 'medieval man', was at the same time a result of and a stimulus towards this process of interiorisation. One's own good works, one's own moral life-style, according to the value system formulated and imposed by the Church, finally led the monastery to disappear as the kindred's insurance contract. Benedictinism survived, but new concepts of religion caused it to be surpassed in the thirteenth century by 'new-wave', that is to say reform, movements. Some of them the established Church was to accept as orthodox, whereas others were condemned. Yes, Benedictines did continue to play a role in the late medieval world, but it was largely limited to politics or economics, as the result of their involvement in great land-ownership and nobility. And that involvement was not why St Benedict wrote his Rule, and not why the upper classes had supported 'their' monks.

relics of their patron saint St Ursmar in order to collect money, the mere presence of the saint operated as a peacemaker. In several towns long-lasting feuds came to an end.

6

The Intellectual Contribution

If there is one field where the role of medieval monks within the evolution of European culture should be highlighted, it is undoubtedly that of intellectual life. The character of and the reason for this interest in the life of the mind, the way in which the monks' ambitions in this direction were fulfilled, and finally its meaning to 'ordinary people' are the themes of this chapter.

THE LEGACY OF ANTIQUITY

What is the truth of the commonplace that the fifteenth- and sixteenth-century Renaissance rediscovered the heritage of classical antiquity, a heritage which was supposedly laid aside by the obscurantist middle ages? A very limited truth indeed, for when one consults modern scholarly editions of classical authors, it is striking that they always turn out to call upon Carolingian copies as their oldest witness to the text. This justifies the statement that 'The classical revival of the late eighth and early ninth centuries, [was] without doubt the most momentous and critical stage in the transmission of the legacy of Rome'.[1] Even for Latin authors who did not appear to fit into medieval thinking, the textual tradition is no different; Ovid, for instance, who was best known for his interest in earthly love, or Lucretius who denied the immortality of the soul.[2]

What does this mean? That regardless of the kind of text, the legacy of Latin literature was secured by copying done in the ninth century. And copying implies selection. Was there any specific and noticeable criterion for the choice which was made? Obviously not. In other words, ninth-century intellectual circles copied indiscriminately whatever they could secure of their classical heritage without *a priori* conditions or any

---

[1] L. D. Reynolds – N. G. Wilson, *Scribes and Scholars. A Guide to the Transmission of Greek and Latin Literature*. London, 1968, pp. 79–93 (esp. p. 79).

[2] Ed. E. J. Kenney, *Amores, Medicamina faciei femineae, Ars amatoria, Remedia amoris*. Oxford, 1961, p. v; C. Bailey, *De rerum natura libri sex*. Oxford, 1922[2], introduction.

particular consensus of opinion. The only restriction on writing in general was its 'eternal' value, and this was guaranteed in this case by Roman origins themselves. But several further questions arise with regard to the limitation to *Latin* texts, the vicissitudes of older manuscripts, the use made of the texts, and finally the involvement of the monks.

Knowledge of Greek was, at least outside those parts of Italy which had contacts with the Byzantine Empire, limited in the medieval West. Few theologians knew Greek, and in normal intellectual activity, only a few words, perhaps only a few alphabetical characters, seem to have been known.

It is remarkable that only a handful of manuscripts older than the ninth century are still in existence. This is a result both of an overall void in the tradition of writing between the sixth and the eighth century and of destruction of the older texts once they had been copied in the uniform and easily readable Carolingian handwriting of the ninth century.

The classical texts were mainly used for educational purposes. As they did not deal with or correspond to the medieval concept of the world, they could hardly have provided material for the comprehensive transcendental system for which that period was looking. Hence classical texts were not commented on in at all the same way as those witnesses of *Christian* antiquity, the so-called 'Fathers', whose writings were ceaselessly re-thought and re-interpreted.

As for the central question of the monks' role, this is easily resolved. When one considers the origin of most of the ninth-century manuscripts, or when one consults the book catalogues of that time which still survive,[3] monks are clearly the agents responsible for the preservation and for the transmission of our classical heritage. But why did they assume this responsibility? Was it a result of the way they put the monastic ideal into practice or was it an activity cohabiting with monasticism but fundamentally alien to it? First, the interest and care for classical texts was a spiritual issue. Monastic life stressed the importance of reading. Cassian had already insisted upon the importance of Bible reading to achieve a 'knowledge of the science of ethics',[4] and through Cassian it slipped into the Benedictine tradition. God had first to be studied, otherwise the purity of contemplation was impossible. This attitude was quite different from later ones which were at once more mystical and more popular, in that they maintained that faith, and not knowledge, shows the way to God, or that faith *is* knowledge.

There was a second issue, an historical one. The ninth century

[3] For example the list of St Riquier (831), in: G. Becker, *Catalogi bibliothecarum antiqui*. Bonn, 1885, pp. 24–29.
[4] *Collationes*, xiv, viiii, p. 191.

exhibited a very great veneration for the Roman past and for the period of Constantine the Great in particular, the early fourth century; this is only to be expected, as it was his reign which saw the triumph of Christianity and the Church over Roman paganism. But this veneration also extended to the heathen imperial period. The idea of ineluctable decay (the decreasing quality of the metals of the prophet Daniel's statue, or the six 'eras' of history), as we have already described it, must be held responsible for this longing for the past. The end of the Roman empire would have meant in fact the end of the world, and therefore the Roman empire *had* to live. A 'fifth metal' did not exist, and as they were living in the 'sixth era' (or 'sixth day' in God's eyes), the 'seventh day' would have been the Day of Judgement.

When we consider all this, we should emphasize the ninth-century eagerness to learn and, moreover, we should reject the existence of obscurantism in intellectual milieus. One should not in fact confuse obscurantism with the prevailing naïveté and with its associative way of thinking and reasoning.

The activity of writing should be looked at from two sides. On the one hand, there was writing itself, a purely automatic procedure of reading a model to transcribe it. On the other hand, there was the comprehension of the text. This activity was by far the most intellectually advanced as it revealed a capacity for reflection. Yet this was not primarily the reason medieval, and especially early medieval, monks wrote. They saw in it above all an activity which complied with the prescription of 'manual labour'. As such, it possessed two spiritual appeals (as has already been stressed), the first being that 'manual labour' helps to guarantee the mental equilibrium of the monk. Too much prayer would eventually become insupportable and would affect the ideal of the monk's life, communion with God. St Benedict's concern in prescribing manual labour was precisely to secure that kind of equilibrium. The second appeal lay in the perception of manual labour as an expression of humility. Only in busying themselves with activities considered more servile than those they would normally have performed 'in the world', could the monks work towards their salvation. Writing was labour, as it was performed in very uncomfortable conditions. Later *Consuetudines* (texts dealing with everyday practices and interpretations of the Rule) often spoke of frozen ink, and to have it warmed, monks were allowed to enter the kitchen.[5] Writing counted as labour, to the same extent as working in the fields. Colophons in manuscripts sometimes show the burden it represented. In the example (chosen at random) 'He who wrote this book was not idle. Let us pray, Brethren, that God might give

---

[5] B. Choisselet – P. Vernet, *Les 'Ecclesiastica Officia' du XIIème siècle*. Reiningue, 1989, c. 72, p. 212–14 (La documentation cistercienne, 22).

him his due',[6] *idle* clearly refers to St Benedict (Ch. xlviii), who said that *Idleness is the enemy of the soul.* Just like writing, reading was considered burdensome. Even though Cassian[7] encouraged his listeners in their eagerness to read, St Benedict was probably more perceptive when he considered that reading should be imposed as an ascetic practice in Lent (Ch. xlviii).

The pursuit of knowledge was equated with the discovery and the availability of manuscripts.[8] This dominated the intellectual policy of Benedictine houses, and of some other religious movements. The scanty diffusion of texts, the unavoidable consequence of expensive parchment and time consuming copying, forced the librarians to be very restrictive about consultation and loan. As a rule severe systems of control were imposed, going from anathematizing formulae in the books in order to frighten thieves or vandals, to chained books. This care had nothing to do with so-called obscurantism, the fear that knowledge, judged to be bad, would be dangerously sown in the simple minds of the readers. It looks much more the result of a genuine feeling of responsibility for a heritage which should be handed over, undamaged, to the next generation.

This rare care for books was reflected in their material form. Early medieval books, at least those which are preserved, are very often richly decorated, in sumptuous bindings with gold, silver, ivory and precious stones. As a matter of fact these rich books had more chance of survival than ordinary ones, even if envy and theft menaced them. Normally they were not kept in the monastic library itself, but in the treasury, among golden chalices, patens and the like. The external aspect certainly suited the eternal value of the contents, and so these manuscripts are normally biblical books. They were not used except on very special occasions. Their purpose was to enhance the magic of writing, according to the attitude of primitive societies where the mastery of letters was

---

6   Ch. Samaran & R. Marichal, *Catalogue des manuscrits en écriture latine portant des indications de date, de lieu ou de copiste*, II. Paris, 1962, p. 13, ms. Paris BN lat. 385, early thirteenth century, from the abbey of Notre-Dame de Foucarmont.

7   *Conférences*, xiv, 9.

8   A nice example is this colophon, from a mid-twelfth century manuscript of Lactantius' *Institutiones divinae* of the abbey of Saint-Benoît-sur-Loire: 'Ego Iulianus armarius, cum hec quatuor folia deessent quesivi ea multis in locis et quia liber hic raro invenitur vix tandem repperi in monasterio clericorum prope Bituricas quod Planipedes dicitur' ('I Julian, the librarian, have searched for these four missing leaves in many places; the book can rarely be found here, but I was at last able to find it in the abbey of regular canons called Plaimpied, near Bourges') (Samaran & Marichal, *op. cit.*, ii, p. 79, Paris BN lat. 1663).

limited to the mediators between ordinary men and the deity. What is written, is fixed, and hence true, and it does not have the unpredictable volatility of the spoken word. Precisely because these people were accustomed to orality and its social function, they were aware of its structural weakness, and they identified eternal values with the written word. Magic, as we have called this, is not too strong a word. Every missionary in the early middle ages, as well as in more recent times, was 'armed' with the 'book', more to impress than to use. No more striking example of such a manuscript exists than the one in the Cathedral Museum of Fulda, Germany with which the eighth-century monk St Boniface tried to parry the Frisian sword, which was to kill him. A heavy, richly decorated book reminded medieval men above all of the Book with the seven seals in Revelation (5:2), enigmatic, threatening, and horrifying: 'and I saw a strong angel proclaiming with a loud voice "Who is worthy to open the scroll and break its seals?" '.

AN EVERLASTING RENAISSANCE

What we have said so far about the legacy of antiquity has been limited almost completely to the ninth century. This is obvious as the period consciously renewed the link with the Roman past. In doing so, however, there was an implication that the present was different, quite different. In this sense, the leading groups cut the umbilical cord to what still survived, if altered and weakened, of the Roman tradition and replaced it with an artificial 'restoration'. But it was not only the ninth century that exhibited such an admiration for the Roman past. In the early years of the twelfth century, Bernard, the chancellor of the schools of Chartres, one of the most esteemed centres of learning, wrote: 'We are dwarfs sitting on the shoulders of [the Ancients as on those of] giants. If we see more things and further than they did, it is not by the perspicacity of our view, nor by our size, but because we are elevated [by them] and brought to a gigantic height.'[9] The appreciation for antiquity which existed in the ninth century, was still alive – or reborn – three centuries later. In fact, throughout the middle ages, there was a nostalgia for Rome. For rather more than half a century historians have been aware that the Renaissance of the fifteenth and sixteenth centuries, *the* Renaissance, was in fact only one of a series, which consciously sought to restore ancient Rome, its empire, and its cultural heritage. This does not signify that any of these movements succeeded in this goal. Is a true

---

[9] Quoted in John of Salisbury, *Metalogicon*, ed. J. B. Hall – K. S. B. Keats-Rohan. Turnhout, 1991, p. 116 (Corpus Christianorum. Continuatio mediaeualis, xcviii).

restoration conceivable at all? The 'genuine' Renaissance of the sixteenth century did no better.

The medieval movements are known respectively as the Carolingian, the Ottonian and the twelfth-century renaissances. Some scholars prefer to limit the expression to intellectual and artistic achievements, whereas others include all aspects of vitality and the socially wider effort to change the Latin Christian world. As for myself, I share the second opinion, but in this chapter I shall deal only with the intellectual contribution, as the economic and social aspects have already been discussed.

We must answer the question of whether and to what extent monasticism played a role in the birth and evolution of these movements, and if any evolution is noticeable. The Bible *versus* antiquity? Answering 'no' to this slogan helps us to approach the problem. I have in fact already implied this on several occasions. The middle ages did not perceive the Bible and Christianity as antagonistic to antiquity. Certainly, they were more sympathetic towards Constantine's time, but the empire, whether pagan or Christian, was considered to have been just one glorious empire, luckily and inevitably converted from illusory idols to the one real, living God. Those within medieval society who reflected on the past and on the evolution of mankind identified themselves with the tradition of the Bible as well as with the heritage of Rome. Yet this identification was eclectic in the sense that what they selected, immediately received the label 'good'. What differed, was rejected: the pagans, the Jews, and the heretics. The monks were precisely the ones who thought about truth and who scrutinized it in books and in their prayers. All of this explains the attention they paid to antiquity.

There are structural differences between the various renaissances of which we have spoken. The first two were undoubtedly the most limited. They were in fact high-level attempts to cast existing society into an ideal mould, composed of St Augustine's 'Two Cities'-doctrine and of the so-called 'renovatio imperii', the renovation of the Roman empire. First the Carolingians, and afterwards the Ottonians, mobilized all the mental and, to a certain extent, material resources they had to accomplish this goal: a well-organized society, ruled by a just emperor, responsible only to God. The theological setting for this policy is more important, so it would seem, than what was actually achieved, for the climax of the Carolingian empire was soon followed by its decay. It could not effectively resist territorial divisions or invasions (especially not those of the Vikings). The vast dimensions of the empire itself were such that the mediocre means of communication available simply could not cope. The aims of the Ottonians in Germany and northern Italy were even less ambitious and their decline faster. Both their dreams were too ambitious to be realizable. Who laid the theoretical basis for the ambitions of these dynasties? As theological opinions were the foundation for such plans, the presence (or at least the influence) of theologians is to be expected. For the Carolingian period the names, and even the careers of a small group of counsellors is known. First of all there was Alcuin, a monk who had come from northern England, from Northumberland, to the Continent, as so many before him had done in the tradition of the Anglo-Irish missionaries. He became the head of the royal palace school in Aachen. The second was Theodulf, a Visigoth who had left Spain to escape the threat of the Muslims who had conquered nearly all of Spain in the early eighth century. He became abbot of St-Benoît-sur-Loire and afterwards bishop of Orleans. Finally, there was Paul the Deacon, a Lombard who had formerly been a monk at Monte Cassino. According to his biographer Einhard, Charlemagne considered them his private teachers. It would be difficult to believe that the great importance which the Emperor and his successor Louis the Pious attached to their legislation of monastic matters, was not the consequence of this, or of an even more widely based monastic influence. Some texts are explicit. Both directly and indirectly the rulers contributed to the structuring of religious life. For monks this meant a monopoly for Benedictine monasticism, and hence the disappearance of other (especially Celtic) observances. For nuns and for clerics too an analogous intervention led to more unified forms of organization. When intellectual activity can be traced in the documents of the Carolingian period, it can be located overwhelmingly in abbeys: Monte Cassino, Corbie, Reichenau, St Gall, Bobbio, Fulda and many others in many countries. Their libraries, especially that of St Gall, continue to bear witness to the riches of their intellectual heritage.

The monastic presence continued to exercise a powerful influence over the Ottonian Renaissance. The most famous of the late tenth-century scholars was Gerbert, who had been a monk in Aurillac in southern France, and spent some years as a student in Catalonia. There he came into contact with Arabic knowledge, mostly mathematics and physical science.[10] His was an outstanding career, as master of the schools in Rheims, and later as pope under the name of Silvester II. As an appointee of Emperor Otto III, and in token of their mutual friendship, he chose as pope the name Silvester, alluding to Constantine the Great and Silvester I, and the fourth-century creation of a Christian society. Gerbert's career, however, was hardly monastic, and cannot really be considered representative of monasticism. Moreover, when Otto and Silvester himself came to power in the last years of the first millennium it was only for a very short time, and the so-called Ottonian

---

[10] U. Lindgren, *Gerbert von Aurillac und das Quadrivium*. Wiesbaden, 1976, pp. 5–12.

Renaissance had already been initiated some decades before. It was to collapse within a few years. Other intellectual stars of the epoch, such as Leo of Vercelli and Bruno of Querfurt, did not belong to the monastic movement at all. The Ottonians were in fact more inclined to turn to the secular clergy for the use they could make of them in the administration of their empire. In so doing they hoped to avoid the centrifugal forces inherent in heritable feudalism. Nevertheless, the names of the great abbeys like Reichenau and St Gall remain central to any traditional field of intellectual achievement. Traditional, we say, as there was a striking lack of response to the experimental sciences, as studied by the exceptional Gerbert.

When we finally consider the so-called twelfth-century renaissance, the period from the late eleventh to the early thirteenth century, its importance far exceeds the bounds of the intellectual sphere. It must be seen as a complete change in every aspect of society, material as well as intellectual, and it should therefore be considered the beginning of a new era. As far as thought is concerned, within its various traditional disciplines (theology, logic, philosophy, and ethics), the names of monks and of monastic centres become steadily rarer, and especially when one considers the rapid development of rational thinking and other innovations. Bec in Normandy apparently the most important monastic educational centre of all in the late eleventh century, had to share its reputation with an increasing number of cathedral and chapter schools. In fact, Orleans, Paris, or even Liège imposed their dominance, soon to be followed or superseded by Bologna, Oxford and Montpellier, that is to say by the rise of the universities. There is no doubt that traditional 'black', and even renewed 'white', Benedictinism were still able to produce 'intellectual monuments'. Peter the Venerable, Benedictine abbot of Cluny, and St Bernard, Cistercian abbot of Clairvaux, are among the leading figures of the twelfth-century renaissance. Yet they and the movements they represented did not project their intellectual achievements into ordinary society, notwithstanding the diffusion of abbeys, their abbeys, all over Latin Christian territory. The reluctance of monasticism to share its knowledge with the 'world', and the eagerness of the secular Church to impose itself upon this same 'world', help to explain the gravitational shift, which asked for greater intellectual creativity. Intellectuals apparently entered Benedictine houses far less than they so patently had done previously. It could also be that their capabilities became less developed, or their achievements less radiant, when they had to compete with the more innovative intellectual attitudes of the secular Church and the 'schools', the result themselves of new and more open structures of society. L. K. Little has underscored how the transmission of traditional and unquestioned sacred literature, through successive generations of Benedictines also hindered their involvement as radical religious reformers, the latter attitude being the result of an education in an urban environment.[11] Although the Cistercians had sprung from the twelfth-century renaissance movement themselves, the restricted dissemination of knowledge was the more understandable with them, as they idealized absolute seclusion.[12]

One last point here. Did the admiration for antiquity not hinder medieval creativity? The answer is undoubtedly in the affirmative. Unlimited esteem led to an exaggerated obedience. The more the ancient achievements were idolized, the more it came to be a goal in itself merely to imitate them. Things were not good because they were good, but because they were handed down from antiquity. A general lack of self-confidence as to its own capabilities on the part of the medieval period long hindered its escape from what it considered its own mediocrity. This attitude went far beyond the monastic precincts. The words of the second-century physician Galen had more value than what medieval and even Renaissance academics observed with their own eyes.

In fact, in the common field of intellectual and pedagogical activity, the two most fundamental characteristics of monasticism reach a culmination: the longing for eternal values and the value placed on obedience. It would therefore seem that monasticism should be held responsible for the positive as well as for the negative side of the medieval period's mental dependence: the preservation of the classical heritage and the low profile of creativity.

WRITING, READING, TEACHING AND THINKING: MONKS AS THE KEEPERS OF COLLECTIVE MEMORY

Writing, reading, teaching and thinking were the components of one and the same intellectual and moral goal: the preservation of the eternal values. In the Rule of St Benedict, and in most other medieval books, the expression 'sicut scriptum est', 'as it is written', referred to 'the Book', the Bible. Here, writing was even more than magic. It was the establishment of God's word. Quite naturally the quality of its manuscript tradition was a continuing preoccupation of medieval monks, as every

---

[11] 'Intellectual Training and Attitudes toward Reform, 1075–1150', in: *Pierre Abélard, Pierre le Vénérable*. Paris, 1975, pp. 235–49 (Colloques internationaux du CNRS 546).

[12] St Bernard himself stressed the example of so many other followers of St Benedict's Rule that 'not teaching, but lamenting is the duty of the monk' (*S. Bernardi Opera*, ed. J. Leclercq – H. Rochais. Rome, 1974, vii, p. 236 (ep. 89); *The Letters of St. Bernard of Clairvaux*. transl. B. S. James. London, 1953, p. 138 (ep. 92)).

copy made implied an increasing number of textual errors. In other texts mistakes might hinder good comprehension, or embarrass one's taste, but for the Bible they constituted a violation of God's Word. One of the most important intellectual performances of the Carolingian renaissance was thus the revision of the Bible for which the most famous scholars of the time, Alcuin as well as Theodulf, were personally responsible.[13] And the fifteenth-century renaissance, too, was initiated by biblical study and printing, Gütenberg's 'Forty-two line Bible' (1452–1456) being one of its most stimulating efforts.

The quality of writing not only depends upon the care (or careless-ness) of the copyist, but also upon the intrinsic quality of the written characters. Here two elements meet: the objective, general letter-type and the subjective, individual handwriting. In most of the medieval period there was no place left for any personalization of writing, al-though palaeographers are able to distinguish 'hands'. Yet the ideal of the copyist was to produce a work where his personality was not ex-posed. To form the letters neatly and to read the model carefully were the two conditions for a good product. The design of the characters must not be ambiguous, and they should be efficient to draw. And, as many abbreviations were used, which could easily lead to misinterpre-tation, the text had to be understood correctly.

Confusion reigned in seventh- and eighth-century handwriting. Partly it recalled the cursive type used in Roman administration, and partly it was created and developed in the *scriptoria* of certain major abbeys. So the copyists' handwriting was determined by the cultural area to which they belonged. When the Carolingian period introduced a new character type, very efficient to write and to read, it immediately spread. The 'Carolingian minuscule', as it is called, meant a tremendous change. Slightly adapted, it was used until gothic and cursive handwrit-ing developed in the later middle ages, and to a certain extent it survives in our modern-day printed characters.

Writing also supposes continuity. A book was so precious a treasure that it had to be preserved for subsequent generations. Its material ap-pearance emphasized the eternal value of its contents. The Bible, the Fathers, the Lives of the Saints were to serve forever. Charters and the like, documents which we perceive as pertaining to the sphere of admin-istration and law, derived their importance from the perennial existence of the abbeys, and from the continuity of common interests. The Rule was so convinced of the value of writing that it wished monks to write, and not just pronounce, their holy vows when they entered into the

---

[13] F. L. Ganshof, 'Alcuin's Revision of the Bible', in: F. L. Ganshof, *The Caroling-ians and the Frankish Monarchy*. Ithaca, NY, 1971, pp. 28–40.

religious community (Ch. lviii; xciii). It was a pledge so solemn that it needed the unalterability of written evidence.

The use of writing depended on several factors and conditions. Was it not to be considered a useless activity? Hermits who were thought to represent a more perfect form of spiritual achievement generally did not write. They were completely detached, and the contact they had with God was expected to be more direct than through books. Yet there was no institutional continuity in hermitages, no material interests to be handed down to the generations to come, and hence no necessity of transmission. Was writing perhaps a luxury for a social group free from material preoccupations, and thus able to spend the day in indolence? Or did the eternal value transcend material preoccupations, and was it thus a sign of self-negation? Within the precincts of the monastery writing was primarily a question of mental equilibrium.

Could monasticism have purposely monopolized writing, in order to preserve its intellectual pre-eminence? The answer is no. In fact, monks were not the only ones to benefit from a kind of monopoly over the centuries. The Church as a whole did so. And, moreover, it was the result of a series of social weaknesses rather than of any conscious planning. The Carolingian rulers had, for example, planned a system of generalized schooling: parish schools open for children of free as well as of servile origin where they were to have learned (elementary) singing, mathematics and grammar.[14] But the speedy collapse of their empire undoubtedly prevented any noticeable realization of these intentions. Its upper class had practised the art of reading in any case. The substantial library which the nobleman Eberhard of Frioul and his wife Gisela bequeathed to their children is the most remarkable, but by no means the only example of lay intellectual activity in the ninth century.[15]

Writing was a structural part of Benedictine life. The vow of poverty precluded possession of private property by monks, who were to rely entirely on their abbot. When the Rule speaks of objects, which may not even be possessed personally, it enumerates as an example (common and ordinary) writing material (Ch. xxxiii; lv).

The picture we have painted here of a high-level, even though traditional, activity of the mind, is probably too optimistic. All abbeys were perhaps not really such intellectual havens, and we might have been deceived, once more, by the splendour of the surviving manuscripts and the letter of the Rule. There were in fact *illiterati* present among the monks, too, meaning those who knew no Latin and hence, since only

---

[14] A. Boretius, *Capitularia Regum Francorum*, i. Hannover, 1883, pp. 59–60 (*Admonitio generalis* of 789) (Monumenta Germaniae Historica. Leges in-4°).

[15] This aspect is stressed by R. McKitterick, *The Carolingians and the Written Word*. Cambridge, 1989, pp. 211–70.

Latin was read and written, were unable to read or to write. In itself, being *literatus* was not a condition imposed by St Benedict on those wishing to enter religious life. Monks, originally just lay people and not clerics, came to the monastery to live in common and to reach self-sanctification. That was their aim. But as time passed, more and more monks were ordained, and as early as the Carolingian period a notice-able percentage of them were priests.[16] Those who remained *illiterati*, at that time and afterwards, were those intellectually incapable of learning Latin. A reliable early thirteenth-century source (already quoted), William of Andres, explicitly complained about noble families who sent their mentally and physically handicapped children into the monas-teries.

There is another reservation to be made with respect to the use of writing. Even in the richest and intellectually most outstanding abbeys, books remained rare and precious. When they were in common use, as were liturgical books, they really had to be shared. The texts were re-hearsed and learned by heart before the liturgical services took place. It was a way of encouraging piety, and of preventing idleness, but most of all it was sheer necessity. The monks simply could not be provided with personal copies in the choir (Ch. xliv). In dark churches they would have needed large and heavy folios, impossible to handle, and much too expensive to produce.

The whole educational process used Latin exclusively. As this lan-guage was no longer spoken as a mother tongue, it had to be taught before the study of any other discipline could be started. Latin was, however, fluently spoken and written by those who had studied, and these mostly belonged to the clergy. In international political relations this language was used as well, at least until it was superseded by French in the later middle ages and especially in the early modern period.

As monasticism so avidly drank in antiquity, and monks copied what-ever they could find, it is quite understandable that the educational tradition of the late Roman epoch continued to be followed, more specifi-cally the study of the Seven Liberal Arts, the *Septem artes liberales*. The system went back to Varro (second century B.C.), and to the adaptation made by Martianus Capella (fifth century A.D.). His book *De nuptiis Philologiae et Mercurii* ('On the Marriage of Philology and Mercury') enumerates and develops all seven disciplines. The first three initiated an overall linguistic training (grammar, dialectic, rhetoric), whereas the

---

16 G. Constable, 'Monasteries, Rural Churches and the Cura Animarum in the Early Middle Ages', in: *Cristianizzazione ed organizzazione ecclesiastica delle campagne nell' alto medioevo*. Spoleto, 1962 (Settimane di Studi, xxviii), pp. 349–89 (more specifically pp. 361–65). Reprinted in G. Constable, *Monks, Hermits and Crusaders in Medieval Europe*. London, 1988.

second four represented a more advanced level. They comprised geometry, arithmetic, astronomy and music. All four sciences dealt with mathematics, since music was seen as harmony. The link between the Arts and monasticism is striking when one considers that there is a ninth-century (once again!) commentary on Martianus' text by the Irish bishop Dunchad (who taught at the monastic school of St Rémy, Rheims) and by the monk John Scotus Erigena. A German translation was made as early as *c*. 1000 by the monk Notker Labeo of St Gall. Catalogues of ninth- or tenth-century abbey libraries, important and less important, mention Martianus, who remained in common use throughout the middle ages. The *Artes* continued to represent a large part of the curriculum even when new educational systems (the universities) were worked out from the twelfth century on. The B.A. and M.A. degrees are a remnant of that situation. That a fifth-century book was still in use after more than half a millennium was, however, not only a symptom of its quality, but mainly of intellectual sclerosis. This stresses what has been already stated: care was certainly taken for the preservation of knowledge, but it was to the detriment of creativity. Those medieval authors familiar with their classical predecessors showily used citations from them in their own writings, but unlike what happened in the case of biblical or patristic excerpts they made them only seldom develop the line of thought. It was above all a question of style or of fashion.

The luxurious appearance of the manuscripts, in the same way as monastic architecture and sculpture, was rejected by the Cistercians.[17] It should be stressed that the pursuit of simplicity in manuscripts applied only to their material production. In the Flemish abbey of Clairmarais for instance, the hair of the goat-skin bindings was not carefully stripped away, and the result was quite different from the sumptuous bindings customarily used. Nevertheless simplicity did not mean either bad taste or rusticity, and it did not at all apply to the content.[18] One of the first decrees of the white monks had been precisely that all their abbeys should have the same liturgical manuscripts, and also that the text itself should correspond.[19] It was more than a hint to the copying monks to work carefully. The ideal of simplicity of mind did not apply to the

---

[17] A. Lawrence, 'English Cistercian Manuscripts of the Twelfth Century', in: C. Norton & D. Park (edd.), *Cistercian Art and Architecture in the British Isles*. Cambridge, 1986, pp. 284–98 (esp. pp. 285–87).

[18] Cf. the miniatures of ms. 170 of the Dijon Municipal Library, reproduced for instance in C. Brooke, *The Monastic World. 1000–1300*, plates 24–29, entrancingly charming, but much simpler than those one would expect in a black Benedictine scriptorium.

[19] J. d. l. C. Bouton & J. B. Van Damme, *Les plus anciens textes de Cîteaux*, Achel, 1974, (Cîteaux. Commentarii Cistercienses. Studia et documenta, ii), p. 122, (Summa Cartae Caritatis, c. 10).

textual quality. Only in copying meticulously could monks guarantee the uniformity of observance.

Books for study, books about eternal values: I have repeated this idea many times. An enlarged application was the care with which monks recorded history. They felt responsible for the transmission of knowledge, and therefore they selected events which they thought eternally interesting. In the preceding chapter we have already dealt with annals in order to show that 'ordinary men' did not enter the monks' horizon. The items recorded indeed deal mostly with the succession of rulers, prelates and their own abbots. Some are related to invasions and battles; others to cosmic, natural or physical events (eclipses, famines, monstrous births), mostly interpreted as omens. In the eyes of modern readers these annals could be, erroneously, considered as so many proofs of obscurantism and narrow-mindedness. In fact this was the result of the inextricability of their religious and cosmic vision. They scrutinized their materially perceivable world for signs given by God.

To us all this seems a very limited amount of knowledge, often borrowed from the Romans and unchanged for many centuries. And so it is. Two reasons have been stressed: admiration and obedience. The third is undoubtedly the material difficulty in the way of any adequate transmission, or, to put it bluntly, the limited availability of manuscripts. Two possible remedies were applied in attempts to cope with the problem: the use of *florilegia*, anthologies, and the training of memory.

Thus far there has not been much study of *florilegia*, their role and diffusion.[20] In most of the medieval catalogues, however, they are mentioned, and the fact that in commentaries or treatises medieval authors very often refer to the same arguments, authorities or excerpts suggests the generalized use of such anthologies.

In the liturgical activities and in the educational process the use and the training of the memory seems to have been the most important way of 'saving data'. Novices for instance, were expected to learn the psalter by heart. The ability to recite it, or not, was often used to distinguish Cistercian monks from lay brethren. As in any other oral society the quality of this transmission was outstandingly important, and was to be verified regularly.[21] This system also necessarily enhanced the static

---

[20] R. H. Rouse & M. A. Rouse, *Preachers, Florilegia and Sermons: Sudies on the Manipulus florum of Thomas of Ireland*. Toronto, 1979 (Studies and Texts, 47) and J. Hamesse, *Auctoritates Aristotelis, Senecae, Boethii, Platonis, Apulei et quorundam aliorum*. Louvain-la-Neuve, 2 vol., 1972–1974 are proofs of how important florilegia were in the transmission of the ancient intellectual heritage.

[21] J. Vansina, *Oral tradition*. Harmondsworth, 1973, pp. 33–34 (Penguin University Books).

character of knowledge and the impact of obedience and authority. The supposed truth of the data must not be corrupted, neither by mistakes, nor by unwanted interpretations or additions. When this attitude could, finally, change, as a result of better writing facilities and a sort of mental renewal (let us say, from the thirteenth century onwards) the Benedictines ended up on a side-track. In the investigation of new knowledge their degree of participation was very scanty. The first travellers to visit the Orient, for instance, and to describe what they saw on their long and perilous journey were Franciscan friars, like John of Pian di Carpine or William of Rubrouck in the middle of the thirteenth century. It was a first, and thus significant indication that what one saw with one's own eyes could from then on at least be compared to what tradition said. The time came, yet slowly, where these eyes also began to scrutinize nature, rather than to contemplate heaven exclusively.

ALLEGORY AND RATIONALISM

The title of this section illustrates and suggests the development of medieval thinking. Let us first return to Isidore of Seville's *Etymologiae*.[22] This early seventh-century compilation was the *summa* of scientific knowledge transmitted from antiquity to the middle ages. In twenty books the author systematically dealt with the seven liberal arts, and with theology, biology, geology, agronomy, and so on. His intellectual aim (as the title indicates) was to explain notions as well as objects through the etymology of their names. It became a very popular textbook in the learned milieus of subsequent centuries, as the numerous mentions in the catalogues and the high number of surviving manuscripts clearly prove.[23] This success once again serves to underline the static character of early medieval scientific knowledge, and its link with respect. It seems to point to an incomprehensible lack of creativity or even, erroneously, to incapacity or intellectual inertia. The *Etymologiae* represent the first of three steps in the intellectual transmission of the middle ages: the preservation of existing knowledge (through copying, or through memorization). The second stage, namely the addition of commentary, can be illustrated by such an author as Hrabanus Maurus. This abbot of Fulda offers a good example of how science (Isidore) and commentary (biblical, which to him seemed common knowledge) were

---

[22] J. Fontaine, *Isidore de Séville et la culture classique dans l'Espagne wisigothique.* Paris, 1959, 2 vol.

[23] More than a thousand manuscripts or references to lost manuscripts have been counted. Cf. *San Isidoro de Sevilla. Etimologías*, ed. J. Oroz Reta & M. A. Marcos Casquero. Madrid, 1982–1983 (especially i, pp. 200–11).

mixed. In his *De universo libri xxii* ('The Twenty-two Books on the Universe') Hrabanus performed what his epoch, the ninth century, was intellectually capable of. He copied Isidore, and added long allegorical explanations which he deduced from the Holy Scripture. In fact, he was convinced that the link Isidore supposed to exist between the name and the definition of notions or things, fitted into the broader context of God's universal and cosmic system. He did not challenge the basic truth of what Isidore said. He just wanted to enlarge his proofs, and to add a supplementary dimension. Hrabanus was, as such, a typical representative of the Carolingian Renaissance with all its eager receptivity, implying admiration and servitude, towards classical tradition.

To a modern reader, Hrabanus' additions do not make much sense, and seem to represent a backward step in rational thinking. In the middle ages, however, the intrinsic difference which we distinguish between scientific truth and the Bible was not perceived. The Bible was the basic text of all truth, and every activity, intellectual or otherwise, had to be gauged according to its standard. This 'comprehensive' vision precluded a distinction between reality and fiction. What we call credulity was nothing more than a way of thinking in which another reality was believed to exist, alongside and above the one the senses could perceive. As a result of centuries of rational thinking, we now refuse to call knowledge everything that cannot be experienced and verified through the senses.

The allegorical form of reasoning continued to exist in the following centuries. A typical example of how it continued in practice was Rupert, the late eleventh- and early twelfth-century Benedictine abbot of Deutz. While most of the scholars of his time studied at the 'schools' of Laon, Paris and the like, and started to use another way to approach truth, he still worked according to the allegorical tradition of his earlier Benedictine confrères.

Step three in this intellectual development was the creation of new knowledge, based upon the integration of traditional knowledge and newly gained data (borrowed from outside one's own cultural territory, or as a result of experiments). This third step was initiated by the 'scholastic method', developed from the late eleventh to the thirteenth century. It juxtaposed contradictory sayings or statements from the past, and then proceeded to add commentary and evaluation, in order to find an explanation for these contradictions, the very existence of which already shocked medieval sensibilities. This reasoning finally led to certain conclusions. Abelard and Peter Lombard in the twelfth century, and St Thomas Aquinas in the thirteenth, were the great names in this evolution. The intellectual progress which was eventually acquired, mainly in the field of theology, implied a systematic approach to the Christian faith by using the rational mind. St Thomas' *Summa theologica* is a most daring performance. Using ancient Greek philosophy, and more especially Aristotle, he evaluated the frequently existing contradictions between the Old and the New Testament, and he defined for many following centuries the content of theology with an authority which could compete with St Augustine's.

In this process the Benedictines were, so to speak, absent. It is true that Abelard, perhaps the greatest thinker of all in the twelfth century, had been a monk, and even an abbot, but much more as a result of personal misfortune than as a result of monastic calling. He was and remained a man of the 'schools', his very first love. Moreover, his philosophical and theological work, the object of suspicion and condemnation, did not reflect upon Benedictine intellectual activity at all. In the whole contemporaneous process of systematization no important model seems to have been the work of a monk.[24]

The striking absence of Benedictines in late medieval thinking can be further underlined by an examination of the encyclopedias three or four centuries after Hrabanus Maurus. When a canon of Our Lady's Chapter in St Omer wrote his *Liber Floridus* (*c.* 1120), and made it a compendium of contemporaneous Western science, his sources were still as traditional as possible. The genre of the encyclopedia was to change drastically only on the eve of the thirteenth century, when it benefited from the importation of scientific treatises of Arabic, or (through this bias) of classical Greek origin. Both influences gave an extremely enriching impetus, indeed the most vigorous since the beginning of the middle ages. Thomas of Cantimpré, a regular canon who afterwards became a Dominican friar, Bartholomeus Anglicus, a Franciscan, and Vincent of Beauvais, also a Dominican, were the most important compilers of the new encyclopedias. No Benedictines were involved.

I do not claim that black or white monks did not play a role in the intellectual achievements of their time. The writings of Peter the Venerable are counted among the stylistic and moral summits of the middle ages. The role of St Bernard and of William of St Thierry in the development of mystic literature, and of mysticism in general is tremendous.

---

[24] The Italian canonist Gratian has been considered traditionally as a monk of the order of Camaldoli, but this opinion has been rejected (J. T. Noonan Jr, 'Gratian slept here. The Changing Identity of the Father of the Systematic Study of Canon Law', in: *Traditio*, xxxv, 1979, pp. 145–72). His *Concordia discordantium canonum* ('Concord of Discordant Canons'), generally known as the *Decretum*, approached Church legislation in the same way that Peter Lombard approached the field of theology, and as St Thomas would in turn do a century later: first opposing the contradictory data, and afterwards formulating his own opinion. So the work breathed the style of the schools, and not that of the monastic houses.

But one is hardly willing to believe that mysticism affected the ordinary medieval man: in his religious feeling, still very rough and superficial, mysticism remained a distant ideal. It was thought to be an unattainable spiritual power, and a life-style for those whom God had called. It did not really interfere in the medieval man's concerns.

However important mysticism was within the religious movements, it was the systematic criticism (thus rationalism) of the 'schools' which changed intellectual behaviour. After a long and steady, but slow evolution in which the scientific experiment steadily became predominant, the aspect of the material and mental world altered. The first representatives who should be mentioned are the thirteenth-century chancellor of Oxford University (and later bishop of Lincoln) Robert Grosseteste, and his pupil Roger Bacon, an astronomer who pleaded for the study of mathematics and physics. Neither of them was a Benedictine. Such a general absence of black monks is quite the opposite of their omnipresence in the learning of earlier centuries. The objection that encyclopedias and *summae*, the achievements of other religious and intellectual traditions, did not affect ordinary people either is substantially correct, yet these texts were steps which made access to knowledge and its popularisation a lot easier in the long run.

Only Hildegard, the Benedictine abbess of Bingen on the Rhine, can be advanced as a twelfth-century example of nature-observation. Her books on nature and on medicine differed completely from what traditional writings taught. Whether her knowledge can be attributed to her own perception, or to oral transmission, is not clear, but there is no doubt that her womanhood gave her an advantage which made all the difference. As a nun, she was not really *literata* (her Latin is very poor indeed), and at the same time she was a visionary (and thus in immediate relation to God).[25] Both these elements gave her a liberty of approach and expression which could not be expected in medieval male abbeys, where the classical authors weighed too heavily on the monks' intellectual creativity.

AS TIMES CHANGED, EDUCATION CHANGED

The two preceding sections have shown that new educational networks were tried out during the second half of the middle ages, more specifically after the eleventh century. The progress in intellectual activity which they represented implied that the Benedictine contribution dim-

---

[25] Cf. among the numerous recent publications B. Newman, *Sister of Wisdom. St. Hildegard's Theology of the Feminine*. Berkeley, Los Angeles, 1987.

inished accordingly in the twelfth century, even in spite of the deserved celebrity of such names as Peter the Venerable or St Bernard.

This educational shift has a multiple explanation. The broad changes in society as a whole led to a greater demand for writing. Social contacts, political as well as economic, became intensified and necessitated more sophisticated structures and organization. The intrinsic quality of writing as it had been perceived up to then (being the unaltered transmission of what had eternal value and truth), inspired its increasing use in administration and in transactions where correctness was also considered a necessity. The twelfth century witnessed the first continuous series of lay government chancery documents, still proudly displayed for example in the astonishingly rich archives of the kings of England in the London Public Record Office.[26] The need for more generalized writing skills increased, and contributed in turn to the formation of a more complex society, based on the written word. The Benedictine houses barely participated in this evolution, even though they had so long been, and continued to be, pre-eminent users of writing. As long as lay seigniorial administration was not adequately organized, monks continued to produce charters mostly when they were personally involved as a contracting party, but they would also make them to order for a third party. This was in fact a survival of a traditional monopoly. As the demand for more writing skill grew, the supply had to follow. This led to a need for 'open' schools, for a broader educational pattern which functioned outside the precincts of the religious houses. One can certainly show examples of black Benedictine, and even of Cistercian houses, which provided education to youngsters who did not plan to embrace monastic life, but this was not a general rule at all. When it occurred, resistance quite generally arose within the monastic movement itself in order to keep their *scholae* closed.[27] The entrance conditions thus differentiated the cathedral and chapter schools (open to all) from the monastic schools (open only to future members). The international attraction of some, long extant but now developing 'schools', such as Paris or Laon, produced top level teachers, scholars and, when they made a career in the Church, bishops. I have John of Salisbury, or Peter Lombard in mind. For celebrated Benedictines of the same type and personality and educated in their own schools, we must seek in an

---

[26] Papal registers were kept since the early middle ages, but they are only continously preserved from *c.* 1200 onwards.

[27] J. Leclercq, 'Textes sur la vocation et la formation des moines au moyen âge', in: *Corona Gratiarum. Miscellanea . . . E. Dekkers . . . oblata*. Bruges, The Hague, 1975, ii, pp. 169–94 (esp. pp. 170–74). P. Johanek, 'Klosterstudien im 12. Jahrhundert', in: J. Fried (ed.), *Schulen und Studium im sozialen Wandel des hohen und späten Mittelalters*, p. 46.

earlier period, and necessarily so. Lanfranc and Anselm, the eleventh-century archbishops of Canterbury, who spent part of their lives in the abbey of Bec in Normandy, are the most illustrious examples of this type.

The purpose of this book, however, is to examine the ordinary people rather than the big names, and normal events rather than exceptional circumstances. Thus the more generalized forms of education interest us more than the exceptionally famous and exclusive schools. More important for our topic thus are those schools where pupils simply learned to read and to write, all in Latin, as we have already stated. It is a pity that evidence concerning this training is so scanty, but one can still justify the presumption that in the many small canons' chapters which were founded and endowed by local lords from the eleventh century onwards, some preliminary schooling was organized. This provided a gradually increasing number of persons with the ability to write. Even if the pupils were not always equally well trained, this type of schools nevertheless explains the more generalized use of writing on a local scale, as is demonstrated by the drastically increased number of lower level charters, especially in the thirteenth century.

There is no doubt that the purpose of education in general, and of writing in particular, became increasingly pragmatic. The sort of education intended to better the performance of the *laus perennis*, the continuous praise of God, or to enhance His glory by what monks called science, faded into the background. Henceforward a career became the primary interest. The study of law and of theology, although initially directed towards the accumulation of pure knowledge became, certainly in the thirteenth century and perhaps already earlier, mainly a professional choice. Law and theology engaged less in scientific thought and speculation than in finding a patron, ecclesiastical or lay, to serve faithfully as good civil servants do. Clerics became clerks that way. The 'closed schools' and the life-style of the monks did not fit into this mentality of pragmatism.

When the universities arose and developed in the twelfth and thirteenth centuries, some of them out of pre-existing chapter schools, the newly founded mendicant orders were swift to flock to them. The monastic orders were generally opposed or at least unenthusiastic. All the great names in thirteenth-century universities were Dominicans, Franciscans or secular clerics, for instance Albertus Magnus, St Thomas Aquinas, St Bonaventura, Henry of Ghent, and Siger of Brabant at the University of Paris. The mendicants built their own colleges in the university towns and were thus integrated into academic life, the social importance of which grew in accordance with the growth of public authority. In Paris the Dominicans had their own college in 1217, the Franciscans some years later, and by 1254 there were Augustinians,

Trinitarians, Premonstratensians, and even Cistercians, but no black Benedictines.[28] In Oxford they appeared as late as 1283 and in Cambridge after 1321, but they were certainly highly esteemed at that time.[29] The statement about the Benedictines' delayed presence neither implies a criticism, nor suggests backwardness. It simply indicates that their seclusion formed a barrier, deliberately sought after, against their integration into intellectual activity of a new type, of a different nature and enlarged in scope. When Pope Benedict XII promulgated reform constitutions for several religious orders in the 1330s, he thought it necessary to impose minimum quotas on the university attendance of the Benedictines, the Cistercians and the regular canons.[30]

TOLERANCE AND INCOMPREHENSION

More than half a century ago the French historian of monasticism Dom F. Cabrol wrote in one of his works: 'St Bernard – that is ascetism; Peter the Venerable and Cluny – that is humanism.'[31] Since then a great deal of scholarly work has been done on the history of both Benedictine movements, black and white. Does Cabrol's opinion still hold? And what is meant by humanism? Is the word to be interpreted in the same sense as one generally does now, as a life-style or philosophical attitude where mankind is central, and where its own fulfilment is the aim, if not the only sense, of life? Or does it mean 'the increase of the total value of the person [in which] the human data and the Christian input cannot be

[28] S. C. Ferruolo, *The origins of the University of Paris and their Critics*. Stanford, 1985, p. 92. R. Schneider, 'Studium und Zisterzienserorden', in: J. Fried (ed.), *Schulen und Studium im sozialen Wandel des hohen und späten Mittelalters*, pp. 321 – 350 (esp. pp. 326–27). C. Obert, 'La promotion des études chez les Cisterciens à travers le recrutement des étudiants du Collège Saint-Bernard de Paris au moyen âge', in: *Cîteaux. Commentarii Cistercienses*, 39, 1988, pp. 65–78. Paris students appear in the Cluny statutes from 1260 onwards (G. Charvin, *Statuts, chapitres généraux et visites de l'Ordre de Cluny*, i. Paris, 1965, p. 253).

[29] Knowles & Hadcock, *Medieval Religious Houses. England and Wales*, pp. 53, 56, 61, 72; W. J. Courtenay, *Schools & Scholars in fourteenth-century England*. Princeton, 1987, pp. 56–87.

[30] *Magnum Bullarium Romanum*. Rome, 1740 (Graz, 1964), iii, pp. 211, 220, 271. Cf. P. Becker, 'Erstrebte und erreichte Ziele benediktinischer Reformen im Spätmittelalter', in: *Reformbemühungen und Observanzbestrebungen im spätmittelalterlichen Ordenswesen*, ed. K. Elm. Berlin, 1989, pp. 23–34 (Berliner Historische Studien, 14).

[31] Quoted in French in the *Dictionnaire d'histoire et de géographie ecclésiastiques*, 8. Paris, 1934, c. 671.

separated'.[32] Humanism in Cabrol's eyes alluded more to understanding for human weakness, and was thus linked to sin and to a transcendental ideal. What Cabrol did was to suggest that asceticism is the antonym of humanism, and hence does not show an understanding for human weakness. This obviously corresponds to St Bernard's opinion on asceticism. In his eyes it is the only means of surpassing human frailty and of meeting God more easily. Was St Bernard then inhuman or superhuman? Or was he simply obstinate in his support of a literal reading of St Benedict's Rule which left no room for compromise?[33] What counted for him and for the founders of the Cistercian order was only their sixth-century spiritual model as it was written, and not as it had been interpreted by monks afterwards. 'Back to the sources' and to their literal meaning was the motto used by St Bernard and other spiritual leaders of his time, in their calls for reform. He was opposed to Cluny, and to the black Benedictines in general, who believed that the monastic tradition, which had grown through the centuries and was observed alongside the Rule, had its own intrinsic value. Throughout the centuries customaries had been composed in which the general directives and the spirituality of the Rule were interpreted in terms of everyday monastic life. Some emphases of the Rule had been changed; some aspects had been emphasized, whereas others had been played down.

Does an attitude of traditional reading suggest more tolerance? If tolerance means acceptance of opposite religious opinions, reformers as well as traditionalists should certainly be called intolerant. Peter the Venerable and St Bernard were convinced of the unique truth of Latin Christendom, like every other person living in the medieval West. That Peter had the Koran translated was by no means a sign of tolerance, but a way of preparing for more scientific warfare. As a warrior should know the weapons of his enemy, a theologian had to take note of the arguments of 'the abominable heresy or sect' that Islam was. Some of Peter's treatises clearly prove that a tolerant attitude towards religious minorities, Jews as well as heretics, was no item of his programme.[34] The

---

[32] This is the definition given by the brilliant Benedictine historian J. Leclercq, 'L'humanisme des moines au moyen âge', in: *A Giuseppe Ermini*. Spoleto, 1970, pp. 69–113 (esp. p. 75): 'c'est l'accroissement de la valeur totale de la personne: les données humaines et l'apport chrétien ne peuvent pas être séparés'. The approach is nearly identical in G. Penco, "Senso dell' uomo e scoperta dell' individuo nel monachesimo dei secoli XI e XII', in: *Benedictina*, 37, 2, 1990, pp. 285–315.

[33] Cf. J. Leclercq, 'Literature and Psychology in Bernard of Clairvaux', in: *The Downside Review*, 93, 1975, pp. 1–20.

[34] *Contra Petrobrusianos hereticos*, ed. J. Fearns. Turnhout, 1968 (Corpus Christianorum. Continuatio mediaeualis, x); *Adversus Iudeorum inveteratam duritiem*,

general conviction that the Latin West was the keeper of the Truth, the Unique Truth, required an attitude, mental and physical, of intransigence. Even if we realize that tolerance formed no part of the medieval religious mind,[35] we have on the eve of the third millennium difficulties with such an attitude and we are shocked when it is practised nowadays in other religions. Since the Enlightenment and, as a result of its political consequences, the eighteenth- and nineteenth-century revolutions in Europe and America, we are used to individual and religious freedom (even if they are often only theoretical). In the middle ages truth was intolerant, whether it was claimed by the established Church or by dissident movements. God is Truth, thus absolute. This demonstrates why the new school systems and the new orders of the second half of the middle ages did not lead to what we would call more respect for others, and thus to more humanism. On the contrary: the truth of the Benedictines was traditionally limited, and protected by their own spiritual isolation, whereas the truth of the academics and of the new orders was easily imposed upon the worldly society they so eagerly infiltrated. They held key functions in the increasingly powerful secular and ecclesiastical courts, expressions of more centralized and even authoritarian ways of government. They both held key functions as well in what we should call the 'mental court', confession, which was imposed in 1215. So the rather benign theoretical intolerance of the monks, more specifically of the black monks (the Cistercians having been involved in the repression of the Cathars in southern France) gave way to the academics' and Dominicans' more cruel applied forms of intolerance for which the later middle ages and the sixteenth century are noted. More open education did not imply thus more comprehension or relativism, the key notions of what we call humanism. Looking towards God (as the monks did) was again succeeded by a scrutinizing of the earthly horizon for human aberration and sin.

ed. Y. Friedman. Turnhout, 1985 (Corpus Christianorum. Continuatio mediaeualis, lviii); *Liber contra sectam sive haeresim Saracenorum*, in: J. Kritzeck, *Peter the Venerable and Islam*. Princeton, 1964, pp. 220–91 (Princeton Oriental Studies).

[35] It is exceptional to meet authors concerned with the place of the 'good heathen' within God's planning. Such an example is the thirteenth-century (lay) author Wolfram von Eschenbach. His *Willehalm* is published by N. J. Schröder & G. Hollandt, *Wolfram von Eschenbach. Willehalm. Titurel*. Darmstadt, 1971, pp. 1–397.

7

Religion, Religious Life and the Church

In dealing earlier with missionary activity, I intended to show how in the first period of the middle ages monks really were involved in converting pagan peoples, but I entered only superficially into the structure which made such an activity possible. In order to do so more thoroughly, I now turn to the different types of monastic observances. When St Benedict says that monks must be 'persevering in [the Lord's] teaching in the monasteries until death' (Prol. 50), only one among many possible religious life-styles is displayed. His text helps to uncover the others. His first chapter (also the first in the Rule of the Master) is entitled 'Of the various Kinds of Monks'. He distinguishes four categories: the cenobites, the anchorites or hermits, the *Sarabaitae*, and finally the *Gyrovagi*. Yet St Benedict is very suspicious, and convinced that only common (thus cenobitical) life under the spiritual guidance of an abbot ('Father') can lead towards perfection. The monks of this category are called 'the strongest race'. He is very negative towards the *sarabaitae*, as they live in small groups and do not practise obedience. He feels the same way towards the *gyrovagi*, who wander around, as the etymology of their name indicates. They live licentiously and do not practise stability. They are bad monks, so we are told, precisely because they do not do so. He evaluates the hermits in a different way. Their form of seclusion is the ultimate step towards perfection, but St Benedict warns his readers that it can only be reached by older monks who are sufficiently experienced through a previous, long-lasting common life to fight off the temptations of the Devil. St Benedict is almost suggesting that if eremitism is a way to heaven, it is a most difficult one indeed.

As I am concerned here with the influence of monasticism upon missionary activity, I do not want to emphasize the eremitical life of the 'Fathers of the Desert' in the Near East. Their story belongs to the history of Eastern Christendom, and it only influenced the West through such intermediary authors and spiritual models as Cassian. What we have to deal with is early medieval Celtic (mainly Irish) monasticism. This was not characterized by stability. Its solution for a perfect life, was exile, a voluntary exile. After a formation period the monk left the abbey to start a life abroad. Only the fulfilment of Christ's saying, 'So therefore, whoever of you does not renounce all that he has cannot be my disciple' (Lk. 14:33), was for them the fundamental way towards perfection and heaven. He was a permanent *peregrinus*, pilgrim, the Latin word for stranger. The monk was not allowed to feel at home anywhere. He was to suffer from homesickness, danger, and hunger. So, from the sixth century onwards, Irish, and later English, monks came to the European continent. They spread a net of what could be called home-base abbeys, from which they were sent out to convert the countryside. For several areas studies clearly show how successive waves of missionary activity finally covered the whole territory, so that by the eighth century, at least for Gaul, the first level of conversion (the change towards a christianized social collective behaviour) was completed. The area east of it, later Germany, was hardly touched at that time. Scandinavia further north, or Slav territory further east had not yet been visited by any missionary at all at that time. Their entry into Christendom only occurred some centuries later.

The contact between Celtic monasticism on the one hand and Benedictine or similar continental observances on the other hand had been growing slowly. They merged with each other, became fused, which meant that the importance of 'stability', the confinement to a single abbey, increased whereas that of perpetual pilgrimage lost its importance. When, finally, in the Carolingian epoch, the Benedictine model achieved a monopoly of monastic observance, stability literally 'cloistered' all the monks. Therefore they only exercised a scanty influence in the further stages of the conversion process (external individual conduct and interior behaviour). The latter stage was especially important, as it needed a continuous and individual repetition and follow-up. It was the field of action for the waxing power of the secular Church and, from the thirteenth century onwards, of the mendicants.

Missionary activity and conversion spring from one basic principle: the conviction that one's own belief is the only true one, and that outside of it, no salvation is possible. That by its elaborate message and theology Christendom could claim its superiority over pagan religions is quite obvious. It believed in a unique God, and therefore it was not at all willing to compromise in order to merge its God into the pagan polytheistic system. Traditional paganism could indeed absorb new gods, with new attributions and new qualifications. The Christian God combined all the 'qualities' in His own deity, and moreover He did so in a perfect way. No place was left for any other Divinity of Good. This explains the intolerant attitude towards paganism, Judaism and Islam. Historically it was translated into the rejection of and only marginal survival of paganism, as well as into the recuperation of pagan elements by and in Christianity. Moreover it explains the anti-semitic attitude of

116

Western Christian civilization and the long-lasting battle against the Muslims on the fringes of the Mediterranean.

In speaking of the medieval attitude towards other religions and their followers, we must examine what monasticism and monastic involvement meant in the very dynamic movement which the Crusades represented. In 1071 Jerusalem, which had already been in Muslim hands since the seventh century, was captured by the Seljuk Turks, who kept Christian pilgrims from worshipping at the holy sites of Palestine, and threatened the security of the Byzantine Empire. As far as its religious aspect was concerned,[1] the Crusader movement was led by the pope. Only a short time before, his predecessors had succeeded in claiming the highest authority within the Church. In fact this had been the issue of the so-called 'Investiture Controversy' which opposed the pope to the 'Emperor of the Roman Empire' (the king of Germany), and this struggle was far from over. In 1095 Urban II summoned the Christian peoples to take the cross, and to fight the infidels. The impetus for the 'Popular Crusade', which preceded the 'Seigniorial Crusade' had been given by a monk, Peter the Hermit.[2]

Even if Peter was originally a Benedictine, one could hardly maintain that his preaching was representative of monasticism. Wandering preachers like him were in fact in sharp contrast to traditional monasticism. It was looking for a re-interpretation of religious life which was more socially committed. These *Wanderprediger* (to use the German term commonly applied to them by modern historians) were mostly hermits at odds with traditional monastic (thus Benedictine) life, and looking for new religious solutions. This does not mean that many abbots and many monks would not leave Europe to go to the Holy Land in the decades to come, even into the thirteenth century. Some participated in the major Crusades. Others left at other times, for as long as the Western presence was secured (that means until the second half of the thirteenth century) there was a continuous reinforcing stream of pilgrims, settlers, and knights. Nevertheless there was no systematic and large-scale presence of black Benedictine monks. Among the many religious houses erected to re-Christianize the area, however, there were a large number which

---

[1] We do not have to deal here with the obvious economic and social aspects of the Crusades.

[2] After his return from the Holy Land Peter became the founder and prior of the monastery of regular canons of Neufmoutier near Liège. Ch. Dereine, *Les chanoines réguliers au diocèse de Liège avant saint Norbert.* Brussels, 1952, pp. 139–59 (Académie royale . . . de Belgique. Classe des Lettres . . . Mémoires 47, 1). For a discussion of his exact role, see E. O. Blake and C. Morris, 'A Hermit goes to War: Peter and the Origins of the First Crusade', in: W. J. Sheils (ed.), *Monks, Hermits and the Ascetic Tradition.* Oxford, 1985, pp. 79–107 (Studies in Church History 22).

belonged to the Cistercian order. Its spread and success were the result of the same general religious dynamism which explained the vitality of the Crusader movement itself.

Much more remarkable for the purpose of this book, however, was the presence and the very existence of the military orders. They can be called a 'monastic translation' of knighthood and as such they help to answer our basic question, the influence of monasticism upon ordinary people. The 'knights of Christ' or *milites Christi*, the metaphorical name these persons were given, combined a cenobitical life-style with that of a real fighting knight. The Cistercian St Bernard played a major role both in the conception and in the legislation of the most important of these military orders, the Templars. He was the author of a treatise on what he called the *new militia*. The half military, half religious status of these knights represents the most striking example of how the monastic ideal came to interfere in the concept of lay society. The victory of God over Evil, and of the Christians over the infidels, seemed at hand. The 'legitimate war' was fought by sacral, monk-like warriors. The two privileged bodies in society, the *ordines* of soldiers and priests (*bellatores* and *oratores*), with their common socio-religious interests, seemed to merge now in their individual members. Cîteaux was, in St Bernard's eyes, divinely called to lead the movement, the centre of a solar system with other militias in orbit.[3] The collapse, however, of the Western presence in the Middle East in the thirteenth century, and the dreadful liquidation of the Templars in the fourteenth, drastically reduced the relevance of the phenomenon. Other religious orders of knights survived (the Hospitallers, the so-called Order of Malta, until the present day), and new ones came to the fore (the Teutonic order). Though the enthusiasm of St Bernard and of his century had died out by that time, both the charity of the military orders and their bloody warfare against the Slav pagans (the two activities were not felt to be contradictory) continued to be considered expressions of the same mental attitude.

St Bernard of Clairvaux himself had preached the Second Crusade of 1147. Even if not reform-minded, black Benedictines were intolerant of and hostile to other religions (forces of Evil!), though none of them were committed to the same extent to the defence and the propagation of their own belief. That Cistercians, still longing for a 'heaven on earth' organized after the image of their own order, were to be active some decades later in the repression of the dualistic Cathars in southern France, then becomes quite easy to understand. That they were removed, in turn, from that battle-field of religious orthodoxy by the

---

[3] Cf. the brilliant paper of J. Leclercq, 'L'Ordine del Tempio: monachesimo guerriero e spiritualità medievale', in: *I Templari: mito e storia*. Siena, 1989, pp. 1–8.

Dominicans, only a few years after their foundation in the early thirteenth century, is one more striking illustration of how the Church, to control the flock, did not need Benedictinism, whether black or white.

When considering Western Christian religious policy *vis-à-vis* Islam in the thirteenth century, the charismatic founder of the Friars minor, St Francis, is the one whose name comes to mind. He went into the Muslim world in an unsuccessful attempt to convert it to his own religion. He neither engaged in dialogue with, nor tried to understand the beliefs of the adherents of Islam. Many more centuries were to pass before a more flexible attitude arose.

And for those at home? People staying in Europe saw the Crusades make the monasteries even wealthier. Even if this was not a substantial increase in their means, the archives of almost all abbeys still have some charters in which crusaders, about to leave and with the conquest of Celestial Jerusalem, Heaven, in mind, bequeathed them earthly goods and rights. Moreover many relics came to swell monastic wealth, both spiritual and material, after the Fall of Constantinople, the capital of the Byzantine Empire. The devastation and pillage of the Christian metropolis was the unexpected but scandalous issue of the Fourth Crusade (1204). Hundreds if not thousands of relics were sent to the West. Even if there was some profit for some abbeys, it did not have any substantial meaning for monasticism as such.

CHARISMA, RULE AND INSTITUTION

This triple heading refers to the triple title of the whole chapter. *Charisma* is a religious feeling; the *rule* translates it into a religious life-style, while this is implemented in an *institution*, namely the abbey. The historian not only needs to consider these three levels themselves, but also their intertwinement. None of them in fact exists on its own. Charisma needs to be made concrete through acts; the rule suggests the way to do so, and this has to fit within the organizational blueprint of the Church, its theology, discipline and traditions.

Which stages lead towards religious life? The answer is threefold. First of all it is to be based upon a conviction, fundamentally the belief in God. Secondly there is a choice, to join God; and finally, there is the way to achieve this choice, mentally as well as materially. Yet this realization is subject to limitations, those imposed by matter ('joining God' is for instance biologically impossible), and those imposed by society.

Charisma is a word whose meaning is difficult to define.[4] I would

---

4 *Webster's Seventh New Collegiate Dictionary*. Springfield, Mass., 1963, gives two meanings: 1. an extraordinary power (as of healing) given a Christian by

describe it as the demonstration of enthusiastic desire to dedicate one's life to God. In this sense charisma seems a necessarily individual phenomenon. The more a society is organized according to collective standards, however, the more this enthusiastic feeling can show social aspects. Ideally charisma implies the refusal of compromise. Its base is absolute Love, and it demands an absolute answer. From the point of view of religious sociology the content of charisma (that which one feels and that which one hopes to fulfil as expressions of charisma) is culturally determined. In other words, even if the Love is conceived as unique and coherent, it is expressed in socially familiar ideas, images, symbols and aims.

Within the history of the religious movements the first and major way to convert charisma into a programme is the 'example of the master'. A spiritual elder guides the young charismatics. He shows them how to translate their feeling into realization, through a system of thoughts as well as of acts. The existing educational networks provide the vocabulary of the relationship. It is the school (St Benedict calls the monastery the 'school of the Lord's service' (Prol. 45)), and it is the link between master and disciple; or, it is the family, and then one stresses the link between the father (the etymological meaning of 'abbot') and the sons. St Benedict mixes both systems when he addresses the readers of his Rule with the words 'Listen, my son, to your master's precepts'. The first expressions of monastic life all belong to the type of the personal example. This stresses a face-to-face relationship, based upon charisma and as such it recalls the first and most simple step of the 'Three pure types of Authority' distinguished by the famous sociologist Max Weber.[5] The direct 'example' is functional only in small-scale communities, and it is moreover characterized by subjectivity. Charisma is not willing to compromise; it is *per se* absolute and subjective (because individual), and as such hardly realizable in that form. Eremitism allows fulfilment of this feeling of charisma in the strictest sense, as it represents an individual life-style, but in a cenobitical environment – a shared common life – every implementation has to be objectified, adapted to a standard. Therefore the basic virtue of the monk's social behaviour is necessarily obedience, in the same way that justice is the primary obligation of the abbot in his relationship with his monks. The 'Rule', every rule,

the Holy Spirit for the good of the Church; 2. a personal magic of leadership arousing special popular loyalty or enthusiasm for a statesman or a military commander.

5 M. Weber, *Wirtschaft und Gesellschaft. Grundriss der verstehenden Soziologie* (ed. J. Winckelmann). Tübingen, 1972[5], pp. 122–76 (translation: *Economy and Society*, ed. G. Roth & C. Wittich. New York, 1968, 3, pp. 1006–69).

describes which acts (or thoughts) are imposed, allowed or forbidden; it reduces charisma to a set of commands and interdictions. Thus a rule implies levelling. As it strives to be objective and functional for the whole of the monastic community, it imposes an accomplishable task on every member of the community. The rule constitutes at once a minimum and a maximum. For the weak, the life-style imposed must remain attainable in order not to discourage them. For the strong-willed it serves as a restraint against heroism, an extravagance generally perceived as dangerous. In other words the Rule, in making charisma functional, suppresses its uncompromising character. It condemns an extreme way of life, and this explains why St Benedict is so reticent on the subject of eremitical practices. Rules which do stress extreme forms of mortification or abstinence (and these do exist) are in fact addressed to hermits. Such a precept as for instance 'Keep not thy meal till it sours. Sleep not till sleep oppresses you'[6] can easily be situated in the early medieval Irish eremitical tradition but it would not adequately function in a cenobitical context.

The monasticism St Benedict prescribed was organized in individual and independent abbeys. When an abbey was founded, some monks left an existing monastery to constitute the nucleus of the new house, a sort of cloning. The system was an expression of, and appealed to, the first stage in Weber's tripartition (face-to-face contact). Within the broader framework of society, however, it caused vulnerability, and this vulnerability constituted a real risk for the abbey. Influence or pressure from outside could easily jeopardize the abbey, its independence and the quality of its religious life, the more so when one takes into consideration the existence of what we have called 'functional reciprocity', serving kinship interests. Their own monastic independence highlighted their social dependence, and this was really a weak point, both materially and religiously. The abbey was, socially speaking, an element of feudalism, and as such it was subject to the same changes undergone by feudalism and the nobility. The most striking proof of this dependence is the fact that the free election of the abbot, foreseen in the Rule, was not normally complied with. The 'owner' of the abbey, king, prince or nobleman, imposed a candidate, usually a member of his own clan, or a reliable collaborator. Afterwards a formal election could take place in order to obey theoretically the precept of the Rule. It explains how the

---

6 Cf. L. Milis, 'Reinheid, sex en zonde' in: L. Milis (ed.), *De Heidense Middeleeuwen*. Brussels, Rome, 1991, p. 151; W. Reeves, 'On the Céli-dé, commonly called Culdees', in: *The Transactions of the Royal Irish Academy*, 24, 1873, p. 211 (quoted from the *Prose Rule of the Céli Dé*).

system of so-called lay abbots could become generalized in the Carolingian period, at least for the greater houses. Faithful counsellors of the emperors became abbots of several abbeys, located at great distances from each other, simultaneously. Even if most of them were highly qualified people with a genuine religious feeling, and not decadent dissipators, as has often been maintained, they did not fulfil what the Rule and St Benedict were asking: the spiritual care and attention of the good shepherd for his 'flock'.[7]

When the Carolingian Empire collapsed in the second half of the ninth century and when the disintegrating aspects of the feudal system became increasingly apparent in the tenth (public authority made private, and exercised at lower levels), abbeys became accordingly more subject to the influence of external rulers who were very often religiously unworthy.

Two major solutions in the shape of institutional reforms (expressions of religious feeling) were worked out. The many smaller ones are not taken into account here, as they basically reflect the major ones. The first is that of Cluny, founded in Burgundy in 909 by William III of Aquitaine. In the first charter the duke already stressed the independence of the abbey *vis-à-vis* himself as its founder, its immediate answerability being to the pope. These two aspects were at that time highly unusual. Nevertheless there appears to be a fundamental contradiction in the Cluniac movement, as it was to develop in the following two centuries. It attempted to maintain and stress its own independence but was nevertheless closely tied to feudalism and the nobility. It was a participant in the dominant social organization, and it was at the same time by its longing for Heaven alien to Earth, as the enhanced importance paid to liturgy and worship so strikingly prove.

In order to structure its religious independence, and to cope with the vulnerability inherent in the small-scale autonomy of individual abbeys, Cluny worked out a very centralized system. All the houses belonging to the movement preserved a direct link with Cluny itself. Its abbot was (at least theoretically) the only abbot within his order, the heads of the dependent houses were called priors, a title traditionally used in monastic terminology to indicate the second-in-command in an abbey. It illustrates the great degree of centralization and the, to some extent effectively workable, answer to lay influence. However, the parallel occasionally perceived between the feudal pyramid (successive degrees

---

7   F. J. Felten, *Äbte und Laienäbte im Frankenreich. Studie zum Verhältnis von Staat und Kirche im früheren Mittelalter.* Stuttgart, 1980 (Monographien zur Geschichte des Mittelalters, 20).

of 'lord and vassal' relations) and a supposed Cluniac pyramidal organization does not appear tenable to us. Cluny constitutes a model of
monocratic or one-ruler authority, and not of a step-by-step gradation of
power. Cluniac monasticism no longer represents the face-to-face relationship between the abbot and his monks in independent abbeys.
Large-scale projects require large-scale solutions to their problems.
Cluniac rulership could be compared with the second step in Weber's
'Three pure types of Authority', namely the 'patrimonial' or 'patriarchal
domination' (also called traditional authority).

Cistercian monasticism grew out of the late eleventh-century 'new-
wave' (i.e. reformed) abbey of Cîteaux, situated, as is Cluny, in Burgundy. It was in search of a more adequate solution, answering to the
literal reading of the Rule. In the minds of its founders and of its most
representative personality, St Bernard, the basic value of the relationship
between the Cistercian abbeys was *caritas* or love. The constitutional text
which explains the links within the order, is called the 'Charter of Love'
(*Carta Caritatis*). The word means here reciprocity and shared responsibility. It was Cîteaux which foresaw a pyramidal structure in which
abbeys continued to remain, to a certain extent at least, dependent on
the abbey from which they were born. The metaphor of mothers and
daughters is used. At the same time the order organized annual General
Chapters, at which the abbots of all the houses were required to be
present. The system of authority exercised was thus partly based upon
collegiate responsibility. It was to a certain extent a prelude to the par-
liamentary systems which were worked out, beginning in the thirteenth
century, in secular politics, though no direct monastic influence can be
traced. Yet the Cistercian General Chapter functioned as a model within
the Church for a great many other religious orders.[8]

Individual charisma can and does fade; shared charisma fades, too.
Over and over again the history of religious movements shows how
successive waves of reform emanate from charismatic impulses. It also
proves that routine always invades religious life. For the religious spirit
to survive when the original enthusiasm disappeared, remedies had to
be found. In my view, the usual solution was a more elaborate administration which kept a closer check on any failure to carry out duties.
When abbots from abroad, for instance, made reluctant by the prospect
of the length and the troubles of the journey, did not show up sponta-

---

8 Cf. The Fourth Lateran Council of 1215 (can. 12) (*Conciliorum Oecumenicorum
   Decreta*. Bologna, 1973, pp. 240–41) imposed the organization of general
   chapters (according to the Cistercian model) for monastic movements which
   lacked them. It was repeated in reform bullae of Benedict XII in the 1330s.

neously at Chapter meetings, they needed to be summoned, and this implied intensified writing and administration.[9]

Utopia became institutionalized.[10] Institutions always betray the expectations of authentic charisma, and thus of monasticism, but this is inherent in mankind itself. Society always compromises.

[9] For monks such a study has not yet been made. We have made such a study for an analogous Order of regular canons: 'Charisma en administratie', in: *Archives et bibliothèques de Belgique – Archief- en Bibliotheekwezen in België*, 46, 1975, pp. 50–69 and 549–66.

[10] J. Seguy, 'Une sociologie des sociétés imaginées: monachisme et utopie', in: *Annales. ESC*, 26, 1971, pp. 328–54.

8

Artistic Expression

It is difficult for those living in the twentieth century to realize what artistic expression meant to medieval people. When travelling in France, Italy or other parts of Europe we are delighted by medieval buildings and sculpture; we are overwhelmed by the riches of miniatures and wall-painting. But usually we are totally ignorant of the deeper sense of these productions. For us, *ars* means art, an expression of aesthetic feeling, of beauty. For medieval people *ars* meant craft, professional skill. It had two applications: it was as much the ordinary skill which the blacksmith or the weaver needed as the more refined skill mastered by the goldsmith or the *tapissier*.

In fact the meaning of the word 'art' has shifted. Originally it pointed to a relationship between producer and product, before coming to stress the relationship between consumer and product. What was once considered craft, the necessary ability involved in making something, eventually became the means of evaluating aesthetic transmission. Even art historians themselves have had difficulties in objectifying this shift. Since the beginning of art history as a discipline, their attention has mainly been focused on aesthetic issues. In doing so 'artistic' and 'aesthetic' became synonymous, erroneously. Nowadays most scholars share other opinions. This change might perhaps be best illustrated by looking at archaeology. The archaeologist no longer digs for sculpture that will enrich, for example, the collection of a museum, that will catch, so to speak, the eye of the visitor in search of beauty. Now the archaeologist digs in order to examine the stratigraphy of the soil and to deduce from it the social context in which the objects he or she encounters, were manufactured and used.

As a result of these divergent meanings of art, the question we are dealing with here, how to evaluate monastic art and its relevance to society, is open to ambiguity. In fact, what do we measure? Skill, or what today we call beauty? Moreover, are we interested in assessing its value for society in the past, or its importance as a legacy to posterity? The anonymity of nearly all the artistic productions which have come down

125

to us from the middle ages,[1] finds its explanation here: the artist is a craftsman, etymologically and mentally. He is convinced of his skill and if he is, for instance, a sculptor, he carves the stone with the same self-confidence shown later by his Renaissance colleagues. His attitude towards his sculpture, however, and its social meaning, is different. The idea of the complete anonymity of the medieval artist has become so much a cliché as to be nearly false. That a sense of collectivity caused the artists to lose their individuality is only partly true. Medieval society, or at least segments of it, distinguished good craftsmen from mediocre ones, to the same extent as happened in other societies. It appreciated individual achievement even though the name of the *artifex*, 'he who makes craft', was seldom transmitted in documents and even more rarely on the object itself. Just as with many literary works, no individual claim was laid on art production. Referring to an earlier chapter, texts once written and circulating could not only be copied, but also compiled, adapted, or plagiarized, without any compunction whatsoever. Thus one could say: the quality of the person mattered, not his name. Unfortunately this same attitude of anonymity obscures the study of the real role played by monks in architecture and the decorative arts.

SPACE AND IMAGE

For our purpose, namely the measuring of the impact of monasticism on society and, more specifically, on 'ordinary people', architecture seems more important than its decoration. In fact, building addresses one of the most fundamental needs of individuals when confronted with their environment. We need shelter against climatological extremes, just as we need safety *vis-à-vis* men and animals. Did monastic architecture merely fulfil this challenge of survival and nothing else? The answer is negative, and hence explains its fundamental difference from the building techniques used for other types of housing. In areas where natural stone was rare, or lacking, and expensive, ecclesiastical buildings were virtually the only buildings in durable materials, at least in the early medieval period. Even though it is not monastic, St Stephen's church in Paris comes to mind, the recently excavated Merovingian precursor to Notre-Dame, the remains of which can be visited beneath the Parvis Notre-Dame. One might reply by stressing the importance of the Carolingian palace at Aachen, also known to us through archaeology, as a witness of civic building activity. It was the most elaborate architectural complex north of the Alps for the period up to the eleventh century. It remains an

---

[1] Exceptions, at least outside twelfth- and thirteenth-century Italy, are rare. A sculptor of Autun, Gislebertus, is therefore in art history a famous name.

exception in the sense that it was the highest expression of the highest royal and imperial wish, and however long the list of such exceptions eventually might be, the architectural landscape was dominated by monastic, or at least ecclesiastical, achievements. Let us recall the Carolingian abbey of St Riquier in northern France. It did not survive later devastations and modifications, but an early modern engraving has been preserved. It displays an extensive monastic complex with three churches and many dwellings, intended to house over three hundred monks and youngsters.[2] An even more striking example of ideal monastic architecture is the ninth-century layout preserved at the abbey of St Gall in what is now Switzerland. The church and the conventual buildings were planned so as to be surrounded by a complete set of workshops, rendering the settlement a self-sufficient manor, one completely cut off from lay society outside. The buildings were to represent monasticism, 'an inner fortress, in which the monks could perform their spiritual offices without being exposed to contamination by the secular world'.[3] A last and, in part, still surviving example is the monastic complex of Reichenau, on Lake Constance: three churches of the tenth century, but no monastic dwellings from that time.[4] One could add to this list many more examples. But they would not significantly modify our statement that only the buildings of monastic origin are generally preserved, and that within this monastic context the survival chances of the churches largely surpassed those of the monks' domestic buildings. Pure chance? No. In fact, if the answer is easy, its explanation is not much more difficult. It seems likely that a combination of external and internal conditions similar to that applicable to written documents was responsible for the survival or destruction of buildings: calamities, continuity of the settlement and of the institution, the function, the material, and so on.

By far the greatest, in fact the only structural, reason for such rich building activity itself was the *Laus Dei*, the Praise of God. In other words, the search for Eternity created buildings for Eternity, just as it used writing to preserve words. Only His House was worthy of stability and solidity. It was as if the monks' observance of their vow of stability was made easier by the durability of the building. A novice could be persuaded when he entered (the insecurity of the time being what it was) that dying in his abbey in the peace of the Lord after a life dedicated to Him was the ideal way to live out one's life.

[2] C. Heitz, 'Saint-Riquier en 800', in: *Revue du Nord*, 69, 1986, pp. 335–44.
[3] W. Horn & E. Born, *The Plan of St. Gall. A study of the architecture & economy of, & life in a paradigmatic Carolingian monastery*. Berkeley, 1979, ii, p. 356.
[4] See A. Zettler, *Die frühen Klosterbauten der Reichenau. Ausgrabungen – Schriftquellen – St. Galler Klosterplan*. Sigmaringen, 1988.

Ordinary housing on the other hand was constructed in ephemeral materials, the more so in regions where stone was lacking or available only after costly transportation. For a long time and for large areas of the European continent the early medieval village itself (a gathering of a number of 'shelters', rather than houses) did not really have any fixed settlement, but followed, so to speak, the biochemical needs of agricultural exploitation.

Permanent building was an exceptional activity in the first centuries of the middle ages, one moreover foreign to the traditions of the Germanic and Slav peoples, and foreign even to much of Celtic civilization. What this implies is a loss of ancient architectural knowledge, due not so much to 'barbaric decadence' as to a shift in priorities. It was the acculturation process between Mediterranean and Continental cultures which made solid building superfluous, unusual and rare. Then practice and skill decreased, so that Carolingian and later building activity was often synonymous with plundering ancient sites in order to re-use the material remnants of an idealized past. Re-use was conspicuous in Italy as well as in southern France.

How then did majestic buildings in Romanesque style arise? Who were their builders? Our information is scanty and the opinion of art historians divided. Cluny is the most striking example which can be put forward. Within a two-hundred-year period, from the tenth to the early twelfth century, three monastic complexes succeeded each other, each larger, more impressive and self-confident than the last.[5] The opinion has been cultivated that a 'Cluniac style' existed, as if the autocratic ruling system of the Cluniac order imposed a unique building style as well. This idea is no longer followed, even if artistic areas with similar features can undoubtedly be delimited.[6] Nineteenth-century opinion, influenced as it was by a romantic exaggeration of medieval religious solidarity, maintained that monasteries had indeed been built by the monks themselves. Nobody actually believes this any longer, at least insofar as the Cluniacs and other black Benedictine monks are concerned. In fact, one does not really see how communities which were by any standards small (ordinarily one consisting of an abbot and twelve or some more monks) could fit ambitious building into the manual labour programme outlined in the Rule. How could the requisite professional skill and physical strength be found among so small a group of socially high-ranking, fasting monks, who were moreover diverse in age? In the case of St Gall, for instance, craftsmen sent by the king are explicitly

---

5 K. J. Conant, *Cluny; les églises et la maison du chef d'Ordre*. Mâcon, 1968.
6 J. Evans, *The Romanesque Architecture of the Order of Cluny*. Cambridge, 1938, pp. 3–15.

mentioned as being present at the building-site.[7] The evidence does not permit us to define more precisely their responsibility and their speciality, although it is highly unlikely that ordinary masons would have been attracted to the monastery from elsewhere. We would expect them to have been hired locally. In fact, knowing whether monks did the building themselves, or whether they had this work done by hired hands, yields only part of the picture. Building activity had one obvious repercussion: that work had to be done by others, completely or partly. Materials, for instance, had to be transported, and this for the entire period during which this construction was taking place. In this sense abbeys undoubtedly played a role as employers, though temporary, for the building campaigns themselves were dependent upon riches, ambition and the incidence of devastating calamities.

Another structural question one needs to address is that of whether the monastic world had a monopoly of architectural skills. This must be answered in the negative. There is no indication of such a monopoly and an attribution of architectural knowledge to lay people rather than to communities of monks practising stability seems much more likely. This is especially applicable to traditional Benedictinism. The attitude of the Cistercians has to be evaluated in another way.[8] There are a number of indications which show very clearly that members of the monastic community built with their own hands, at least in the twelfth century, whereas other evidence proves the presence of hired workers. Among the first, the lay brethren or *conversi* should be taken into account, that special group of semi-religious persons who worked in the shadow of the monks and secured the self-sufficiency of the abbey. Even if it is plausible that *conversi* moved from one abbey to another (there are protests within the order against this practice!), only specialized workers were mobile. In other words, the shift from a non-typical (Benedictine or Cluniac) to a typical architecture (Cistercian abbeys did have a common style), indicated a shift in the employment structure. Local workers were to a certain extent replaced by the abbey's own lay brethren. The assumption that their recruitment pool was mostly local too, except perhaps in the beginning, means that the impact of abbeys on a more general employment of workers (ordinary lay people with their families) was replaced by a more restricted one, limited to *conversi*. The needs of Cistercian communities and the way in which they functioned

---

7 Horn & Born, *op. cit.*, ii, p. 332.
8 P. Fergusson, *Architecture of Solitude. Cistercian Abbeys in Twelfth-Century England*. Princeton, 1984, pp. 165–72; C. Brooke, 'St Bernard, the Patrons and Monastic Planning', in: C. Norton & D. Park (ed.), *Cistercian Art and Architecture in the British Isles*, pp. 11–23.

were such as to bring about a lessening of the monastic impact on society outside its precincts.

Fundamental questions, such as the identity and social milieu of the designers, are unfortunately difficult to answer. There is no doubt that these were sometimes monks, or abbots, and there is even less doubt that the spiritual structure which had to be given to the buildings (more particularly to the churches), had to be dictated by a monk or (for the Cistercians) by the order. By spiritual structure we mean then the architecture and decoration as determined by the implementation of the monastic ideal through liturgy, conventual life, symbolism and the like.

What monastic building activity meant to society may now be addressed. To a certain extent it had obvious local repercussions upon the employment of lay people, but it apparently decreased when the Cistercians appeared, since they had their own lay brethren at hand. Monastic examples did not stimulate private building. The huts of the peasants did not refer in any way to the skill displayed for abbeys. And public building activity? There was no need whatsoever for comparably large edifices, concomitant with and illustrative of public authority, as central power was so weak. When churches, sometimes used for secular purposes, were already built in stone, castles and fortifications often continued to consist of wooden constructions and earthworks. Hence they were vulnerable, the more apparently as the function they fulfilled was to restrain violence. Eternal life meant so much more than earthly death, and that antagonism needed to be expressed in reality. In times of danger the gates of the abbeys certainly opened so that people could be rescued, referring to the virtue of 'loving thy neighbour'. The documents of Vézelay are very explicit in this regard.[9] Economic considerations, too, were undoubtedly part of this issue: the protection of useful human, as well as animal, life.

Sculpture, painting and goldsmiths' work constitute the decorative elements of the architectural setting; they are the products of the imagination. St Bernard, in his *Apologia*, criticised traditional monastic art which diverted the attention of the monks from the essential (the unifying prayer with God) to a world of hybrid monsters and animals.[10] He asked if one was not ashamed of this absurdity. Did the decoration, in other words, achieve its goal, enhance the meaning of the building, this being the glorification of the Lord? Both attitudes, that which stresses as well as that which refuses decoration are clear, though contradictory, expressions of that same medieval mentality of searching for God and

---

[9] Huygens, *Monumenta Vizeliacensia*, nr. 5, p. 264, anno 897 (and some later ones).

[10] C. Rudolph, 'Bernard of Clairvaux' Apologia as a Description of Cluny, and the Controversy over Monastic Art', in: *Gesta*, xxvii, 1–2, 1988, pp. 125–32.

the transcendental world. The denial of worldly matters which St Bernard wanted, pointed towards the restoration of an ideal, the unity between God and man, which in his view had been lost. The weird characters on the sculptured capitals testified in their turn to a primitive world, one which was not as yet able to distinguish reality from fiction; one for which scientific knowledge was not sufficiently developed so as to be able to separate the real and the really threatening world from another threatening, but (to us) imaginary, meta-world, both expected to intermingle. I, for one, believe that the menacing atmosphere of the Book of Revelation, seen as containing the divine truth, contributed in large measure, and for a long time, to the survival of a belief in a world where reality and fiction merged. People believed in the existence and the omnipresence of ugly devils and of eccentric monsters. This was a fundamentally different attitude from that of the Renaissance, where no one accepted the existence of the ancient gods whom the painters so realistically portrayed.

'ART FOR ART'S SAKE' OR FUNCTIONAL ART?

Medieval *ars* meant craft, skill. This linguistic statement implies that 'art for art's sake' cannot have been the creative force in medieval *ars*. Craft is more concerned with a final result, a product, which is intended to be used. Decorative art highlights the object on which it is to be seen: the capital and the keystone as structured elements of architecture, or the baptismal font and the chalice as necessary accompaniments to liturgical functions. Decoration stresses the essence, as for instance in the case of the superb bronze font cast by Reinier of Huy, now in the church of St Bartholomew in Liège. It represents the baptism of Jesus in the purifying waters of the Jordan.

Decoration can also be instructive. It helps the viewer to imagine words and to picture images. It showed how God, the Holy Trinity, the Virgin Mary and the saints were to be thought of, and also what Hell and its devils were expected to be like in their horrifying reality. When it comes to measuring to what extent the viewing of these works of art had a social impact (and here we mean by social impact a reiterative religious stimulus) one becomes rather sceptical.[11] To be sure, some decorative 'messages' were highly visible, such as the ones on fonts, but the majority of them could not really achieve a pedagogic aim. The capitals were too high and churches too badly lit. The liturgical office was

---

[11] A socio-economic dimension is obvious, to the same extent in fact, as it is with the specialized workers in building activity. I refer to the places where I have dealt with this aspect.

An example of a luxurious ninth-century Carolingian manuscript: the *Liber evangeliorum* of St Vaast, Arras (France, Pas-de-Calais)

(Arras, Bibliothèque municipale, ms. 233/1045)

performed in the concealing seclusion of the choir, far away from people's eyes, if they were allowed to be present at all. Moreover people did not wear glasses until the fifteenth century (and even then it was a luxury), and how many times in their lives did ordinary men and women have occasion to view the great monastic churches and their decorative treasures? And for those who were so fortunate, what did they feel? Fear above all, one would suppose, for this imaginary world of monsters, conceived as real, and this fear was expected to bring them nearer to God by the intercession of the saints. What did they understand? Not very much, one is willing to believe, for the symbolism used was too esoteric. What were they reminded of? The atmosphere of a single moment, even if intense and perhaps unforgettable, felt while walking around a saint's shrine, for instance, that of Ste. Foy of Conques in southern France, a golden manikin dotted with precious stones.

In his *Apologia* St Bernard deplored the cost of church decoration when he exclaimed: 'Why is one not at least troubled by the expense?'.[12] There, too, two opposing aspects of one and the same medieval religious feeling and thinking meet: for one, unlimited Praise had to be paralleled by unlimited allusive beauty (castles were not decorated, or only later and less sumptuously, when they became palaces); for the other, nothing should be allowed to distract one from the essential unification with God. Yet ordinary people knew only their own church: they were confined to the static illustrated message they saw there in sculpture or stained glass, and yet further restricted by other factors ranging from their eye-level or the simplicity of their minds to the direct and simplistic explanation given by the local priest (as a result of his deficient training). But where was monasticism in all this? Both thematic and stylistic influences were usually exerted regionally. The artistic language of far-away models had little or no diffusion.[13]

A DEEPER SENSE

In the preceding pages the impact of monasticism on society has implicitly been interpreted from the perspective of contemporaneous society and not from that of any posterior legacy whatsoever. This explains why nothing has been said, for instance, about book illustrations, as part of manuscripts, and also of their scarcity, their preciousness and hence of their inaccessibility in general. Rich books with miniatures belonged to the treasury or to the library, themselves shrines within the precincts of shrines for the abbeys were already shrines. Although we have no doubt at all as to their value as delightful witnesses to the fluctuating evolution of art, we do not believe in any impact, in the sense either of craft or of beauty, on contemporary 'ordinary people'. However sceptical one can be, buildings could at least be seen and walked through, sculptures and stained glass could be 'read' on occasion, but not miniatures. The exhausting, sometimes literally painstaking labour and care with which such art was executed, and undoubtedly mostly by monks as part of their manual labour programme, was proof of the very praise of God it gave. Miniatures underscored both the content and the writing activity in their reach for Eternity.

Moreover, another fundamental handicap impeded the social impact

---

12 Rudolph, *op. cit.*, p. 127.
13 Cf. J. Williams, 'Cluny and Spain', in: *Gesta*, xxvii, 1–2, 1988, pp. 93–101, who identifies with great precision some Spanish works of art as a result of Cluniac intervention, stressing at the same time the limitations of its influence.

of the decorative arts, and in part even of architecture: symbolism. Reading medieval treatises immediately indicates how much concern there was with a deeper meaning. By means of numerical conventions, colours, signs and configurations, not only building and decoration breathed symbolism, but even more generally speaking, so did a medieval mind-set. The conviction was alive that the fundamental structure of Creation could be understood and re-interpreted; that it could be 'captured' in a system of symbols. The verse 'Thou hast ordered all things in measure, number and weight' (Wisd. 11:21), quoted by St Augustine in his *De Civitate Dei*, constituted the biblical backing for this intellectual approach.[14] Popular among Benedictine monks, the seventh-century author Isidore of Seville as well as the ninth-century Benedictine Hrabanus Maurus had written treatises on this subject. The use of symbolic numbers as essential features in architectural design, for instance, can be proved very effectively by referring to the plan of St Gall, the layout of an ideal monastic complex.[15] A contemporaneous manual, written by an exceptional noblewoman, Dhuoda, is another example of the importance attributed to symbolic numbers. It addresses a lay milieu as well as serving an 'educational mirror' for her son, trained to be a knight.[16]

There is no doubt that most, if not all, decorative art was the expression of a 'symbolic language'. This means that scenes on capitals, for example, could (and can) be read at different levels of understanding. There were at least two: the obvious, external one, in which the scene is viewed in its own terms, and a deeper one, symbolic, which was understood only by those who had learned to understand. When tourists now walk around such sublime monastic churches as Vézelay and Moissac, or other marvels of Romanesque architecture and sculpture, they are indeed struck by what could be called the naïve and touching beauty of the sculptures, or they laugh at the childish horror of the threatening Afterlife. For the ordinary visitor of eight centuries or so ago terror was certainly real, but that visitor was, like ourselves, only able to understand the first level of meaning. Symbolism in itself was a difficult intellectual craft, even a science in the opinion of medieval men. It was much more so than what we would think now of symbolism, judged from the few symbolic remnants we still understand and perhaps believe in, such as lucky or unlucky numbers. We can summarize by affirming that while there is little certainty as to whether monks were the

---

[14] *Sancti Aurelii Augustini De Civitate Dei libri*, ed. B. Dombart – A. Kalb. Turnhout, 1955, p. 350 (Corpus Christianorum. Series Latina, xiv 2).
[15] Horn & Born, *op. cit.*, pp. 119–25.
[16] Dhuoda, *Manuel pour mon fils*, ed. P. Riché. Paris, 1975 (1990^2), iv, 4, pp. 290–96 and ix, pp. 326–36.

architects of the monastic churches or not, there is no doubt at all that the symbolism employed was decided upon by the monks. Thus the concept of the building was theirs, as well as that of the decoration. Nor is there doubt that the material layout was subordinate to the spiritual one: the more symbolism, the more monastic influence. The major problem now, even for art historians, is how to penetrate that system.

It is time now to conclude. Generally speaking, monasticism had no significant impact on the way in which contemporaneous ordinary people implemented architectural needs and its decorative accompaniment, either materially, spiritually, or functionally. Building techniques used by abbeys were poorly applied to civic purposes, unless perhaps for complex houses and palaces in the late middle ages; the esoterica of the decorative message was not understood by the public and, finally, building as well as decoration underscored monastic seclusion and its search for the Divine. This does not mean that examples of monastic art, unlocked to a broader public, which contradict this thesis, such as wall-paintings in priories open to the parochial community, cannot be found. In history antinomous white and black do not exist.

Monastic building activity had a social and economic impact on ordinary lay people when, and to the extent that, monks themselves were not engaged.

9

Monastic Life

Historians who are familiar with the chronicles and annals of medieval monasteries know how regularly violence occurred within the walls of the abbeys: monks injuring or even killing their abbots and confrères. Does that mean that the general vision of monasticism expressed in this book as the attempt to realize Heaven on Earth is naïve? That we over-stress the quality of its life-style, oriented towards God, even if its social impact is consequently reduced? That instead, monks were just ordinary men with all the usual hatred and envy, and sometimes perhaps a greater aggressiveness, since they were living in an abnormal social context? We should be aware of the discrepancy which exists between ideal structures and everyday individuals, and moreover of the metho-dological problem this involves. How should the historian, for example, evaluate some story or other of sexual aberration such as can really be found in the documents of any abbey: as an exception, implying that everything was fine for the rest of the community and for the rest of the time, or on the contrary as an indication of general moral decay? Or is it possible that the historian is not even aware of the existence of these two poles, and that he or she only states facts, merely 're-telling' what the documents themselves tell? I wish to point out here one of the most difficult aspects of medieval studies. Unable to work statistically, at least for the early middle ages, the medievalist seems condemned to the use of analytical description, and too often he takes into account only events, and not the intertwining of interacting and evolving social structures.

The 'bird's eye view' with which I try to consider the social relevance of monasticism, has the advantage that it does not permit particular, incidental, events to be stressed. From the sky the bird sees only colonies of busy ants, and the monastery is such a colony. It represents that type of structure, aiming specifically at the fulfilment of the link between Heaven and Earth. It is evidently a social structure as it organizes its members' behaviour.

The monastery where monks or nuns share a 'common life' is thus one of the possible solutions worked out to fulfil the goal of linking

Heaven to Earth. Life is considered and called 'common' when it is characterized by some shared activities, usually eating (in the refectory), sleeping (in the dormitory) and praying and celebrating the Divine Office (in the church). As these activities are in common, and as they are spread over all twenty-four hours of the day, organizational forms are needed, for the in-between periods as well. What time is left is devoted to manual labour, reading, and other forms of private devotion.

Eremitism constituted another solution with pre-Christian roots in the Near East. After Christianity was publicly tolerated in 313 and became the state religion of the Roman Empire late in the same century, the number of the new religion's adherents rapidly increased, and consequently the previous risk attached to involvement in it decreased. Zealots then left 'society' for the desert of Syria and Egypt, in order to live an individual saintly life. All through the centuries, from late antiquity to the early modern period, hermits existed (and continue to exist to this day), although more frequently in some centuries than in others. The late eleventh and early twelfth centuries were in that respect very important, as the revival of eremitism was a heavy blow to the long-standing monopoly of Benedictine monasticism. It constituted, at least to a certain extent, a reaction against classical Benedictinism, and it was one of the developments which made the rise of the new Cistercian movement possible. As we have already said, St Benedict's Rule had warned against the dangers of eremitism. The loneliness of 'the Desert' (even if in reality it was not a desert, but merely a remote site) was a frightening, yet attractive, prospect. It was frightening, as the ambushes of the 'Great Enemy' (as the Devil was often called) were numerous. One could imagine how dangerous these could be since Christ Himself had been tempted during the forty days He spent in the Desert.[1] There was the example of St John the Baptist and of the repentant St Mary Magdalene. Religious people also knew of the temptations of St Anthony the Abbot and of other hermits, according to the stories in the *Lives of the Fathers*, which were part of the compulsory reading in Benedictine monasteries (Ch. xlii; lxxiii). In painting, the 'Temptation of St Anthony' as well as 'St Jerome in the Desert' were popular themes throughout the late middle ages and the early modern period.

On the other hand the desert attracted the hermit, as he could practise there his challenging combative heroism in ideal circumstances. That

---

[1] A nice example of what the moral image of religious orders was can be deduced from Juan de Flandes' painting 'Christ and the tempting Devil', *c.* 1500. The latter is disguised as a Franciscan friar. He is meant to be at the same time 'trying to seduce' and 'bad', an image more often applied to these and other mendicants in the later middle ages. (Washington, National Art Gallery).

was precisely what frightened St Benedict. In his eyes the battle against Evil was so ferocious that the devil could only be overcome when all forces were joined. The 'knights of Christ', as monks were called, had to form one army.

Cenobitism, another word for common-life monasticism, had to ensure that the Heaven on Earth which the abbey was intended to be, did not deteriorate into a human hell as a result of the 'evil nature' of all men and thus, too, of monks. On three levels the position of the monk therefore had to be established: with respect to his equals, to his superiors, and to himself. Real equality, however, is non-existent as there is even among ordinary fellow-brethren a distinction based upon age. This does not mean biological age, but the time since entrance into monastic life. This fact shows that horizontal relations are not mentally conceived of, and hence not organized. All the relations are cast into vertical functional systems. So 'equality' in the sense of the right to obtain as much as one's colleagues, is absent from the rule of St Benedict,[2] and from any other religious normative text. The life of the monk is egocentric in the sense that he is not expected to care about the spiritual fulfilment of his 'neighbour' although no one should follow 'what he considers useful for himself, but rather what benefits another' (Ch. lxxii). He has only to care about his own salvation and perhaps about that of those for whom he is held responsible by a decision of his superior (implying then a vertical relationship). Monastic life is certainly common, but this word must not be misinterpreted. As far as possible the whole monastic system avoids horizontal intrusion. When they are said 'to obey one another' (Ch. lxxi), juniors are expected to obey seniors. The Rule makes use of heavy keys for vertical control. As one of the principles is not to disturb the 'peace of the other', silence was imposed as a major element of long-term workable social behaviour.[3] Silence moreover is a reminder of the desert, and as such it is the only survival of the 'horror of solitude' at which eremitical life was aimed. So monasticism created an artificial desert, a loneliness amid the crowd.

---

[2] Cf. the title of ch. xxxiiii 'Whether all should receive in *equal* measure what is necessary', implying a negative answer. But as a counterweight ch. ii, 22 says: 'Therefore let the abbot show *equal* love to all . . .'.

[3] C. L. Kruithof, 'De institutionalisering van de stilte: een aantekening over heremitisme en cenobitisme', in: *Tijdschrift voor sociale wetenschappen*, 28, 1983, pp. 214–18. P. Fuchs, 'Die Weltflucht der Mönche. Anmerkungen zur Funktion des monastisch-aszetischen Schweigens', in: *Zeitschrift für Soziologie*, 15, 1986, pp. 393–405.

A PYRAMID OF SELF-NEGATION: THE INDIVIDUAL
AND THE COMMUNITY

Silence was moreover a sign of obedience, and thus of humility. The virtue of obedience governed the behaviour of the monks, in the same way that in ordinary society it compelled the poor and the weak. Monastic life reflected astonishingly well the general ideal of a society organized according to static hierarchic levels. This is naturally not an accidental parallelism, but the obvious result of the purpose of monastic life itself, namely the creation on Earth of a heavenly society, whereby heavenly means (from a scientific viewpoint), conceived (or constructed) in accordance with human ideals. Paradise was thought to be organized as a hierarchic sequence of beings: the Trinity, the several groups of angels, the several groups of men.[4] It is in this way that Heaven is so very often represented in medieval painting.[5]

Obedience asks for consolation. We have already stressed in another chapter how Christ's message itself provided this feeling. Self-negation was the ideal which made obedience practicable, and as a social ideal it was nearer to realization in the transcendent atmosphere of monastic life than in society itself. When he entered the abbey the new monk had to take off his secular clothes as a symbol of renunciation of his former personality (Ch. lviii), an act which referred to St Paul's metaphorical language 'that you have put off the old nature with its practices and have put on the new nature' (Col. 3:9–10; Ephes. 4:22–24). Henceforward the hierarchic structure of the monastery would take care of his whole being. He becomes the child whose problems are solved and whose needs are fulfilled by his 'father', the abbot. Obedience is what the monk gives in return. Mechanisms control his behaviour, and when he transgresses the command, a series of corrections and punishments will constrain him to a stricter observance.

From the abbot one expects justice, the correlative of obedience. To

---

4   Cf. Hildegardis (of Bingen), *Scivias*, ed. A. Führkötter – A. Carlevaris. Turnhout, 1978 (Corpus Christianorum. Continuatio mediaeualis, xliii A), pp. 604–13 (with miniatures of the Day of Judgement and of Heaven). Joachim of Fiore, a former Cistercian abbot and known for his apocalyptic spirituality, made a concept of an ideal abbey, called 'the New People of God pertaining to the third State after the Model of the Heavenly Jerusalem' (see H. Grundmann, *Neue Forschungen über Joachim von Fiore"*. Marburg, 1950, pp. 116–21 (Latin text); pp. 85–115 (comments), and *Apocalyptic Spirituality*, transl. B. McGinn. New York, Ramsey, Toronto, 1979, pp. 142–48).
5   The most remarkable among these paintings is undoubtedly the Ghent Altarpiece of Hubert and Jan van Eyck in the St Bavo's Cathedral in Ghent, painted in the 1420s.

A father offering his son as an oblate
(Brussels, Royal Libr., ms. 5668–5669)

provide every monk with an equal quality or quantity of goods is not part of his policy. Monasticism is, as we already know, in no way the expression of an egalitarian ideology. St Benedict says that the needs of the monks differ individually, and the abbot has to take that into account (Ch. xxxiiii).

To 'put on the new nature' also implies abandoning the past: private property should be given to the poor or become part of the common property of the monastery. The monk belongs to a new family, his community, which will determine his whole life, until death. Even that death will be celebrated in common. The dying monk will be surrounded by his brethren, and their prayer and songs will conduct him from Heavenly Earth to Heaven. He will live in their memory for ever, as his name and that of the benefactors of the abbey are registered in 'necrologies' and 'obituaries'. Every year on the anniversary of his death he will be commemorated, and if he was important enough in the eyes of the community, a special pittance will be added to the monks' food ration for that day.

How can the contradiction be explained between self-negation and the loss of the biological family-link on the one hand and our earlier indication of a pronounced functional reciprocity between clan and monastery on the other hand? In fact, it is a contradiction in appearance only. The first point (self-negation) refers to the ideology of monastic life, monasticism, whereas the second refers to the everyday reality and to the use or abuse mighty men made of it.

The power of the abbot was not just vertical. It is partly pyramidal, which means that even though he was the only one responsible before God, some activities of control and organization were entrusted to officials. The most important among them was the prior. In periods when abbots combined several dignities and were not able to reside in the monastery (a situation which is usually interpreted as proof of decay), the prior functioned as the acting head of the community. Other officials were (or might be) the sub-prior, the chanter, the provost, and so on. They were normally appointed by the abbot, who was also able to withdraw the mandate. This system shows considerable parallels with what medieval secular government was intended to be, and with what every government all over the world presumably hopes for: good 'officers'. Feudalism, however, with its inborn weakness with respect to hereditary succession and infidelity, one reason for which was the limited amounts of money in circulation, had prevented the development of such an administrative staff. The monastic organization could then have functioned as an example for the remedy of this problem, but there are no indications at all that it actually did so.

The abbot's power was also bound by a double control, in order to avoid its turning the virtue of justice into the vice of pride. For some decisions the abbot had to consult the elders, the *seniores*, at the same time those with the greatest wisdom, the *saniores*. Other decisions had to be submitted to the complete convent in its daily gathering in the chapter-house. Although forms of 'democratic consultation' with respect to the administration and the decision-making of the abbot existed, they were not meant to be expressions of democracy, majority, or participation in the exercise of power as such. Rather they corresponded to St Benedict's saying that God could often reveal to the younger ones what is best (Ch. iii). It was a system designed to make an autocratic government function righteously, from God to abbot and from abbot to monk.

Once again one might argue that what is said here depends much more upon the ideal than upon reality. It certainly does, but a study of the meaning of monasticism has to be based upon its spiritual model and not upon the institutions which the abbeys constituted in everyday life (always imperfect emanations and thus to a certain extent betrayals of the ideals). How monks evaluated monastic life can best be studied by looking at the image left by their leaders. What is the 'good abbot' in the monastic historiography of the time?[6] The adjective is often reserved for those abbots who gather possessions, or build. It would be wrong, however, to reduce the interest of a monastic community (insofar as it is reflected in the historiography) as being oriented only towards these material aspects. Certainly, religious people were very much aware of the wealth they thought necessary to increase and preserve. As their institution was meant to be perennial, its survival had to be secured. So the thirteenth-century author Thomas of Cantimpré could (positively) compare the Church with organized and prudent bees,[7] just as some centuries later his Low Countries' fellow-countryman, the protestant Philip of St Aldegonde (negatively) referred to the Roman Catholic Church as an intolerably rich beehive.[8] Both focused in a different way on the 'savings' of the Church, one of its major weaknesses *vis-à-vis* Jesus Christ's authentic message. On closer investigation, however, the link between a good abbot and a good administrator very often turns out to be a later interpretation. Contemporaneous or nearly contemporaneous chronicles and annals, indeed, more frequently stress spiritual qualities, such as 'the good example' or piety. In the evaluation of monastic

---

6 P. Van Daele, *De goede en de slechte kwaliteiten van de middeleeuwse abt, bezien door de ogen van zijn monniken.* Ghent, 1984 (Unpublished thesis State University Ghent).

7 *Bonum universale de apibus.* Cologne, (1480); Den Haag, 1902; C. M. Stutvoet – Joanknecht, *Der Byen Boeck. De Middelnederlandse vertalingen van Bonum universale de apibus van Thomas van Cantimpré en hun achtergrond.* Amsterdam, 1990.

8 *Den Biënkorf der H. Roomsche Kercke.* S.l., (1569).

behaviour one has once again to take into account the specific features of the historical documents themselves. As the span between the abbot's lifetime and the moment of writing increased, oral information had less chance of surviving. At that time, only materially verifiable acts (such as buildings or the content of charters) could bear witness to any activity. The memory of such characteristics as piety had (and have) only in very exceptional circumstances, or for very extraordinary persons, a chance of surviving much beyond their lifetime. It implies a context of saint-hood. In the same way as later generations of monks, the outside world considered an abbot to be important when he was able to display riches and splendour. For monasticism itself, however, the 'good abbot' was the one who succeeded optimally in his task of being a just and caring father, stimulating them in the only goal, spiritual self- fulfilment.

SPIRIT AND FLESH: THE BATTLE OF THE INDIVIDUAL

People entering monastic life were said to undergo a *conversio*, which literally means that they were turned upside down. We have stressed how the changing of clothes on the occasion of the entrance symbolized the birth of a 'new man'. According to the spiritual goal of monasticism the monk should transcend the Earth. In proper terms he had to leave his own flesh which was, like all matter, a reminder of the Fall and a source of sin. The sense of cenobitical life was that evil should be over-come by the stimulus and the support of the whole community. Besides the already stressed interaction of the values of justice and obedience, another element of psychological control played a major role in common life: the *scandalum*. Monks should not be scandalized by any conduct of their fellow-brethren. This feeling extended even beyond the precincts of the monastery and was an important regulator of Christian behaviour in general. In the first stages of conversion from paganism (namely the adaptation of the external collective, and afterwards of the external individual behaviour) scandal was an element of social control. Later on, when the conversion reached the inner individual behaviour, and even tried to insinuate itself further into the subconscious, being scan-dalized by one's own thoughts, feelings and dreams became an element of self-control, in conjunction with the general system of contrition, penance and shame.

To avoid this omnipresent risk of causing scandal, the religious prac-tices were levelled from two sides. Thas is, the brethren should not be shocked either by the carelessness of the light-hearted monk, or by the exaggeration of the scrupulous and zealous one. Rules and explanatory customaries were automatically aware of this risk, and imposed optimal (which means levelling) ascetic practices. Within the abbey there was indeed no place for the 'heroic' type of asceticism, characteristic of the hermits. Fasting to the point of starvation, or rolling in nettles when sexual desire awoke, could not be tolerated in a community where a regular scheme outlined daily life. Such ferocious battles should only be fought by experienced monks, those whom St Benedict allowed to go 'into the desert'.

The entrance of a new recruit into the monastery was poised between two extreme systems, both of which had been in existence during the medieval period. As they were opposite, their acceptance or rejection reflect different stages of varying underlying opinions. The first system was the *oblatio*, the entrance of children, offered by their parents normally at the age of five to seven. The second was when adults entered.

For us the *oblatio* is certainly a shocking phenomenon, as it does not take into account the person's free will, an emanation of the individual rights we take for granted.[9] Moreover, free will had always been an important issue in Christian theology, even if it implied the possibility of a certain opposition to God, and hence of a limitation to His omnipotence. The medieval social structure, as we have already pointed out, was heavily dominated by the family structure. The right of the individual was subject to that of his clan. The emancipation of the individual (the low-ranking man as well as the woman) only began in the second half of the middle ages, in correlation with the disruption of the clan-system, and its steady substitution by the (as yet partially ineffective) nuclear family. In the eyes of those who offered their children, their act had nothing offensive about it. In socio-religious terms it was an element of what I have called 'functional reciprocity'. Even from the purely religious point of view there was no impediment. Had not Abraham been willing to offer his only son Isaac to the Lord (Gen. 22)? Moreover, from the viewpoint of monastic ideology aiming at sinless perfection, what could have been better for the service of God than to receive innocent children who had not yet been spoiled by contact with the evil world? They could be perfectly cast into the ideal matrix of virtues, so as to constitute a militia of angelic monks. Moreover children were considered to possess a potential for closeness to God and the transcendental world.[10] The belief in the power of children's purity was widespread.

---

[9] Cf. G. Constable, 'Liberty and Free Choice in Monastic Thought and Life, especially in the Eleventh and Twelfth Centuries', in: *La notion de liberté au Moyen Age*, ed. G. Makdisi, D. Sourdel & J. Sourdel – Toumine. Paris, 1985, pp. 99–118 (reprinted in: G. Constable, *Monks, Hermits and Crusaders in Medieval Europe*. London, 1988).

[10] J. Kroll, 'The Concept of Childhood in the Middle Ages', in: *Journal of the History of the Behavioral Sciences*, 13, 1977, pp. 384–93.

It was, for instance, very much alive in the thirteenth century when contrary to all common sense a Children's Crusade was organized against Islam, spiritually pure but in military terms condemned to fail, as indeed it did. As the Carolingians above all had emphasized the 'Two Cities' ideology, and as they had generalized the Rule of St Benedict for whom the *oblatio* was obvious (Ch. xxx; xxxvii), the entrance of young children represented the current system in the ninth century.[11] The custom of accepting oblates was subject to changes and to criticism. The advantage of the 'angelic' character of the children was challenged by the problem of free will. What was a religious life worth when it was not the result of a self-chosen option?

Monastic life could also start in adulthood. The candidates of this type 'knew the world' and had already experienced its badness. So their *conversio* represented an individual and free choice, and a way of repenting for the sins they had committed. This explains the cases where former knights, for example, entered monastic life.[12] Generally speaking, the oblate system met with opposition during periods of religious fervour. In the eyes of the late eleventh- and early twelfth-century reform movement the entrance of adults meant much more than the entrance of young children. The religious sense of the adults was expected to be more genuine and strong, even if the expectation of moulding the character and life-style of adults is likely to be a contradiction in terms. In customaries a minimum entrance age would henceforward be required, usually eighteen or even older. Nevertheless the *oblatio*-system did not disappear until the thirteenth century. The new religious movements of that time did not practise it any longer, and also within the Benedictine monasteries it seems to have died out by that time. This disappearance meant that voluntary seclusion and the personal fight against Evil were considered by the Church to be, with respect to spirituality, more fruitful than angelic innocence, won and preserved by imposed isolation. Some doubts remain, however, as to the effectiveness of this free choice. In the religious reform movement some documents report cases of whole families entering newly founded abbeys. It is hard to believe that every individual could really have expressed his will freely under those

---

[11] M. de Jong, *Kind en klooster in de vroege middeleeuwen. Aspecten van de schenking van kinderen aan kloosters in het Frankische Rijk (500–900)*. Amsterdam, 1986 (Amsterdamse historische reeks, 8); J. Boswell, *The Kindness of Strangers*, pp. 298–321.

[12] A well documented example is the foundation of the Benedictine abbey of Affligem in Flanders. Cf. A. Despy – Meyer & C. Gérard, 'Abbaye d'Affligem à Hekelgem', in: *Monasticon belge. Tome IV. Province de Brabant. Premier volume*. Liège, 1964, pp. 21–24. Moreover the 'repenting knights' are a well known topic.

circumstances.[13] The speed of the religious and institutional evolution within those new houses, and the number of failures, probably imply some prompt abandonment, as a price to be paid for the apparent improvement of the religious feeling.

It is striking that two renaissances, those of the ninth and of the twelfth centuries, responded in distinct ways to the quest for heavenly life. The explanation may be found in their contrasting characters. The first was marked by élitism, the second by a greater mass appeal. The Carolingian renaissance was the result of a planned and outlined policy, imposed from the peak of the social pyramid downwards. It was too weak to spread and unable to be effective over the whole of society. The twelfth-century renaissance started from a much broader general base of demographic and economical changes, and hence displayed an ample range of social challenges and possibilities.

Non docere, sed lugere, 'not teaching, but lamenting', was the programme of the black Benedictine monks, influenced by St Jerome[14] and St Gregory the Great, and it was insistently reiterated by the Cistercian St Bernard of Clairvaux. Life on earth had to prefigure life in heaven. That could be simulated by the quality of the Divine Office. Life also had to win Heaven, and that could only be attained by the restraint of the flesh and by pious works. A regime of fasting, of interrupted sleep and of a total denial of sexuality knitted together the days and the years in the abbey. The daily reunions of the community in the chapter-house regulated and controlled this behaviour as far as trespasses against the prescriptions of the Rule were concerned. Other transgressions belonged to the domain of private confession.

Quite a number of the monastic implementations in this field (for instance the fasting and sexual denial) were more generally imposed by the Church as norms upon the other segments of the population, secular clergy as well as on the whole of lay society. Is not this a clear proof of the role monasticism exercised? Certainly, monastic values were presented as the solution for an ideal behaviour 'in the world', and as time went on, they were formulated with more and more insistence. Yet the monks themselves did not play a role of any importance in the

[13] Very explicit examples can be found in L. Milis, 'Ermites et chanoines réguliers au douzième siècle', in: *Cahiers de Civilisation médiévale*, xxii, 1979, pp. 39–80 (although it refers to canons regular and not to monks). Specifically on monastic eremitism, see G. Constable, 'Eremitical forms of monastic life', in: *Istituzioni monastiche e istituzioni canonicali in Occidente, 1123–1215.* Milano, 1980, pp. 239–64 (reprinted in: *Monks, Hermits and Crusaders in Medieval Europe.* London, 1988). See also H. Grundmann, 'Adelsbekehrungen im Hochmittelalter', in: *Adel und Kirche,* ed. J. Fleckenstein & K. Schmid. Freiburg, 1968, pp. 325–45.

[14] *Liber contra Vigilantium* (*Patrologia Latina*, xxiii, c. 351).

attempt to have these values realized. The increased quality of religious life among lay people, that is a more profound and internalized religious life, was an achievement of the late middle ages, when success in the field of the 'inner conversion' must be attributed to the secular Church or to the mendicant friars, and not to the monks.

THE EASY WAY OR THE DIFFICULT WAY? COMPARISON WITH THE WORLD OUTSIDE

When dealing with monasticism and society, one cannot avoid the question of how monks perceived their life and how this should be evaluated. It is scarcely of any help to quote from highly spiritual texts evoking monastic life as the ideal way to join God. In fact, a series of texts, opposite in scope and origin, could at once be proposed, which would stress real anger, escape, and violence, or other forms of opposition to monastic life. Individual monks undoubtedly lived their life of seclusion in such disparate ways that the whole range of possibilities between extreme happiness and extreme unhappiness was to be found in any place and at any time.

Let us once more examine the *oblatio*-system. From a modern point of view, we would believe that a career imposed by the clan or the family, and thus considered as contrary to the individual will, automatically created unhappiness, and was felt as a restriction to personal fulfilment. This way of thinking is not appropriate for the middle ages, and in fact for none of the cultures where the whole social system was or is based on family decision-making. As A. Molho has so suggestively said: 'free choice and coercion were part of the same framework'.[15] So the imposed reclusion fitted into a general pattern. The notion 'vocation', as we understand it now, as God's call to religious life, rarely entered medieval monastic documents. The word itself was hardly known whereas the generally used expression *conversio* did not have the same meaning. It indicated in fact the actual step of entering religious life. Books for the medieval and modern periods (even at a time when a person's own will was supposed to determine more largely his own acts) clearly show that vocations occurred much more often in 'predisposed families' than elsewhere. Predisposed families were those which already had contacts with the order or the monastery which their youngsters entered. In other words, vocation can be interpreted very generally as a socially based phenomenon.

To the young children who entered the medieval abbey, the world

---

[15] 'Tamquam vere mortua', in: *Società e storia*, 43, 1989, p. 71: 'libera scelta e coercizione erano parte di uno stesso quadro'.

outside soon became a strange world, and even when they came into contact with it, it was no longer the normal social environment in which they felt at ease.[16] The abbey was their home; the search for Heaven was their profession. For those who entered as adults, the situation was quite different. The commitment of both groups, however, expressed as it was in the vows of obedience, chastity, poverty and stability, was generally irreversible. Nevertheless later customaries started to foresee procedures allowing for a possible return to the secular world. The original system of unique solemn vows, made once and for all, was replaced in the modern period by successive stages from temporary to eternal vows.

The way back to the world, as well as the way down to an easier formula of monastic life, was difficult. According to canon law (and more specifically papal legislation) religious persons were only allowed to switch from one order to another when the new one was known to be stricter and more austere than the one they left. The texts call it the passage to an *arctior vita*. Thus regular canons could become Benedictines, and black Benedictines could pass to the Cistercian order, but to take these steps in the opposite direction was not permitted.

Was material life in a monastery easier than it was outside? Let us try to answer this question by visualizing the medieval human landscape with the help of archaeological, monumental and documentary evidence. We then see before our eyes, or in our minds, the huge abbeys with their thick walls and their high towers, and we can imagine the (relative) luxury of the large housing facilities, even of their sanitary equipment. We then see, too, the small houses of the farmers, in wattle and daub, timber, or rubble. Yet it would be unfair and incorrect to compare the good housing of the monks with such 'shelters' and the difficult life outside. Servile, or even lower-class people who lived in this type of house, did not have a chance to enter monastic life. It was a life-style reserved for the nobility or, at the most and in the periods of easier access, for wealthy people. When the Cistercians recruited their *conversi* among the lower classes, and made of 'lay brotherhood' a common feature of their organization, it certainly implied for the people involved easier material circumstances than they were used to outside. That lay brethren frequently rose against monks in the late twelfth and thirteenth centuries, is more likely to be the result of protest against the discriminatory behaviour of the monks than of a revolt against any objectively measured low standard of living.

---

[16] A nice example of such an oblate is the author Orderic Vitalis, born in 'the remote parts of the region of the Mercians' in 1075 as the son of an English mother and a French father. He was received in the Norman abbey of Saint-Evroult at the age of ten (M. Chibnall, *The World of Orderic Vitalis*. Oxford, 1984, pp. 3–41).

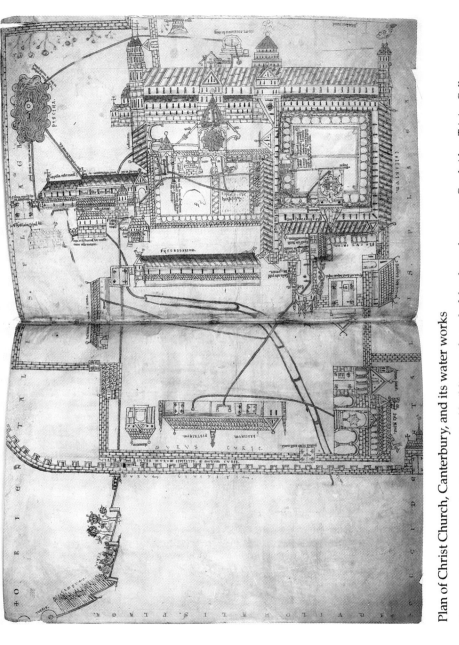

Plan of Christ Church, Canterbury, and its water works

(Drawn c.1165 and showing the conventual buildings at the end of the eleventh century. Cambridge, Trinity College ms. R.17.1., ff. 284v/285. Courtesy of the Master and Fellows of Trinity College Cambridge)

The landscape as we have just sketched it has to be completed with the presence of castles. Within their protecting walls, they sometimes included an abbey, a priory or a chapter, and there is no doubt that the material life-style of either population reached about the same level. According to the standards of the time, the abbey offered good protection against the hostility of man and climate, and it guaranteed the food supply of its inhabitants. Fasting was part of the obligations of monastic life, but in reality it did not imply hunger. When monastic annals describe famines (they paid a lot of attention to them as indications of God's wrath), they never lamented the hunger of monks.[17] Hunger rarely struck monastic houses and precisely in such moments of distress their stocks sometimes helped the Works of Mercy, normally ritualized and marginal, to respond to a genuine concern. Fasting did not imply bad food either. Even if it was voluntarily limited and the consumption of meat mostly avoided, the variety of fishes, for instance, which the Cluniacs could refer to in their special sign language (to cope with the imposed silence), was astonishingly rich.[18] This example has the advantage of not being related to decay, but being part of an imposed normative pattern. Proof of decadence of the authentic monastic life can easily be found, at any place or time,[19] but I said from the outset that I would not mix general with anecdotal evidence, nor consider the oscillations between vigour and decay.

When in the future archaeologists apply more precise scientific methods than they presently can, they will be able to resolve remaining problems of direct interest to social history, such as relative longevity and health. The study of skeletons permits historical pathology to establish the sex, the age, the medical and sanitary past of individuals, and hence of groups. Data of any importance, however, which would allow a comparison between monastic and secular populations, their differences in life-style and possible differences in life-expectancy and comfort, are

---

[17] According to Raoul Glaber hunger is so terrible in 1033 that even nobles die, but he does not mention monks (Raoul Glaber, *Historiarum libri quinque. The five books of the Histories*, (ed.) J. France & N. Bulst. Oxford, 1989, pp. 184–87 (Oxford Medieval Texts)). P. Spitz, 'Silent Violence: Famine and Inequality', in: *International Social Science Journal*, 30, 1978, pp. 867–92 stresses that food producers themselves are the people who are most directly struck by famines, whereas people in armies, businesses, or monasteries seldom are.

[18] See W. Jarnecki, *Signa loquendi. Die cluniacensischen Signa-Listen*. Baden-Baden, 1981 (Saecula spiritalia, 4); J. Sebeok, *Monastic Sign Language*. Berlin, 1987 (Approaches to Semiotics, 76).

[19] G. Jaritz, 'The Standard of Living in German and Austrian Cistercian Monasteries in the Late Middle Ages', in: E. R. Elder (ed.), *Goad and Nail*. Kalamazoo, MI, 1985, pp. 56–70 (Cistercian Studies Series 84) (with many references to earlier publications).

seldom available as yet, but when available at all they are very convincing indeed.[20] Some historians take it for granted that in fourteenth-century England monasteries, though severely affected by the 'Black Death' which ravaged Europe, were less hard hit than the ordinary population. If this opinion were to receive more general approval,[21] it would emphasize biologically what we have advanced historically throughout the book, namely that isolation and a reluctance to participate in society, rather than social involvement, were the most characteristic, and in fact essential, features of medieval monasticism.

[20] Cf. S. Bonde & C. Maines, 'The Archaeology of Monasticism: a Survey of recent Work in France, 1970–1987', in: *Speculum*, 63, 1988, pp. 794–825 (esp. pp. 807–08); G. Billy, 'Les restes humains de l'abbaye de Saint-Martial de Limoges (Fouilles de 1966–1967)', in: *Bulletin de la société archéologique et historique du Limousin*, ciii, 1976, pp. 63–74, calls the longevity of the medieval and late medieval persons buried there 'abnormal' and explains it by 'its character as [the burial place of] a religious community, and the sedentary life-style of its members in undoubtedly privileged conditions when compared with [those of] the populations living in the same period' (p. 69).

[21] J. Hatcher, *Plague, Population and the English Economy. 1348 –1530*. London, 1977, pp. 21–26 (Studies in Economic and Social History) suggests a mortality rate of about 45% in monasteries and over 50% among the peasant population. Ph. Ziegler, *The Black Death*. London, 1969, pp. 224–31 advances a rate ranging between 23% and 45%, while that of monks would have been about 44%. Hatcher makes us believe that noble persons moved in order to escape from the epidemic. As monks were bound by stability, common life enhanced the risk. So, a lower mortality rate of monks allows proof of their isolation, whereas a higher figure does not prove the opposite.

Epilogue

From its very beginnings in the late Roman epoch and throughout the ages, the primary goal of monasticism has been to offer monks on Earth the image of Heaven. Those who proposed this ideal life-style praised the virtues of transcendental life and condemned the vices of sinful matter. Arduous denial of the body and will was the fragile weapon with which victory was won. It was reserved for an élite, a spiritual élite which largely corresponded with the social élite.

What I have tried to gauge in this book is to what extent monasticism influenced the conditions of life and behaviour of the vast mass, the silent body of the medieval population. In several areas of life monks came into contact with 'ordinary people', when for instance the monks were landlords or wealthy consumers and the 'ordinary people' were peasants or craftsmen. In such a relationship, however, the monks were not acting specifically as monks, and that is precisely what I have been trying to appraise. In other areas, such as literacy, they looked up to God, or they looked back to antiquity, but in both cases they looked away from the pre-occupations of simple people. According to biblical precept Christians were expected to care about the poor and the weak and, as the most perfect among Christians, monks followed this precept that way. Generally speaking, however, their aid was limited even if their means were great. The praise of God and its price far exceeded philanthropic concern.

Monasticism certainly exercised an influence on how the moral value system was formulated; this was normally through the bias of the secular Church. But monasticism proved too transcendental to rule Christian society. Society never became that 'generalized abbey' foreseen by some theoreticians in their blueprint of a *civitas terrena* resembling Heaven on Earth. The aim of monasticism was perfection, because Heaven was perfect, but perfection is unreachable *per se*, as its limits are automatically moved a step further away once it seems to come nearer to realization. Monasticism, and especially Benedictine monasticism, offered an adequate answer to personal sanctification by self-denial, probably the best and the most balanced solution ever worked out within the borders of our cultural area. It was an adequate escape from Earth and from the evil of mankind. But could mankind as a whole be expected to escape from itself?

List of Works Cited

Sources

Ambrosius Autpertus, *De conflictu vitiorum et virtutum*, ed. J. P. Migne, *Patrologia Latina*, 40, Paris, 1845, cc. 1091–106.

Annales abbatum monasterii Eenamensis, ed. U. Berlière, in: *Documents inédits pour servir à l'histoire ecclésiastique de la Belgique*. Maredsous, 1894, i, p. 120–29.

Apologia de barbis, ed. R. B. C. Huygens, introd. G. Constable, *Apologiae duae*. Turnhout, 1985 (Corpus Christianorum. Continuatio mediaeualis, lxii).

Apophtegmata Patrum, ed. J. P. Migne, *Patrologia Graeca*, 65, Paris, 1864, col. 71–440.

Augustine of Hippo, *De Civitate Dei libri*, ed. B. Dombart & A. Kalb. Turnhout, 1955 (Corpus Christianorum. Series Latina, xiv, 2).

Becker G., *Catalogi bibliothecarum antiqui*. Bonn, 1885.

Benedict of Nursia, *La Règle de saint Benoît*, ed. A. de Vogüé. Paris, 1971, 6 vols (Sources chrétiennes, 181–86).

Benedict of Nursia, transl. Doyle, L. J., *St. Benedict's Rule for Monasteries*, Collegeville, MN, 1948.

Bernard of Clairvaux, *Five Books on Consideration. Advice to a Pope*. Kalamazoo, MI, 1976 (Cistercian Father Series).

Bernard of Clairvaux, *Opera*, ed. J. Leclercq & H. Rochais, vii. Rome, 1974.

Bernard of Clairvaux, *The Letters of St. Bernard of Clairvaux*, transl. B. Scott James. London, 1953.

Book of William Morton, almoner of Peterborough Monastery. 1448–67 (The), ed. W. T. Mellows, P. I. Kings & C. N. L. Brooke. Oxford, 1954 (Northamptonshire Record Society 16).

Boretius A., *Capitularia Regum Francorum*, i. Hannover, 1883 (Monumenta Germaniae Historica. Leges in-4°).

Bouton J. de la Croix & Van Damme J. B., *Les plus anciens textes de Cîteaux*. Achel, 1974 (Cîteaux. Commentarii Cistercienses. Studia et Documenta ii).

Breviarium Caeremoniarum monasterii Mellicensis, ed. J. F. Angerer. Siegburg, 1987 (Corpus Consuetudinum Monasticarum xi 2).

Cesarius of Arles, *Sermones*, ed. G. Morin, Turnhout, 1953, 2 vol. (Corpus Christianorum. Series Latina, ciii, civ).

Charvin G., *Statuts, chapitres généraux et visites de l'Ordre de Cluny*, i. Paris, 1965.

Choisselet B. & Vernet P., *Les 'Ecclesiastica Officia' du XIIème siècle*. Reiningue, 1989 (La documentation cistercienne, 22).

Conciliorum Oecumenicorum Decreta. Bologna, 1973.

Corpus Iuris Canonici, ed. A. Friedberg. Leipzig, 1879 (Graz, 1959), 2 vols.

Cronica et cartularium monasterii de Dunis. Bruges, 1864.

Customary of the Benedictine Abbey of Eynsham in Oxfordshire (The), ed. A. Gransden. Siegburg, 1963 (Corpus Consuetudinum Monasticarum ii).

Dhuoda, *Manuel pour mon fils*, ed. P. Riché. Paris, 1975 (1990[2]) (Sources chrétiennes, 225).

Disticha Catonis, ed. M. Boas & H. J. Botschuyver. Amsterdam, 1952.

Francis of Assisi, *Écrits*, ed. Th. Desbonnets *et al.* Paris, 1981 (Sources chrétiennes 285).

Gregory the Great, *Dialogues*, ed. A. de Vogüé. Paris, 1978–1979 (Sources chrétiennes, 251, 260).

Gregory the Great, *Moralia in Iob. Libri XXIII–XXXV*, ed. M. Adriaen. Turnhout, 1985 (Corpus Christianorum. Series Latina, cxliii B).

Hildegard of Bingen, *Scivias*, ed. A. Führkötter & A. Carlevaris. Turnhout, 1978, 2 vols (Corpus Christianorum. Continuatio mediaeualis, xliii, xliii A).

Historia miraculorum in circumlatione per Flandriam, ed. J. Ghesquierus & I. Thysius, *Acta Sanctorum Belgii*. Tongerlo, 1794, vi, pp. 295–309.

Hockey S. F. (ed.), *The Cartulary of Carisbrooke Priory*. S.l., 1981.

Isidore of Sevilla, *Etimologías*, ed. J. Oroz Reta & M. A. Marcos Casquero. Madrid, 1982–1983, 2 vols.

Jerome, *Liber contra Vigilantium*, ed. J. F. Migne, *Patrologia Latina*, xxiii, cc. 353–68

Jocqué L. & Milis L., *Liber Ordinis Sancti Victoris Parisiensis*. Turnhout, 1984 (Corpus Christianorum. Continuatio mediaeualis, lxi).

John Cassian, *Conférences*, ed. E. Pichery. Paris, 1955–1959, 2 vols (Sources chrétiennes, 42–62).

John Cassian, *Institutions cénobitiques*, ed. J.-C. Guy. Paris, 1965 (Sources chrétiennes, 109).

John of Salisbury, *Metalogicon*, ed. J. B. Hall – K. S. B. Keats-Rohan. Turnhout, 1991, p. 116 (Corpus Christianorum. Continuatio mediaeualis, xcviii).

Lucretius, *De rerum natura libri sex*, ed. C. Bailey. Oxford, 1922[2].

Magnum Bullarium Romanum, ii. Rome, 1740 (Graz, 1964).

Margery Kempe, *Memoirs of a Medieval Woman. The Life and Times of Margery Kempe*, ed. L. Collins. New York, 1983[2].

Master, *La Règle du Maître*, ed. A. de Vogüé. Paris, 1964–1965, 3 vols (Sources chrétiennes, 105–07).

Monumenta Vizeliacensia, ed. R. B. C. Huygens. Turnhout, 1976, 2 vols (Corpus Christianorum. Continuatio Mediaeualis, xlii).

Ovid, *Amores, Medicamina faciei femineae, Ars amatoria, Remedia amoris*, ed. E. J. Kenney. Oxford, 1961.

Peter the Venerable, *Adversus Iudeorum inveteratam duritiem*, ed. Y. Friedman. Turnhout, 1985 (Corpus Christianorum. Continuatio mediaeualis, lviii).

Peter the Venerable, *Contra Petrobrusianos hereticos*, ed. J. Fearns. Turnhout, 1968 (Corpus Christianorum. Continuatio mediaeualis, x).

Peter the Venerable, *Liber contra sectam sive haeresim Saracenorum*, in: J. Kritzeck, *Peter the Venerable and Islam*. Princeton, 1964, pp. 220–91 (Princeton Oriental Studies).

Peter the Venerable, *The Letters of Peter the Venerable*, ed. G. Constable. Cambridge, Mass., 1967, 2 vols.

Prose Role of the Céli Dé, in: Reeves W., 'On the Céli-dé, commonly called Culdees', in: *The Transactions of the Royal Irish Academy*, 24, 1873, pp. 202–15.

Raoul Glaber, *Historiarum libri quinque. The five books of the Histories*, ed. J. France & N. Bulst. Oxford, 1989 (Oxford Medieval Texts).

Statuta seu Brevia Adalhardi abbatis Corbeiensis, ed. J. Semmler. Siegburg, 1963, pp. 365–408 (Corpus Consuetudinum Monasticarum i).

Thomas of Cantimpré, *Bonum universale de apibus*. Cologne, (1480), (The Hague, 1902).

Udalric, *Antiquiores consuetudines Cluniacensis monasterii*, ed. J. P. Migne, *Patrologia Latina*, 149. Paris, 1882, cc. 635–778.

Walter of Arrouaise, *Fundatio monasterii Arroasiensis*, ed. O. Holder-Egger, *Monumenta Germaniae Historica, Scriptores*. Hannover, 1888, xv, 2, pp. 1117–25.

William of Andres, *Chronica Andrensis*, ed. I. Heller, *Monumenta Germaniae historica, Scriptores*, xxiv, Hannover, 1879, pp. 684–773.

Wolfram von Eschenbach. *Willehalm. Titurel*, ed. Schröder N. J. & Hollandt G., Darmstadt, 1971.

Ysengrimus, ed. J. Mann. Leyden, 1987 (Mittellateinische Studien und Texte xii).

Secondary Works

Apocalyptic Spirituality, transl. B. McGinn. New York, Ramsey, Toronto, 1979.

Auberger J.-B., 'Spiritualité de l'architecture cistercienne du XIIe siècle', in: *Visages cisterciens*. Paris, 1990, pp. 64–72 (Sources vives, 33).

Aubrun M., *La paroisse en France des origines au XVe siècle*. Paris, 1986.

Avril J., 'Moines, chanoines et encadrement religieux des campagnes de l'Ouest de la France (fin XIIe – début XIIIe siècle)', in: *Istituzioni monastiche e istituzioni canonicali in Occidente (1123–1215)*. Milan, 1980, pp. 660–78.

Avril J., 'Recherches sur la politique paroissiale des établissements monastiques et canoniaux (XIe–XIIIe s.)', in: *Revue Mabillon*, 59, 1980, pp. 453–517.

Batselier P. (ed.), *Benedictus Pater Europae*. Antwerp, 1980.

Becker A., *Papst Urban II. (1088–1099). Teil 2. Der Papst, die griechische Christenheit und der Kreuzzug*, Stuttgart, 1988.

Becker P., 'Erstrebte und erreichte Ziele benediktinischer Reformen im Spätmittelalter', in: *Reformbemühungen und Observanzbestrebungen im spätmittelalterlichen Ordenswesen*, ed. K. Elm. Berlin, 1989, pp. 23–34 (Berliner Historische Studien, 14).

Bell D. N., 'The English Cistercians and the Practice of Medicine', in: *Cîteaux. Commentarii Cistercienses*, 40, 1989, pp. 139–74.

Berings G., 'Transport and Communication in the Middle Ages', in: *Kommunikation und Alltag in Spätmittelalter und Frühneuzeit*, ed. H. Kühnel, Krems, 1992 (in press).

Berlière U., 'Le nombre des moines dans les anciens monastères', in: *Revue bénédictine*, 41, 1929, pp. 231–61 et 42, 1930, pp. 19–42.

Berman C. H., *Medieval Agriculture, the Southern French Countryside, and the early Cistercians. A Study of Forty-three Monasteries*. Philadelphia, 1986 (Transactions of the American Philosophical Society, 76, 5).

Billy G., 'Les restes humains de l'abbaye de Saint-Martial de Limoges (Fouilles de 1966–1967)', in: *Bulletin de la société archéologique et historique du Limousin*, ciii, 1976, pp. 63–74.

Blake E. O. & Morris C., 'A Hermit goes to War: Peter and the Origins of the First Crusade', in: W. J. Sheils (ed.), *Monks, Hermits and the Ascetic Tradition*. Oxford, 1985, pp. 79–107 (Studies in Church History 22).

Blockmans W. P. & Prevenier W., 'Poverty in Flanders and Brabant from the fourteenth to the mid-sixteenth century: sources and problems', in: *Acta historiae Neerlandicae*, x, 1978, pp. 19-57.

Bloomfield M. W., *The Seven Deadly Sins: An Introduction to the History of a Religious Concept*. East Lansing, 1952.

Boeren P. C., *Étude sur les tributaires d'Église dans le comté de Flandre du IXe au XIVe siècle*. Amsterdam, 1936.

Bonde S. & Maines C., 'The Archaeology of Monasticism: a Survey of recent Work in France, 1970–1987', in: *Speculum*, 63, 1988, pp. 794–825.

Bosl K., *Armut Christi, Ideal der Mönche und Ketzer, Ideologie der aufsteigenden Gesellschaftsschichten vom 11. bis zum 13. Jahrhundert*. Munich, 1981 (Bayerische Akademie der Wissenschaften. Philosophisch-Historische Klasse. Sitzungsberichte 1981, 1).

Boswell J., *The Kindness of Strangers. The Abandonment of Children in Western Europe from Late Antiquity to the Renaissance*. New York, 1988.

Bouchard C. B., *Sword, Miter, and Cloister. Nobility and the Church in Burgundy, 980–1198*. Ithaca, London, 1987.

Boyd C. E., *Tithes and Parishes in Medieval Italy. The Historical Roots of a Modern Problem*. Ithaca, NY, 1952.

Brooke C., 'Priest, deacon and layman, from St Peter Damian to St Francis', in: Sheils W. J. & Wood D. (edd.), *The Ministry: Clerical and Lay*. Oxford, 1989, pp. 65–97 (Studies in Church History, 26).

Brooke C., 'St Bernard, the Patrons and Monastic Planning', in: C. Norton and D. Park (edd.), *Cistercian Art and Architecture in the British Isles*. Cambridge, 1986.

Brooke C., *The Medieval Idea of Marriage*. Oxford, 1989, pp. 186–202.

Brooke C., *The Monastic World*. London (1974). The second edition (New York, 1982) was published under the title *Monasteries of the World*.

Brooke R. & C., *Popular Religion in the Middle Ages, Western Europe, 1000–1300*. London, 1984.

Brown P., *The Body and Society*. New York, 1988.

Chadwick O., *Western Asceticism*. London, 1958 (Library of Christian Classics, 12).

Chibnall M., *The World of Orderic Vitalis*. Oxford, 1984.

Clanchy M. T., *From Memory to Written Record. England 1066–1307*. London, 1979.

Clark C., *Population Growth and Land Use*. New York, 1977.

Coleman E., 'Medieval Marriage Characteristics: A Neglected Factor in the History of Medieval Serfdom', in: *The Journal of Interdisciplinary History*, ii, 1971–1972, pp. 205–19.

Conant K. J., *Cluny; les églises et la maison du chef d'Ordre*. Mâcon, 1968.

Constable G., 'Eremitical forms of monastic life', in: *Istituzioni monastiche e istituzioni canonicali in Occidente, 1123–1215*. Milano, 1980, pp. 239–64 (reprinted in: *Monks, Hermits and Crusaders in Medieval Europe*. London, 1988).

Constable G., 'Liberty and Free Choice in Monastic Thought and Life, especially in the Eleventh and Twelfth Centuries', in: *La notion de liberté au Moyen Age*, ed. G. Makdisi, D. Sourdel & J. Sourdel-Toumine. Paris, 1985, pp. 99–118 (reprinted in: G. Constable, *Monks, Hermits and Crusaders in Medieval Europe*. London, 1988).

Constable G., 'Monasteries, Rural Churches and the Cura Animarum in the Early Middle Ages', in: *Cristianizzazione ed organizzazione ecclesiastica delle campagne nell' alto medioevo*. Spoleto, 1962 (Settimane di Studi, XXVIII), pp. 349–89 (reprinted in G. Constable, *Monks, Hermits and Crusaders in Medieval Europe*. London, 1988).

Constable G., 'Suger's Monastic Administration', in: *Abbot Suger and Saint-Denis. A Symposium*, ed. P. L. Gerson. New York, 1986, pp. 18–32 (reprinted in G. Constable, *Monks, Hermits and Crusaders in Medieval Europe*. Oxford, 1988).

Constable G. & Smith B., *Libellus de diversis ordinibus et professionibus qui sunt in Aecclesia*. Oxford, 1972 (Oxford Medieval Texts).

Constable G., *Medieval monasticism: a select bibliography*. Toronto, Buffalo, 1976 (Toronto Medieval Bibliographies 6).

Constable G., *Monastic Tithes from their Origins to the Twelfth Century*. Cambridge, 1964.

Constable G., *Monks, Hermits and Crusaders in Medieval Europe*. London, 1988.

Contamine Ph., 'The French Nobility and the War', in: *The Hundred Years War*, ed. K. Fowler. London, 1971, pp. 137–45. (reprinted in: *La France au [sic] XIVe et XVe siècles. Hommes, mentalités, guerre et paix*. London, 1981).

Coulton G. G., *Five Centuries of Religion*, New York, 1923–1950 (1979), 4 vols.

Courtenay W. J., *Schools & Scholars in fourteenth-century England*. Princeton, 1987.

D'Haenens A., 'La quotidienneté monastique au Moyen-Age', in: *Klösterliche Sachkultur des Spätmittelalters*. Vienna, 1980, pp. 31–42 (Österreichische Akademie der Wissenschaften. Philologisch-Historische Klasse. Sitzungsberichte, 367).

de Jong M., *Kind en klooster in de vroege middeleeuwen. Aspecten van de schenking van kinderen aan kloosters in het Frankische Rijk (500–900)*. Amsterdam, 1986 (Amsterdamse historische reeks, 8).

de Vogüé A., *The Rule of St. Benedict. A Doctrinal and Spiritual Commentary*. Kalamazoo, MI, 1983 (Cistercian Studies Series 54).

Décarreaux J., *Les moines et la civilisation en Occident. Des invasions à Charlemagne*. Paris, 1962 (Signes des temps, xiii)

Dereine Ch., *Les chanoines réguliers au diocèse de Liège avant saint Norbert*. Brussels, 1952 (Académie royale . . . de Belgique. Classe des Lettres . . . Mémoires 47, 1).

Despy G., 'Les richesses de la terre: Cîteaux et Prémontré devant l'économie de profit au XIIe et XIIIe siècles', in: *Problèmes d'histoire du Christianisme*. Brussels, 1976, pp. 58–80.

Despy-Meyer A. & Gérard C., 'Abbaye d' Affligem à Hekelgem', in: *Monasticon belge. Tome IV. Province de Brabant. Premier volume*. Liège, 1964, pp. 17–80.

Donkin R. A., 'Settlement and Depopulation on Cistercian Estates during the twelfth and the thirteenth Centuries', in: *Bulletin of the Institute of Historical Research*, xxxiii, 1960, pp. 141–64.

Duby G., 'Le monachisme et l' économie rurale', in: *Il monachesimo e la riforma ecclesiastica (1049–1122)*. Milano, 1971, pp. 336–49.

Duby G. (dir.), *Histoire de la France urbaine*. Paris, 1980–1985, 5 vols.

157

Duby G., *Guerriers et paysans*. Paris, 1973, pp. 240–48.

Duby G., *The Three Orders, Feudal Society imagined*. Chicago, London, 1980 (*Les trois ordres ou l'imaginaire du féodalisme*. Paris, 1978).

Dunn M., 'Mastering Benedict: Monastic Rules and their Authors in the Early Medieval West', in: *The English Historical Review*, cv, 1990, pp. 567–94.

Dwyer P. O., *Céli Dé. Spiritual Reform in Ireland. 750–900*. Dublin, 1981.

Evans J., *The Romanesque Architecture of the Order of Cluny*. Cambridge, 1938, pp. 3–15.

Felten F. J., *Äbte und Laienäbte im Frankenreich. Studie zum Verhältnis von Staat und Kirche im früheren Mittelalter*. Stuttgart, 1980 (Monographien zur Geschichte des Mittelalters, 20).

Fergusson P., *Architecture of Solitude. Cistercian Abbeys in Twelfth-Century England*. Princeton, 1984.

Ferruolo S. C., *The origins of the University of Paris and their Critics*. Stanford, 1985.

Fontaine J., *Isidore de Séville et la culture classique dans l'Espagne wisigothique*. Paris, 1959, 2 vols.

Foot S., 'Parochial Ministry in Early Anglo-Saxon England: The Role of Monastic Communities', in: W. J. Sheils & D. Wood (edd.), *The Ministry: Clerical and Lay*. Oxford, 1989, pp. 43–54.

Fossier R., *La terre et les hommes en Picardie jusqu' à la fin du XIIIe siècle*. Paris, Louvain, 1968, 2 vols.

Fuchs P., 'Die Weltflucht der Mönche. Anmerkungen zur Funktion des monastisch-aszetischen Schweigens', in: *Zeitschrift für Soziologie*, 15, 1986, pp. 393–405.

Ganshof F. L., 'Alcuin's Revision of the Bible', in: Ganshof F. L., *The Carolingians and the Frankish Monarchy*. Ithaca, NY, 1971.

Ganshof F. L. & Verhulst A. E., 'Medieval Agrarian Society in its Prime. France, The Low Countries, and Western Germany', in: *The Cambridge Economic History of Europe*, i. Cambridge, 1966[2], pp. 291–339.

Genicot L. & Tombeur P. (dir.), *Index Scriptorum Latino-Belgicorum Medii Aevi*. Brussels, 1973–1979, 4 vols.

Gottfried R. S., *Bury St. Edmunds and the Urban Crisis: 1290–1539*. Princeton, 1982.

Graves C. V., 'The Economic Activities of the Cistercians in Medieval England (1128–1307)', in: *Analecta Sacri Ordinis Cisterciensis*, 13, 1957, pp. 3–60.

Grégoire R., 'La place de la pauvreté dans la conception et la pratique de la vie monastique médiévale latine', in: *Il monachesimo e la riforma ecclesiastica (1049–1122)*. Milano, 1971, pp. 172–92.

Grundmann H., 'Adelsbekehrungen im Hochmittelalter', in: *Adel und Kirche*, ed. J. Fleckenstein & K. Schmid. Freiburg, 1968, pp. 325–45.

Grundmann H., *Neue Forschungen über Joachim von Fiore*. Marburg, 1950.

Gyon G. D., 'L'état et l'exploitation du temporel de l'abbaye bénédictine Sainte-Croix de Bordeaux (XIe–XIVe siècles)', in: *Revue Mabillon*, n.s. 1 (vol. 62), 1990, pp. 241–83.

Hahn A., 'Sakramentelle Kontrolle', in: W. Schluchter (ed.), *Max Webers Sicht des okzidentalen Christentums*. Frankfurt-am-Main, 1988, pp. 229–53.

Hamesse J., *Auctoritates Aristotelis, Senecae, Boethii, Platonis, Apulei et quorundam aliorum*. Louvain-la-Neuve, 2 vols, 1972–1974.

Hamilton B., *Religion in the Medieval West*. Sevenoaks, Kent, 1986.

Hartridge R. A. R., *A History of Vicarages in the Middle Ages*. New York, 1930 (1968).

Harvey B., *Westminster Abbey and its Estates in the Middle Ages*. Oxford, 1977.

Hatcher J., *Plague, Population and the English Economy. 1348–1530*. London, 1977, (Studies in Economic and Social History).

Heinzelmann H., 'Sanctitas und "Tugendadel". Zu Konzeptionen von "Heiligkeit" im 5. und 10. Jahrhundert', in: *Francia*, 5, 1977, pp. 741–52.

Heitz C., 'Saint-Riquier en 800', in: *Revue du Nord*, 69, 1986, pp. 335–44.

Hillery Jr G. A., 'Monastic Occupations: A Study of Values', in: *Research in the Sociology of Work*, 2, 1983, pp. 191–210.

Horn W. & Born E., *The Plan of St. Gall. A study of the architecture & economy of, & life in a paradigmatic Carolingian monastery*. Berkeley, 1979, 3 vols.

Hubert J., 'La place faite aux laïcs dans les églises monastiques et dans les cathédrales aux XIe et XIIe siècles', in: *I laici nella 'societas christiana' dei secoli XI e XII*. Milano, 1968, pp. 470–87 (Pubblicazioni dell' Università cattolica del Sacro Cuore. Contributi. Serie terza. Varia. 5).

Il Monachesimo nell'alto medioevo e la formazione della civiltà occidentale, 8–14 aprile 1956. Spoleto, 1957 (Settimane di Studio, iv).

International Encyclopedia of the Social Sciences, x. S. l., 1968.

Jaritz G., 'The Standard of Living in German and Austrian Cistercian Monasteries in the Late Middle Ages', in: E. R. Elder (ed.), *Goad and Nail*. Kalamazoo, MI, 1985, pp. 56–70 (Cistercian Studies Series 84).

Jarnecki W., *Signa loquendi. Die cluniacensischen Signa-Listen*. Baden-Baden, 1981 (Saecula spiritalia, 4).

Johanek P., 'Klosterstudien im 12. Jahrhundert', in: J. Fried (ed.), *Schulen und Studium im sozialen Wandel des hohen und späten Mittelalters*. Sigmaringen, 1986 (Vorträge und Forschungen, 30).

Johnson P. D., *Prayer, Patronage, and Power. The Abbey of la Trinité, Vendôme, 1032–1187*. New York, London, 1981.

Kieser A., 'From Asceticism to Administration of Wealth. Medieval Monasteries and the Pitfalls of Rationalization', in: *Organization Studies*, 8, 1987, pp. 103–23.

Klösterliche Sachkultur des Spätmittelalters. Vienna, 1980 (Österreichische Akademie der Wissenschaften. Philologisch-Historische Klasse. Sitzungsberichte, 367).

Knowles D. & Hadcock R. N., *Medieval Religious Houses. England and Wales*. London, 1971².

Knowles D. & St John J. K. S., *Monastic Sites from the Air*. Cambridge, 1952.

Knowles D., *The Monastic Order in England*. Cambridge, 1940 (1963²).

Knowles D., *The Religious Orders in England*. Cambridge, 1956–1959, 3 vols.

Kroll J., 'The Concept of Childhood in the Middle Ages', in: *Journal of the History of the Behavioral Sciences*, 13, 1977, pp. 384–93.

Krüger K. H., *Die Universalchroniken*. Turnhout, 1976 (Typologie des sources du moyen âge occidental, 16).

Kruithof C. L., 'De institutionalisering van de stilte: een aantekening over here-mitisme en cenobitisme', in: *Tijdschrift voor sociale wetenschappen*, 28, 1983, pp. 214–18.

Kuchenbuch L., 'Die Klostergrundherrschaft im Frühmittelalter. Eine Zwi-schenbalanz', in: *Herrschaft und Kirche*, ed. F. Prinz. Stuttgart, 1988, pp. 297–343 (Monographien zur Geschichte des Mittelalters, 33).

Kühnel H., 'Beiträge der Orden zur materiellen Kultur des Mittelalters und weltliche Einflüsse auf die klösterliche Sachkultur', in: *Klösterliche Sachkultur des Spätmittelalters*. Vienna, 1980, pp. 9–29 (Österreichische Akademie der Wissenschaften. Philologisch-Historische Klasse. Sitzungsberichte, 367).

Lackner B. K., *The Eleventh-Century Background of Cîteaux*. Washington DC, 1972 (Cistercian Studies Series 8).

Lawrence A., 'English Cistercian Manuscripts of the Twelfth Century', in: Chr. Norton & D. Park (edd.), *Cistercian Art and Architecture in the British Isles*. Cambridge, 1986, pp. 284–98.

Lawrence C. H., *Medieval Monasticism. Forms of Religious Life in Western Europe in the Middle Ages*. London, New York, 1984.

Leclercq J., 'Comment vivaient les frères convers?', in: *I laici nella 'societas christiana' dei secoli XI e XII*. Milano, 1968, pp. 152–176 (Pubblicazioni dell' Università cattolica del Sacro Cuore. Contributi. Serie terza. Varia. 5).

Leclercq J., 'L'humanisme des moines au moyen âge', in: *A Giuseppe Ermini*. Spoleto, 1970, pp. 69–113.

Leclercq J., 'L'Ordine del Tempio: monachesimo guerriero e spiritualità medi-evale', in: *I Templari: mito e storia*. Siena, 1989, pp. 1–8.

Leclercq J., 'Literature and Psychology in Bernard of Clairvaux', in: The Down-side Review, 93, 1975, pp. 1–20.

Leclercq J., 'Textes sur la vocation et la formation des moines au moyen âge', in: *Corona Gratiarum. Miscellanea . . . E. Dekkers . . . oblata*. Bruges, The Hague, 1975, ii, pp. 169–94.

Leclercq J., *L'amour des lettres et le desir de Dieu: initiation aux auteurs monastiques du moyen âge*. Paris, 1957.

Lekai L. J., *The Cistercians. Ideals and Reality*. Kent Ohio, 1977.

Lemarignier J.-F., 'Structures monastiques et structures politiques dans la France de la fin du Xe et des débuts du XIe siècle', in: *Il monachesimo nell' alto medioevo e la formazione della civiltà occidentale*. Spoleto, 1957, pp. 357–400.

Lennard R., *Rural England. 1086–1135. A Study of Social and Agrarian Conditions*. Oxford, 1959.

Lerner R., 'Refreshment of the Saints: the Time after Antichrist as a Station for earthly Progress in Medieval Thought', in: *Traditio*, 32, 1976, pp. 97–144.

Lesne E., *Histoire de la propriété ecclésiastique en France*. Lille, 1922–1943, 6 vols.

Leyser H., *Hermits and the New Monasticism. A Study of Religious Communities in Western Europe, 1000–1150*. London, 1984 (New Studies in Medieval History).

Lindgren U., *Gerbert von Aurillac und das Quadrivium*. Wiesbaden, 1976.

Little L. K., 'Intellectual Training and Attitudes toward Reform, 1075–1150', in: *Pierre Abélard, Pierre le Vénérable*. Paris, 1975, pp. 235–49 (Colloques inter-nationaux du CNRS 546).

Little L. K., *Religious Poverty and the Profit Economy in Medieval Europe*. Ithaca, NY, 1978.

Lohrmann D., *Le moulin à eau dans le cadre de l'économie rurale de la Neustrie (VIIe–IXe siècles)*, in: *La Neustrie. Les pays au nord de la Loire de 650 à 850*, ed. H. Atsma. Sigmaringen, 1989, pp. 367–404 (Beihefte der Francia 16/1).

Longère J., 'La fonction pastorale de Saint-Victor à la fin du XIIe et au début du XIIIe siècle', in: *L'abbaye parisienne de Saint-Victor au moyen âge*. Paris, Turnhout, 1991, pp. 291–313 (Bibliotheca victorina, i).

Lynch J. H., *Simoniacal Entry into Religious Life from 1000 to 1260. A Social, Economic and Legal Study*. Columbus, 1976.

Madden J. E., 'Business Monks, Banker Monks, Bankrupt Monks: the English Cistercians in the Thirteenth Century', in: *The Catholic Historical Review*, 49, 1963, pp. 341–64.

Maréchal G., *De sociale en politieke gebondenheid van het Brugse hospitaalwezen in de middeleeuwen*. Kortrijk, 1978 (English summary on pp. 309–12) (Anciens Pays et Assemblées d'États – Standen en Landen, lxxiii).

Marnix van St. Aldegonde Ph., *Den Biënkorf der H. Roomsche Kercke*. S.l., (1569) (Zutphen, 1974).

Marsch E., *Biblische Prophetie und chronographische Dichtung. Stoff- und Wirkungsgeschichte der Vision des Propheten Daniels nach Dan. VII*. Berlin, 1972.

McCrank L. J., 'The Cistercians of Poblet as Landlords: Protection, Litigation and Violence on the Medieval Catalan Frontier', in: *Cîteaux. Commentarii Cistercienses*, xxvi, 1975, pp. 255–83.

McDonald J. & Snooks G. D., *Domesday Economy. A New Approach to Anglo-Norman History*. Oxford, 1986.

McKitterick R., 'Town and Monastery in the Carolingian Period', in: D. Baker (ed.), *The Church in Town and Countryside*. Oxford, 1979, pp. 93–102 (Studies in Church History 16).

McKitterick R., *The Carolingians and the Written Word*. Cambridge, 1989.

Milis L., 'Charisma en administratie', in: *Archives et bibliothèques de Belgique – Archief- en Bibliotheekwezen in België*, 46, 1975, pp. 50–69 and 549–66.

Milis L., 'Dispute and Settlement in Medieval Cenobitical Rules', in: *Bulletin de l'Institut historique belge de Rome – Bulletin van het Belgisch Historisch Instituut te Rome*, lx, 1990, pp. 43–63.

Milis L., 'Ermites et chanoines réguliers au douzième siècle', in: *Cahiers de Civilisation médiévale*, xxii, 1979, pp. 39–80.

Milis L., 'La conversion en profondeur: un processus sans fin', in: *Revue du Nord*, 69, 1986, pp. 487–98.

Milis L., 'Monks, Mission, Culture and Society in Willibrord's time', in: P. Bange & A. G. Weiler (edd.), *Willibrord, zijn wereld en zijn werk*, pp. 82–92.

Milis L., 'Pureté et sexualité', in: *Villes et campagnes au moyen âge. Mélanges Georges Despy*, ed. J.-M. Duvosquel & A. Dierkens. Liège, 1991, pp. 503–14.

Milis L., 'Reinheid, sex en zonde', in: Milis L. (ed.), *De Heidense Middeleeuwen*. Brussels, Rome, 1991, pp. 143–166 (Institut historique belge de Rome. Bibliothèque, xxxii).

Molho A., 'Tamquam vera mortua. Le professioni religiose femminili nella Firenze del tardo medieovo', in: *Società e storia*, 43, 1989, pp. 1–44.

Mollat M., 'Les moines et les pauvres', in: *Il monachesimo e la riforma ecclesiastica (1049–1122)*. Milano, 1971, pp. 193–215.

Moorhouse S., 'Monastic Estates: their Composition and Development', in: *The Archaeology of Rural Monasteries*, ed. R. Gilchrist & H. Mytum. Oxford, 1989, pp. 29–81 (BAR British Series 203).

Morimoto Y., 'État et perspectives des recherches sur les polyptyques carolingiens', in: *Annales de l'Est*, 40, 1988, pp. 99–149.

Moulin, L., *La vie quotidienne des religieux au moyen âge. Xe–XVe siècle*. [Paris], 1978.

New Catholic Encyclopedia, ix. New York, 1967.

Newman B., *Sister of Wisdom. St. Hildegard's Theology of the Feminine*. Berkeley, Los Angeles, 1987.

Noonan Jr J. T., 'Gratian slept here. The Changing Identity of the Father of the Systematic Study of Canon Law', in: *Traditio*, xxxv, 1979, pp. 145–72.

Nouveau Wauters. Brussels, Louvain-la-Neuve, 1989, 4 vols.

Obert C., 'La promotion des études chez les Cisterciens à travers le recrutement des étudiants du Collège Saint-Bernard de Paris au moyen âge', in: *Cîteaux. Commentarii Cistercienses*, 39, 1988, pp. 65–78.

Pacaut M., *Les Ordres monastiques et religieux au Moyen Age*. Paris, 1970.

Pagels E., *Adam, Eve, and the Serpent*. New York, 1988.

Peaudecerf M., 'La pauvreté à l'abbaye de Cluny d'après son cartulaire', in: M. Mollat (ed.), *Études sur l'histoire de la pauvreté*, Paris, 1974, i, pp. 217–27.

Penco G., 'Senso dell' uomo e scoperta dell' individuo nel monachesimo dei secoli XI e XII', in: *Benedictina*, 37, 2, 1990, pp. 285–315.

Penco G., *Medioevo monastico*. Roma, 1988 (Studia Anselmiana 96).

Poirier-Coutansais F., *Les abbayes bénédictines du diocèse de Reims*. Paris, 1974 (Gallia Monastica. i).

Prevenier W., 'En marge de l'assistance aux pauvres: l'aumônerie des comtes de Flandre et des ducs de Bourgogne (13e–début 16e siècle)', in: *Recht en instellingen in de Oude Nederlanden tijdens de middeleeuwen en de Nieuwe Tijd. Liber amicorum Jan Buntinx*. Louvain, 1981, pp. 97–120 (Symbolae A 10).

Religion dans les manuels scolaires d'histoire en Europe (La). Actes . . . Strasbourg, 1974, p. 111.

Reynolds L. D. & Wilson N. G., *Scribes and Scholars. A Guide to the Transmission of Greek and Latin Literature*. London, 1968.

Richter M., 'England and Ireland in the Time of Willibrord', in: P. Bange & A. G. Weiler (edd.), *Willibrord, zijn wereld en zijn werk*. Nijmegen, 1990, pp. 35–50 (Middeleeuwse studies, vi).

Rosenwein B. H., 'Reformmönchtum und der Aufstieg Clunys', in: W. Schluchter (ed.), *Max Webers Sicht des okzidentalen Christentums*, pp. 276–311.

Rosenwein B. H. & Little L. K., 'Social Meaning in the Monastic and Mendicant Spiritualities', in: *Past and Present*, 63, 1974, pp. 4–32.

R. H. Rouse & M. A. Rouse, *Preachers, Florilegia and Sermons: Sudies on the Manipulus florum of Thomas of Ireland*. Toronto, 1979 (Studies and Texts, 47).

Roussel H. & Trotin J., 'Invective aux clercs et satire anti-cléricale dans la littérature du moyen âge', in: *Acta Universitatis Wratislaviensis*, 265, 1975, pp. 3–36.

Rubin M., *Charity and Community in Medieval Cambridge*. Cambridge, 1987 (Cambridge Studies in Medieval Life and Thought. Fourth Series).

Rudolph C., 'Bernard of Clairvaux' Apologia as a Description of Cluny, and the Controversy over Monastic Art', in: *Gesta*, xxvii, 1–2, 1988, pp. 125–32.

Samaran Ch. & Marichal R., *Catalogue des manuscrits en écriture latine portant des indications de date, de lieu ou de copiste*, ii. Paris, 1962.

Schama S., *The Embarrassment of Riches*. New York, 1987.

Schneider R., 'Studium und Zisterzienserorden', in: J. Fried (ed.), *Schulen und Studium im sozialen Wandel des hohen und späten Mittelalters*, pp. 321–50.

Schwarz G. M., 'Village Populations according to the polyptyque of the Abbey of St. Bertin', in: *Journal of Medieval History*, 11, 1985, pp. 31–41.

Searle E., *Lordship and Community. Battle Abbey and its Banlieu. 1066–1538*. Toronto, 1974.

Sebeok J., *Monastic Sign Language*. Berlin, 1987 (Approaches to Semiotics, 76).

Seguy J., 'Une sociologie des sociétés imaginées: monachisme et utopie', in: *Annales. ESC*, 26, 1971, pp. 328–54.

Sheehan M. M., 'Choice of Marriage Partner in the Middle Ages: Development and Mode of Application of a Theory of Marriage', in: *Studies in Medieval and Renaissance History*, i, 1978, pp. 1–33.

Sheils W. J. (ed.), *Monks, Hermits and the Ascetic Tradition*. Oxford, 1985 (Studies in Church History, 22).

Sheils W. J. & Wood D. (edd.), *The Ministry: Clerical and Lay*. Oxford, 1989 (Studies in Church History, 26).

Simons W., 'The Beguine Movement in the Southern Low Countries: A Reassessment', in: *Bulletin de l'Institut historique belge de Rome – Bulletin van het Belgisch Historisch Instituut te Rome*, lix, 1989, pp. 63–105.

Smalley B., 'Ecclesiastical Attitudes to Novelty *c*. 1100–*c*. 1250', in: D. Baker (ed.), *Church Society and Politics*. Oxford, 1975, pp. 113–31 (Studies in Church History, 12).

Smith R. A. L., *Canterbury Cathedral Priory. A Study in Monastic Administration*. Cambridge, 1969.

Snape R., *English Monastic Finances in the Later Middle Ages*. Cambridge, 1926.

Sous la Règle de Saint Benoît: structures monastiques et sociétés en France du moyen âge à l'époque moderne. Genève, Paris, 1982.

Spitz P., 'Silent Violence: Famine and Inequality', in: *International Social Science Journal*, 30, 1978, pp. 867–92.

Stock B., 'Schriftgebrauch und Rationalität im Mittelalter', in: W. Schluchter (ed.), *Max Webers Sicht des okzidentalen Christentums*. Frankfurt-am-Main, 1988, pp. 165–83.

Stutvoet-Joanknecht C. M., *Der Byen Boeck. De Middelnederlandse vertalingen van Bonum universale de apibus van Thomas van Cantimpré en hun achtergrond*. Amsterdam, 1990.

Sullivan L. M., 'Workers, Policy-makers and Labor Ideals in Cistercian Legislation', in: *Cîteaux. Commentarii Cistercienses*, 40, 1989, pp. 175–99.

Thoen H. & Milis L., 'Het site Ten Duinen te Koksijde: archeologisch, geologisch, historisch', in: *Handelingen van de Maatschappij voor geschiedenis en oudheidkunde te Gent*, 28, 1974, pp. 1–35.

Toepfer M., *Die Konversen der Zisterzienser*. Berlin, 1983 (Berliner Historische Studien, 10, Ordensstudien iv).

Tombeur P., *Thesaurus Linguae Scriptorum Operumque Latino-Belgicorum Medii Aevi. Première partie. Le vocabulaire des origines à l'an mil.* Brussels, 1986, 5 vols.

Trio P., *De Gentse Broederschappen (1182–1580).* Gent, 1990 (Verhandelingen der Maatschappij voor geschiedenis en oudheidkunde van Gent, xvi).

Van Acker G., 'Abbaye de la Byloque à Gand', in: *Monasticon belge. Tome VII. Province de Flandre orientale,* 3. Liège, 1980, pp. 329–53.

Van Daele P., *De goede en de slechte kwaliteiten van de middeleeuwse abt, bezien door de ogen van zijn monniken.* Ghent, 1984 (Unpubl. thesis State University Ghent).

Van Engen J., 'The "Crisis of Cenobitism" reconsidered: Benedictine Monasticism in the Years 1050–1150', in: *Speculum,* 61, 1986, pp. 269–304.

Van Engen J., *Rupert von Deutz.* Berkeley, 1983.

Vansina J., *Oral tradition.* Harmondsworth, 1973 (Penguin University Books).

Verhulst A., 'Agrarische revolutie: mythe of werkelijkheid', in: *Mededelingen Faculteit Landbouwwetenschappen Rijksuniversiteit Gent,* 53, 1, 1988.

Verhulst A. & Semmler J., 'Les statuts d'Adalhard de Corbie de l'an 822', in: *Le Moyen Age,* 68, 1962, pp. 91–123, 233–69.

Ward B., 'The Desert Myth. Reflections on the Desert Ideal in early Cistercian Monasticism', in: M. B. Pennington (ed.), *One yet Two. Monastic Tradition East and West.* Kalamazoo, MI, 1976, pp. 183–99 (Cistercian Studies Series 29).

Weber M., *Protestant Asceticism and the Spirit of Capitalism,* in Max Weber, *Selections in translation.* Ed. W. G. Runciman, transl. E. Matthews. Cambridge, 1978, pp. 138–73 (Translation of *Die Protestantische Ethik und der 'Geist' des Kapitalismus.* 1905).

Weber M., *Wirtschaft und Gesellschaft. Grundriss der verstehenden Soziologie* (ed. J. Winckelmann). Tübingen, 1972[5], pp. 122–76 (translation: *Economy and Society,* ed. G. Roth & C. Wittich. New York, 1968, 3, pp. 1006–69).

White jr L., *Medieval Technology and Social Change.* Oxford, 1962, (New York, 1966[2]).

Williams J., 'Cluny and Spain', in: *Gesta,* xxvii, 1–2, 1988, pp. 93–101.

Witters W., 'Pauvres et pauvreté dans les coutumes monastiques du moyen-âge', in: M. Mollat (ed.), *Études sur l'histoire de la pauvreté (Moyen Age – XVIe siècle).* Paris, 1974, I, pp. 177–215 (Publications de la Sorbonne. Série Études, 8).

Wollasch J., 'Konventsstärke und Armensorge in mittelalterlichen Klöstern. Zeugnisse und Fragen', in: *Saeculum,* 39, 1988, pp. 184–99.

Wollasch J., 'Parenté noble et monachisme réformateur', in: *Revue historique,* 104, 1980, pp. 3–24.

Wollasch J., *Mönchtum des Mittelalters zwischen Kirche und Welt.* Munich, 1973.

Zarnecki G., *The Monastic Achievement.* London, New York, 1972.

Zettler A., *Die frühen Klosterbauten der Reichenau. Ausgrabungen – Schriftquellen – St. Galler Klosterplan.* Sigmaringen, 1988.

Ziegler Ph., *The Black Death.* London, 1969.

INDEX